HERBERT BEERBOHM TREE

HERBERT BEERBOHM
TREE   BY
J. S. SARGENT, R.A.

HERBERT BEERBOHM TREE

SOME MEMORIES
OF HIM AND OF HIS ART
COLLECTED BY
MAX BEERBOHM

SECOND EDITION

BENJAMIN BLOM New York/London

First Published 1920
Reissued 1969 by
Benjamin Blom, Inc., Bronx, New York 10452
and 56 Doughty Street, London, W.C. 1

Library of Congress Catalog Card Number 75-91895

Printed in United States of America
at Westbrook Lithographers, Inc.
Westbury, New York

CONTENTS

LIST OF ILLUSTRATIONS

NOTE.—As it has been impossible to trace the origin of some of these illustrations, the usual acknowledgments have been unavoidably omitted in a few cases.

NOTE

FORMAL and elaborate biographies of actors are apt to be not the most inspiring kind of literature. When Herbert Tree died, it seemed to those who knew him best that of such a biography he would not have cared to be the subject. There was, however, a clear need that one who had so distinguished himself in his art, and had been in himself so interesting a character and so unusual a figure, should not go unrecorded. Off the stage, as on it, he was a man of much variety. He was many-sided, impressing different people in very different ways. And it has seemed that perhaps the best, perhaps indeed the only adequate book about him might be such a book as this is, comprising the views of some different people who had good opportunities for observing him.

TABLE OF FACTS AND DATES

HERBERT DRAPER BEERBOHM, better known as Herbert Tree, was born in London, December 17th, 1853. He was the second son of Julius Ewald Beerbohm and Constantia Draper. (His father, who had been born at Memel, in 1811, was of German and Dutch and Lithuanian extraction, had settled in England when he was twenty-three, and had become a naturalized British subject some years before his marriage.)

He was educated first at a school at Frant, in Kent, and afterwards, with his two brothers, at Schnepfenthal College, Thuringia, where his father had been educated.

At the age of seventeen or eighteen he " went into the City " as a clerk in the office of his father, who was a grain merchant.

Soon afterwards he began to be well known as an amateur actor ; and in 1878 he went upon the stage professionally, as Herbert Beerbohm Tree, playing many parts in London and the provinces.

Among his chief successes in the early 'eighties were his impersonations of the Rev. Robert Spalding, in *The Private Secretary*, and Macari, in *Called Back*.

On September 16th, 1882, he married Miss Maud Holt. Their first child, Viola, was born in 1884 ; their second, Felicity, in 1895 ; and their third, Iris, in 1897.

In April, 1887, he became manager of the Comedy Theatre, where he produced *The Red Lamp*.

Later in that year he became manager of the Haymarket Theatre. Among his chief productions here were *Captain Swift* (1888), *The Merry Wives of Windsor* (1889), *A Village Priest* (1890), *The Dancing Girl* (1891), *Hamlet* (1892), *A Woman of No Importance* (1893), *A Bunch of Violets* (1894), *Trilby* (1896), and *The First Part of Henry IV.* (1896).

In 1895 he conceived the idea of building Her Majesty's Theatre, which was completed early in 1897. In April of that year he opened the theatre with a production of *The Seats of the Mighty*. Among his chief subsequent productions were *Julius Cæsar* (1898), *The Musketeers* (1898), *King John* (1899), *A Midsummer Night's Dream* (1900), *Herod* (1900), *Twelfth Night* (1901), *The Last of the Dandies* (1901), *Ulysses* (1902), *The Eternal City* (1902), *Resurrection* (1903), *Richard II.* (1903), *The Darling of the Gods* (1903), *The Tempest* (1904), *Much Ado About Nothing* (1905), *Nero* (1906), *Colonel Newcome* (1906), *The Winter's Tale* (1906), *Antony and Cleopatra* (1906), *Edwin Drood* (1907), *The Beloved Vagabond* (1908), *The Merchant of Venice* (1908), *Faust* (1908), *The School for Scandal* (1909), *Drake* (1912), *Othello* (1912), *Joseph and his Brethren* (1913), *Pygmalion* (1914), and *David Copperfield* (1914).

Late in 1915, and again in 1916, he visited America, to fulfil a contract with a " film " company in Los Angeles. During his stay in America he travelled much and was very active in war propaganda.

In the summer of 1917 he was once more in England. On June 16th he had an accident to his knee. This necessitated an operation, which was successfully performed by Sir Alfred Fripp. On July 2nd he died quite suddenly, owing to the formation of a clot of blood on the lungs.

His body was cremated on July 6th, and on July 7th the ashes were buried in the churchyard of the Parish Church, Hampstead.

Herbert Tree had received the honour of Knighthood in 1909.

He was author of three books : " An Essay on the Imaginative Faculty " (1893), " Thoughts and Afterthoughts " (1913), and " Nothing Matters " (1917).

MY FATHER

I CANNOT think that you have gone away :
   You loved the earth—and life lit up your eyes,
   And flickered in your smile that would surmise
Death as a song, a poem, or a play.
You were reborn afresh with every day,
   And baffled fortune in some new disguise.
   Ah ! can it perish when the body dies,
Such youth, such love, such passion to be gay ?

We shall not see you come to us and leave
   A conqueror—nor catch on fairy wing
Some slender fancy—nor new wonders weave
   Upon the loom of your imagining.
The world is wearier, grown dark to grieve
   Her child that was a pilgrim and a king.

IRIS TREE.

July 4th, 1917.

HERBERT BEERBOHM TREE

HERBERT AND I

A TRIVIAL, FOND RECORD

CHAPTER I

" My whole heart rises up to bless your name, in pride and thankfulness."

September 16th, 1917.

THIS is the anniversary of our marriage, and it is more than two months since Herbert blotted out the world for me by leaving it. I recall the unmemorable, sacred incidents of our wedding-day. A country vicarage : a warm September sunshine brooding over the garden—the hum of bees among the asters and late sweet-peas—the little procession of loving parents, brothers and sisters, along petal-strewn paths and under flowery arches, through lych-gate to church porch—and then two very young people kneeling in love and simplicity to thank God for one another. And I live to thank God upon every remembrance of you, Herbert, from that day to this.

Yet these many married years have left me with but kaleidoscopic memories of my dear and great husband. I wish—how fondly I wish !—that I had retained some written records of such large design as adorned Herbert's vivid life ; but no diary exists.

There is only my memory, casting flashes here and there on the glad, good days made momentous by him.

Let me try and recollect our first meeting. It was early in 1881, at a fancy dress party—the last function in the world to attract Herbert's presence ; but I believe his coming there was the result of a conspiracy that he and I should meet. " But you cannot possibly be the old man who acts in *Forget-Me-Not ?* " was my unpremeditated but not untactful greeting to the tall, pale, youthful creature who was introduced to me as Mr. Beerbohm Tree, and who assured me, in a voice whose wistful cadence haunted the hearer then as now, that he was none other. I can remember nothing as to our themes of conversation, or how much we were together, or whether there was held out any chance that we should ever meet again. I only know that for a long time I lived upon the hope that a combination of Fate and friends would one day bring me face to face once more with that gentle, compelling personality.

Goaded by this aspiration, my footsteps during the early summer were led over and over again from Queen's College, when study ended, to a far-off street, where, according to my childish belief, all actors congregated at the windows and upon the steps of the Garrick Club. It is a score of years since then, and I may be permitted to say that in hundreds of passings and haltings near that historic, histrionic pile, I have only once caught a glimpse of a notability ; this, an eminent divine, seated at a table in the window, discussing lunch with his lawyer.

The Garrick Club—how Herbert loved it ! And how proud he was when he became a member ! And how many thousand times have I taken him, or called for him, there ! " I like its glare," said Disraeli of Brighton. " I like its gloom," said Herbert of the Garrick.

More with the intention of recalling myself to his memory than of following his advice should it be vouchsafed, I wrote to him— in May, perhaps—asking him if my petty successes on the amateur stage were an earnest of great things to come, were I to decide on leaving the Cloister of learning for the Hearth of the green-room. I watched for his answer day after day, still ever and anon penetrating to the purlieus of Covent Garden with the idea of a chance encounter. Vain hopes, both ! No letter came —and no vision. He was all but banished from my category

of possible excitements when, towards the end of summer—while
I was away on a visit—his long-delayed answer reached me.

"MY DEAR MISS HOLT,
    "Don't go on the stage unless you feel you *must*. How
are you ? We shall meet in the autumn.
      "Yours sincerely,
        "H. B. T."

And in the winter he came to see me. I had rather nice big
rooms over a shop in Orchard Street, and he came more and more
often as the days drew in. "A young man to tea," was rather a
departure ; and Mrs. Newman—bless her !—with whom I lived,
used to think it incumbent upon her to preside ; but on the whole
we were left alone, and he used to tell me stories, and to say
poetry to me : " Jim," " In the Mission Garden " and " *Aux
Italiens.*" There was one song (" Rest," by J. S. Payne) that
he loved and used often dreamily to murmur :

> " Silence sleeping on a waste of ocean—
>   Sun down—westward traileth a red streak—
> One white sea-bird, poised with scarce a motion,
>   Challenges the stillness with a shriek,
> Challenges the stillness, upward wheeling
>   Where some rocky peak containeth her rude nest ;
> For the shadows o'er the waters they come stealing,
>   And they whisper to the silence, ' There is Rest.'

> " Down where the broad Zambesi river
>   Glides away into some shadowy lagoon,
> Lies the antelope, and hears the leaflets quiver,
>   Shaken by the sultry breath of noon ;
> Hears the sluggish water ripple in its flowing ;
>   Feels the atmosphere, with fragrance all-opprest ;
> Dreams his dreams, and the sweetest is the knowing
>   That above him, and around him, there is Rest.

> " Centuries have faded into shadow ;
>   Earth is fertile with the dust of man's decay ;
> Pilgrims all they were to some bright El Dorado,
>   But they wearied, and they fainted, by the way.
> Some were sick with the surfeiture of pleasure ;
>   Some were bowed beneath a care-encumber'd breast ;
> But they all trod in turn Life's stately measure,
>   And all paused betimes to wonder, ' Is there Rest ? '

" Look, O man ! to the limitless Hereafter,
   When thy Sense shall be lifted from its dust,
When thy Anguish shall be melted into Laughter,
   When thy Love shall be sever'd from its Lust.
Then thy Spirit shall be sanctified with seeing
   The Ultimate dim Thule of the Blest,
And the Passion-haunted fever of thy being
   Shall be drifted in a Universe of Rest."

I fancy he wrote to me while I was away for the Christmas holidays, but I suppose neither of us was seriously thinking about the other—though, " remembering how I love thy company," it is certain that I looked forward with intense excitement to seeing him again. And he comes—once a week, perhaps, and then more often. He tells me of his work and his ambitions, while I neglect my Greek to listen to him. (In those days my grail was a University degree.)

An excuse for his frequent visits was the discussion of à one-act tragedy, *Merely Players*, which he thought wonderful, and whose leading part, Pantaleone, appealed strongly to him. The story was practically that of *Pagliacci*, and there was a vague idea of producing it at a matinée, and of my acting the heroine in it. I cannot remember that his hopes of it ever came to fruition, even in after-years ; but a great deal of time was spent, delightfully, over the incomplete and densely-annotated manuscript.

One evening—it must have been the 12th of February, 1882 —Herbert asked me to be his wife. We were standing over the fire, leaning on the mantelpiece, and he took my hand and kept it while he spoke. I was dismayed and bewildered—not in the least realizing the great and wonderful honour paid me. I thought of puny things : What would College say ? An actor ! What would my sister say—she who until then had ruled my destiny ? But I cannot have hesitated long, for on Valentine's Day we walked together the two miles from my home to the home of Herbert's people, to declare ourselves engaged. It was magic weather—" bare winter suddenly was changed to spring " —and there were daffodils and jonquils all the way. Our hearts sang ; we were absolutely happy.

Herbert's relations and friends received me with open arms, and it became a custom for us to lunch at his father's house every

Sunday. (His love and veneration for his father were boundless.) From there we used often to go to the Routledges', who
lived opposite. Edmund Routledge dallied, in the intervals of
book-publishing, with amateur acting. He and I had already
met and exchanged vows as Benedick and Beatrice at St.
George's Hall. His family—wife, sons and beautiful daughters
—were already intimate friends. Dear Edmund Routledge,
of kind memory, you cherished the belief that it was you who
brought Herbert and me together; and I like to think it was
so. At all events, you were a beloved friend to us, and when
you died we mourned you very sorrowfully.

There were two charming little girls—babies almost—who
used to come to play in the Routledges' big drawing-room. It
was in his romps and games with them that I first saw Herbert's
wonderful love for little children; his sympathy, his alertness,
his delightful fancies and frolics: all his life he was the light of
childish eyes.

Sunday dinner-parties took place at the houses of various
friends in our honour, and Herbert himself, who lived in rooms
in Maddox Street, gave feasts to celebrate our engagement.
Among those who came—some of his closest associates in those
days, I remember—were Edwin Godwin, Herman Vezin, Norman
Forbes, Justin Huntly McCarthy, A. K. Moore, Edmund Bell,
Hamilton Synge and George Alexander. Herbert loved my
singing, and I used to go through my repertoire every time there
was a piano—" The Creole Love-Song," " Echo," " Crépuscule,"
" Es war ein Traum." When I bewailed my lack of voice he
consoled me: " You *act* the songs so wonderfully—sing that
again; " and he would murmur with me the refrain:

> "Lean low, speak low,
> Oh, Memory, Hope, Love of long ago! "

One day he brought me my engagement ring. It had a
history. A little tiny boy, when his own mother was alive, he
was playing in the garden of their Kensington home, and he came
upon a bauble deep below the ground. He took it into the house,
to his mother, and said, " That is yours, because you have a
headache." (Herbert cherished the most devoted memory of
his mother; but she died when her four children were scarcely
out of babyhood.) The stones in the ring turned out to be

diamonds. Had it dropped from the slender hand of some fine lady in the days when Kensington Palace had its deer-park? Herbert's mother bequeathed it to whomsoever he in after years should marry. So it was re-set and (incidentally) enlarged—and he put it on my " engaged " finger. Alas! many years later, in using on the stage a so-called dramatic gesture with my left hand, the ring, which I always wore, sprang from my hand, described an arc in the air, rolled—and was never found again. Will it be unearthed, I wonder, in days to come, from the foundations of the Haymarket Theatre?

Herbert was acting in *The Colonel* at this time (the spring of 1882), and he used to come and see me on his way to the theatre. Once or twice Florence Théleur, who was engaged to George Alexander, came to see me. I hope she will not mind my saying that it was of her that I experienced my first pang of jealousy! Herbert brought me a little song which he had heard sung by Miss St. John (an artist for whom he had an immense and abiding admiration). The words were: " Oh! my love, she is a kitten, and my heart a ball of string." I tried very hard to do justice to the refrain and music. He decided, rather sadly, that they did not suit me. " Florence (Alexander) could sing that," he said, unconsciously delivering a terrible blow. I remember another, a similar blow, that he dealt me. He arrived radiant, with a parcel: " It is Myra Holme's birthday " (Myra Holme was the heroine in *The Colonel* and married Arthur Pinero), " and I have got her a scarf from Liberty's. Isn't it lovely? " " Too lovely," I answered, with ill-concealed acerbity; and he added insult to injury by using my writing-paper, which had a large M upon it, to wreathe " Dear Myra " round my initial. Darling Herbert, you hadn't the slightest idea how cross I was for that one afternoon, or you would have been unhappy. There never was so gentle and tender a heart: thoughtless sometimes, but the moment you realized another's pain or difficulty, " consideration like an angel came."

So the early spring passed, and we were glad as birds. My few relations, who knew nothing of the theatre world, were only mildly sympathetic over my engagement. Herbert went to lunch with my eldest brother, Willie, to talk things over; and a dreadful verdict was pronounced—" How can Maud marry him?

His shirt-cuffs were frayed ! " I might have replied, " Fielding's were inked." My sister Emmie, a divine woman, whose judgment and approbation were of real moment to me, wrote from Italy to say she only wanted my happiness ; but had I, she asked, considered what might be the torment and the fret of marrying an actor, who must necessarily belong to the Public and not to the Home ? Emmie did not realize that Herbert was destined to lift her little sister out of the small things of life into the great world of Art that he made his own—his own and, because I belonged to him, ours.

In May, Herbert had lodgings at Hampstead Heath, which he shared with George Alexander. Florence, " Alec's " fiancée, tells me that she and I used to arrange with each other when we should go to their cottage in Heath Street, a modest dwelling now no longer to be found. I know I went there early one Sunday morning in spring—that day, May 6th, when England had heard of the Phœnix Park murders. I found Herbert in the little garden of his lodgings, reading *The Observer ;* and I remember his wild indignation and horrified eloquence, and his firing me to feel that the whole world was disgraced for ever and ever.

Soon after this there came the little rift that all but made our music mute. Some kind and dear friends of mine, to whom I owed great gratitude from childhood, who knew little of the world, and nothing of a world such as Herbert's, came between us with the usual arguments—" Wait until you know one another "—" Try a long sea-voyage "—" Time will show." I was weak and easily influenced, and I thought it my duty to break off our engagement. " And the letter that brought me back my ring," caused Herbert the deepest resentment and sorrow. I need not dwell upon my own despair. We bore our separation for a week or two : he with fierce impatience and a raging and never-conquered resentment against my intervening friends (" a little less than kin and less than kind," he called them) which used to reach me in the bitter blots and savage dashes of many a beseeching note. If I revelled a little in my misery and gloried in his grief, it must be forgiven to one unused to adoration and unaccustomed to power. I soon capitulated.

Early one Sunday morning in June, or at the end of May, a letter arrived from Hampstead by hansom, and my answer was to get into the cab and go to him.   Oh ! the divine morning—the buttercups, the sunshine, the May ! (This is more than thirty years ago, when as yet there were Hampstead fields ablaze with buttercups.)   Everything was happy after that : my work at Queen's College—his at the theatre—and daily meetings of incomparable and unimpaired delight.

In July there came a sudden summons for me and my sister Harrie to go to Aix-les-Bains, where my eldest sister lay seriously ill.   That ended our wonderful summer, which I can only remember as a sea of gold—Herbert and I wading through it hand-in-hand.   Sadly we said good-bye to each other and to those sweet days.   But our separation did not last long.   One morning in Aix, instead of the post bringing me a letter from him, a little scrawled note reached me—I know it by heart : " Am here. Have already bathed in Sulphur.   When can I see you ?—H."

Gladness and astonishment were drowned in dismay, for all my life I had been in awe of my brilliant sister, and I dreaded her disapproval of my " young man " who had followed me to France.   I hate to remember my dear Herbert's disappointment that I met his eager greeting with coldness and scolding words.   His love was bounteous, and his soul sincere—he could not understand my complex questionings.   In the afternoon I gathered together sufficient courage to tell my sister that my lover had arrived.   How could I have so misjudged that wisest and most understanding of women ?   The moment they met they were close friends—their spirits rushed together.   Their worlds were wide apart, but their minds had everything in common, and Herbert spent many hours by her bed, hours that lightened the dreariness of her days of pain.   He stayed two weeks—two wonderful weeks.   As we wandered in the woods there was always the sound of rushing streams—a sweet accompaniment to our happy talk and laughter and to the scraps of poetry that bubbled from our lips.

> " All along the valley, where thy waters flow,
>   I walked with one I loved two-and-thirty years ago "—

so used I to quote with him—alas ! alas !

MAUD TREE
IN 1882.
From a pencil drawing by the Duchess of Rutland

Herbert's holiday came to an end, and with it those halcyon days. He returned to work : I stayed on while my poor sister's hopeless illness dragged on its sorrowful course. In September we brought her to London, and the moment Herbert met me he told me that the fashion, the hour and the place of our wedding were fixed—only the actual day remained for my decision. I chose my sister Emmie's birthday—" then I'm certain not to forget it "—and the sixteenth of September it was.

Fate had arranged it after the hearts of both of us. Herbert's people had a house in Kent for the summer, a sweet house—I suppose it was the Vicarage—in whose garden there suddenly happened a church—a lovely little old church, which seemed to have been planted there on purpose for Herbert and Maud's wedding. I went to stay with his people the day before, and Herbert arrived on the day itself. He was disappointed, I remember to my sorrow, that I was too engrossed in wreathing and adorning to talk quietly to him about the new life we were entering upon together. Even when we did meet, I was full of waywardness and frivolity—utterly disinclined to think or talk seriously over the present or the future. The contrast of our moods that marriage morning has often recurred to me as laying bare the lightness of my temperament and the unguessed, ungauged depths of his. I remember how touching and simple was the Service ; and I remember that as I listened to the dear voice calling me his wife there crept into my heart a new kind of love—a protecting love—the passionate longing to guard from harm that one feels towards a little child.

There followed a feast, at which bride and bridegroom were enthroned in huge chairs that seemed made entirely of flowers ; these had been woven and fashioned and decked by the loving hands of Herbert's little sisters, Agnes and Dora. We were surrounded with tenderness and kindness and love and rejoicing, and in our own two hearts there was the fullness of joy.

Our first home was in delightful rooms in Old Burlington Street, and one of our first visitors was Edmund Routledge, who entered, bringing a large silver salver—a present from the Philothespian Amateur Actors. I did not attempt any house-keeping, but I did set up a system by which every penny that we spent should be written down, considered, added up and balanced. A very expensive book was bought for this purpose, and I have it to this day—with exactly three weeks' accounts elaborately entered. By it I learn that Herbert entrusted to me every week the whole of his salary (twenty pounds, as a matter of fact), and I seem to have spent a great deal in nuts and handkerchiefs (for him), and to have doled out to him each day little sums as pocket-money—sums varying from ten shillings to eighteenpence ; while sometimes there are extravagances to record, such as " tickets to Brighton," and daily and hourly hansoms, bearing witness to Herbert's inveterate driving habit. He was acting in a farcical comedy at the Criterion Theatre, and, except that he loved reading Shakespeare, I cannot recall that he had any great ambitions or plans for his career. He was boyish and full of fun and laughter—eager, though a little shy— loving life and people.

It was in the autumn of 1882 that I first met Julius, Herbert's younger brother (Max, their half-brother, was then a little boy of ten). Julius was a brilliant creature, exquisite and elusive : a poet and a dreamer. His poetry was of the soul ; his dreams, alas ! were of the earth. He was a potential millionaire, and from time to time, one would have said, an actual one. But, over and over again, some bright El Dorado would fade before his vision. Fortunes came quickly, and as quickly were engulfed in new and more glittering enterprises. Throughout his eager, hunted life triumph and disaster followed one another in quick succession ; but I never saw him—even when misfortunes were huddling on his back—otherwise than calm, perfectly accoutred and equipped, fastidious, fantastic, fascinating and debonair. When I first knew him he was either engaged to that graceful and gracious being, Mrs. Younghusband, or they were just married. He brought her, Evelyn, to see us at Old Burlington Street. She had (has to this day) great beauty, charm and distinction, a lovely way of speaking, lovely manners, a gentle and rare disposition. After their marriage, they lived in great splendour at Almond's Hotel, and I remember dinner-parties where not the decoration but the tablecloth itself was fashioned of Parma violets, and where food and wine were of the nature of a Sybarite's dream. After such Lucullus' feasts, we would sometimes repair to our rooms, where Julius would make me sing " Crépuscule," and where he also would sing, read us his poems, or tell us stories of his travels. His was an enchanting personality, and Herbert's pride and joy in him were immense. In their stern and cruel school-days Herbert had been the stronger of the two, the most able to endure ; therefore his had been the task to temper hardships to his little brother ; and who would accomplish this task so tenderly or with such love and understanding as Herbert ? Both brothers, while remembering with delight the beauty of the Thuringian land in spring and summer, recalled with shuddering dislike the iron system of their German school.

While we were in our first home there came, close upon our own, another wedding—that of the beautiful and radiant Violet Lindsay to Mr. Henry Manners. My sister Emmie had been for the preceding five years the guide, philosopher and friend of this adorable and gifted girl. Thus when I was hardly more than a child had I come to know her, and a close friendship has existed ever since between her and hers and between us and ours. Henry Manners, then private secretary to Lord Salisbury, was one of the most remarkably handsome and well-favoured of men, and I recall the amazing spectacle of those two peerless creatures as they stood side by side at the altar—with Violet's splendid father, Colonel Charles Lindsay, that *preux chevalier, sans peur et sans reproche*, on one side, and on the other Henry's father, the great Lord John Manners, of Victorian history. Violet's beauty was the theme of contemporary painters : Watts, Millais, Burne-Jones and Poynter, all delighted to immortalize it.

As winter advanced, my health was not good, and Herbert indulged the restlessness that possessed me by taking me from place to place, in the hope that my half-imaginary *malaise* might be allayed. We left Old Burlington Street to sojourn at various hotels, each one less sympathetic to our souls than the last. But in the end, we found—and actually stayed in (except for a few weeks of financial crisis) for more than a year—a charming little house, 4, Wilton Street. There, with two servants, Leah and Mrs. Pellatt, I set up housekeeping—and once more the expensive note-book has the tale to tell of three weeks' thrift.

Herbert's birthday was on December 17th. I try in vain
to remember what we did to celebrate it. It is quite certain to
have been observed as a feast-day, for that was always so ; and
my birthday gift is sure to have taken the form of something
that *I* longed to possess and so presented to him. Oh, and I
suddenly remember what it was ! I gave him the reproduction
of that wax Head of a Woman, attributed to Raphael, in the
Museum at Lille. This treasure, outliving a few cracks and one
tragic cleaning at the hands of an " Obliger," has remained the
head (and front) of our Lares to this day.

Hardly had we settled in Wilton Street than I broke down
under a real illness—serious perhaps for a few hours. How can
I describe Herbert's wonderful care and devotion, his flood of
grief over the slightest weakness and pain, his tears of self-
reproach lest he should have been lacking in love ? He, who
from the first had never ceased to lavish love and tenderness !

Early in the New Year came my sister Emmie's death.
Herbert dreaded the blow for me, for I was not yet strong ; but
I was so hedged in by his consideration and his efforts to distract
my mind from grieving that the sorrow touched me but lightly.
On the other hand, my little sister Harrie, nearest to Emmie, and
inseparable from her in their girlhood, was utterly weighed down
with the grief of her going. She came to stay with us for a night
or two, and Herbert's tenderness and thoughtfulness for her
in her unspeakable anguish laid the foundations of her huge,
unchanging love for him—the passionate, adoring admiration
and devotion of a heart that Herbert recognized to be the
simplest, most tender, most pitiful in the world.

The following is a letter which he wrote to her during our
engagement as a " Collins " after leaving Aix-les-Bains.

" Kent,
" *The 24nd August.*

" (My dear Rarrie)
" if I may so turm you. I trust i am not acting
derogittary to the *ettiquette* of the walk of Life to wich we have
respectually been called by ' one who knows ' in so adressing
you previusly to recevin such incurrieregiment from you so to
do. I am quite cognizant of the fact that wenn a gentleman

meet a lady friend in a street it is her not him as is deputyd to make the furst reckonisement that it is agreable he should raze his at her to. But I trust simular cerrymoneyall is not Here desirubbell though nun the lest Respeck is intended in so doin your near and Dere relutif having keptcompny with him whoo, now, adress you ? How are yer 'Rarrie old pal parding for what I truss you will not reggard as fumilliarity (but mear relashunship though not blood) parding the menshunning off suche verb (thou not on riggle). Kent is inn the country and is a verry rurrial spot ; wich is siroundit by ills one on side hence pressumable the addage Surry ills. This day the whether is rainin(g) wich is bad for the bluming cropps. This is not my mark but uninttensual accident. And now avin finnishe the pagge I will artst youre per misshun to bid fair well to ɪ whosse remembrance will never fade ass long as Brittins never will bee slaves and (this mackine arry is too him) ass Hamlick expostlethwaited, evenn mad turn over youre lawfull brother (ass his too bee).

" D.V. has the sayin goes.   " BILL.

" Pleese remember mee to my fine nancy as furreneers turm it."

One day, soon after Emmie's death, Herbert arrived home, bringing with him Hamilton Aïdé—that gifted dilettante of a poet, musician, writer of novels and playwright ; that virtuoso of a water-colour painter ; that last word on distinguished and cultivated manners, on lovable and high-minded disposition. Herbert knew him already, but he and I had never met. Mr. Aïdé told me afterwards that my little black dress and wan face made instant appeal to him, and that, as I rose to greet him, his affection for us and his interest in us began and never changed. So was initiated a vivid friendship that ended only with that dear comrade's death.

He had, when we first knew him, beautiful rooms in a long, low house called Garden Mansion (since demolished) in Queen Anne's Gate—stately rooms leading from one to another, such as one sees in Italy, and furnished with dim and costly things. We were often at his house, where all the interesting people of the day were to be met—Kings, Princes, Governors and (wellbehaved) Bohemians.

and is a verry
curcial ❚ ; wich
is siroundit by
ills one on side
hence pressumable
the addage Surry
Ills. This day the
whether is rainin=
(g) wich is bad
. for the bluming
cropps ✻

This is not my may
but uninttensual

Facsimile of part of the letter printed on pp. 12-13.

Youre lawfull brother
(as his too bee)
D. V. has the
sayin goes.

Bill

Please remember me
to my fine nancy
as furreners turm it

son gilding of
the ills, coppered
from Natur
in every mow.

To know Mr. Aïdé was to know his cousin, Mrs. Tennant, and her two beautiful daughters—one of whom married the great H. M. Stanley ; the other, Frederick Myers. Mrs. Tennant, kind, hospitable, cultivated, also gave parties, though quite of a different order, at her big house in Richmond Terrace. Those were the days—now of course obsolete !—when certain hostesses would have an amiable weakness for lions and would love the roar of the King of Beasts to reverberate through their rooms. Hamilton Aïdé looked rather for the heart than for the mane ; whence it came that he was sought after and beloved by many a great one of the earth.

It was through him that we knew the Cecil Clays ; and, indirectly, it was through him and them that I ever " went on the stage." Cecil Clay had married that delightful embodiment of mirth, Rosina Vokes, the youngest and the greatest jewel of the celebrated Vokes family. The Clays held open house for lunch on Sundays, and over and over again Herbert and I found ourselves at their hospitable board in Park Street. Rosie Clay, having left the stage, occasionally acted in amateur performances, and very soon I was enmeshed in a network of these.

New Men and Old Acres was a favourite play, and Rosie Clay and I, Herbert Gardner, Augustus Spalding and Captain Gooch used to appear in them to our own and an indulgent audience's intense satisfaction. The Shelley Theatre—a charming little Temple of Thespis which Sir John Shelley added to their house in Chelsea—was often the scene of our efforts. Lady Shelley was a delightful woman, devoted to Herbert, but—as it seemed to me—only mildly interested in Sir Percy's theatrical dabblings. They were both sweet friends to us.

Scarcely was winter past when an awful, an utterly unexpected calamity overtook us : Herbert had no engagement ! The easy, delightful twenty pounds poured automatically into my lap on Friday and spent as soon as poured, suddenly ceased. This was an appalling state of things : we were as Babes in the Wood—but where were the robins ? Where were even the leaves to cover us ?

Two good fairies did actually alight to save us from starva-

tion, in the form of Messrs. Curtis and Henson, who let our " desir-
able " little house for us at a large rent, and thus enabled us,
though but as wanderers upon the face of the earth, to subsist.
My third sister, Bertha, lent us rooms at first—not very smart
ones, for she was as poor as we ; and afterwards we took horrible
lodgings in a forlorn house, down a forlorn turning in that forlorn
neighbourhood where Haverstock Hill pretends to be Hampstead
Heath. Here we sounded the depths and shoals of discomfort
and " disgruntlement," though to our little world, where we
were more and more in demand, we had to appear white-tied
and be-velveted as usual. How I used to dread the gentle-
voiced, courteous overtures of great ladies demanding : " May
I come and see you ? " It must have been a time of terrible
discomfort and disturbance for my dear, gentle Herbert. But
he never uttered one word of complaint. Indeed, in all our
years of varying fortunes, eddying luxuries and movable feasts,
I can remember nothing but cheerful and patient acceptance of
the inevitable. He did not know the art of grumbling, though
no one had a keener sense of what is sweet and good in life :
no one had a more delicate, a more fastidious taste. He deprecated poverty because he thought it stifling to ambition.
" Starvation causes stagnation," I heard him say in after years.
On the other hand, he loathed the kind of self-indulgence which
I once heard him warn a beautiful woman would lead to " the
Carlton Chin."

So daily we walked light-heartedly down the Haverstock
Hill of life together, singing, laughing, and buying clean collars
and snowdrops on the way. Of course, we got into debt, and
it hung long and heavily over our heads. Herbert's sister
Constance, his own and his well-beloved sister Constance, used
to lend me money at times when Marshall and Snelgrove were
more than usually " surprised " (they would have been astonished,
indeed, had they known the real state of our exchequer). I used
to keep an elaborate account of my debts to Constance, and
gradually, though it took years, I repaid her to my own satisfaction, though perhaps not altogether to hers. I daresay she
thought a five-pound note would have been more satisfactory
than a Sheraton chair *worth* five pounds ; yet I remember
perfectly well that I did pay some of that loving loan not in

money but in chairs—doubtless to prevent its becoming a standing debt.

Herbert loved Constance very dearly : she had been all-in-all to him when his mother died, and he looked up to her with the utmost devotion and reverence. He wrote to me once of her : " She has indeed a pure and beautiful soul : she is one of those who will see God."

Since Herbert was not acting, it must have been now that we were able to go to theatres together ; and we saw Mary Anderson, the beautiful girl-actress, who had taken the town by storm, in *Ingomar, Pygmalion and Galatea* and *Romeo and Juliet* —lovely experience which we never forgot. There were amateur theatricals, too, at Lady Freake's house in which we both took part—but an extract from the *Athenæum* will show their nature :

> " A classical representation, entitled *The Tale of Troy*, will be given on the afternoon of May 29th and evening of May 30th, for the benefit of the Building Fund which is being raised to provide better accommodation for the King's College Lectures for Ladies at Kensington. The performance has been organized by Professor G. C. Warr, of King's College, in conjunction with Professor C. T. Newton, C.B., of the British Museum. It will consist of some of the most interesting portions of Homer's *Iliad* and *Odyssey*, arranged in a dramatic form and combined with various tableaux in such a way as to give a connected view of the two poems. . . . Mr. Samuel Brandram will play Priam and Mrs. Beerbohm Tree Andromache. The first performance will be given in English ; the second in the original Greek."

I remember nothing except that sometimes I was Andromache in Greek, and sometimes Helen of Troy (save the mark !) in English—or *vice versâ*—and that beautiful Miss Sellars was Helen of Troy when I was not, and that Herbert Paul was Hector when Herbert was not Hector—and that we all loved to be the willing slaves of all the great artists of the day : Leighton and Watts and Millais, Tadema, Poynter and Burne-Jones ; to such as these one was accustomed to say, " What about my χίτων ? "

and " Please drape the folds of my ἱμάτιον." It was now for the first time that I came to know Mr. Godwin, the famous architect. Though he had been Herbert's friend long before this, and Herbert had an immense admiration and affection for him, I had a stupid, narrow-minded kind of jealousy about him. I wanted Herbert in a glass case, and I used to think that Mr. Godwin tried to get him out. So he did—thank Heaven ! But I regret immeasurably all that I missed in hiding my hands behind my back, when I should have stretched them out with affection and gratitude to a great artist.

Our penury and exile did not last for ever, and by the end of June we were once more back in Wilton Street. All I remember of the waning summer is a performance of *A Midsummer Night's Dream*, which was given by the Labouchères in their garden at Pope's Villa, Twickenham. I remember vividly our getting into a large two-horsed carriage, and driving, in sweet weather, to lunch with the distinguished parents of Edward Bell, painter and poet—a beloved boyhood's friend of Herbert. I remember their house, half-way between Richmond and Twickenham ; I remember almost the food we ate, the wine we drank. Then I remember, dimly, Herbert's enchantment at the performance, in the sweet June twilight that deepened into blue night, of *A Midsummer Night's Dream*. I remember his ecstasies and my torpor. I remember Rose Norreys as Puck, swinging sweetly in the branches ; then an interminable drive home, with our carriage full of joyous, hilarious enthusiasts ; then the mists and darkness of a serious illness which laid me low that very night, and from which it was thought I could not recover—oh, cruel, anxious ending to Herbert's happy summer day ! His devotion ; his tears ; his reiterated cries, " I have not loved you enough ! "—these should be too sacred to let out of one's heart ; but I cannot bear that they should be utterly unrecorded.

When I was well enough, we went to Freshwater, on a visit to Lady Kenmare, whose delicious cottage, The Briary, was our model for many years of all a country home should be. Herbert was obliged to leave me there, for he was rehearsing a new play, and not all the delights of The Briary or of Faringford (where I stayed with Mrs. Lionel Tennyson) could reconcile me to my first separation from him. A far-off glimpse of the Poet Laureate, seated under a cedar-tree, and shrouded in an overwhelming sombrero, hardly entitles me to boast in later life that I knew Alfred Tennyson well—yet I have seen it boasted for me.

> " And did you once see Shelley plain,
>   And did he speak to you ? "

The answer is a decided negative.

September found Herbert acting at the Globe Theatre in *The Glass of Fashion*, with Miss Lingard as the heroine, and Lottie Venne as the *ingénue*. I remember little of the play, beyond his easy, brilliant Prince Borowski, his brown plush smoking-jacket, which set a fashion for stage adventurers, and Lottie Venne's intonation in " Ready, Prince ? " when the jealous husband happily discovered her, instead of his wife, in the rooms of the wicked Polish potentate. The play had a long run, and I often saw it ; indeed, to my astonishment, I find, from an old press-cutting, that I actually appeared in a little curtain-raiser to it—a play called *Elsie*—though why Elsie, whence Elsie, with whom Elsie, I have not the slightest recollection. I imagine it was a sort of preparation to my first real professional engagement, which was at the Court Theatre in October.

Herbert always adhered to his preference for my not going on the stage. " There is so much else you could do," was ever his too-flattering comment. Fate and John Clayton (those two great teachers and great actors) willed it otherwise. I appeared as Hester Gould in *The Millionaire ;* and by dint of donning scarlet hair and of modelling my demeanour on that of Wilkie Collins's immortal adventuress, Miss Gwilt, I made a successful start. I remember the next morning, when a somewhat flaming article appeared about my performance, Herbert rushed in to me, shaving-brush in hand, his razor dangerously near his throat, crying, " I hope it doesn't mean that you will be more famous than I !—because "—with reproachful gravity—" I couldn't have that."

Nothing is more characteristic, both of his *naïveté* and of his humility than this. On much more important occasions, and

HERBERT TREE
ABOUT 1882.

in instances where there might be possible ground for his uneasiness, he would speak his thought like a disquieted child ; thoughts that come to every man, but to which only the child-like in heart give utterance.

We must have had a busy, happy autumn ; success, heaps of friends, money (I think my salary was ten pounds a week, which I spent entirely on hansoms and flowers), little suppers in the " small house in Wilton Street," parties, music, flights by late Saturday night trains to the country or the sea.

Early in 1884 our tenancy of Wilton Street came to an end, and we took a delicious little house in Cheyne Walk. Nothing in the world could be so sweet as Chelsea in earliest spring—the almond-blossom, the brimming river, the seagulls, the lovely lights of morning and evening skies. We revelled in it and in our dear little panelled house.

By this time we had acquired a dog—a beautiful collie, the gift of Professor George Warr, who christened him Argus, in remembrance of our Homeric feats in Lady Freake's tableaux. Argus was a perfect creature, who shared our walks, our hansoms, our restaurant meals, our excursions, and who was only just so much of a sweet, unconscious bore as an adored dog inevitably is. We used to make up odes to him—" Odes to Odour and Others "—which we set to music ; the dance-music tunes of the day. All our dogs have had songs, from Argus to Bruce, the retriever who is still living.

In March was produced *The Private Secretary* at the Globe Theatre, Herbert wandering into his part and inventing it as he rehearsed. Every catchword, every action, every " bit of business " is Herbert's own—indeed, if ever character was created and made immortal by actor rather than author, the Rev. Robert Spalding by Herbert was such.

On the first night of the play I was in the wings, waiting with him till he went on the stage. " Quick, quick ! I must have a bit of blue ribbon in my button-hole," he cried, with sudden inspiration. No one had anything of the desired colour, so I quickly tore something white from my sleeve, rushed to the painting room, and returned with the badge, duly blued, just in time for his entrance. Of course, that blue ribbon became

historic. The play was a failure at first, and I used to sit in the
stalls nearly every night to help to conceal their emptiness. I
remember the last time that the " free list " was thus open to
me (about the fourteenth night of the play). The scanty
audience rocked with laughter throughout, but we all became
hysterical when Mrs. Leigh Murray, having accidentally shed an
underskirt, which she blushingly threw away, in sight of the
audience, Herbert put his head in at the door through which
it had been hurled (it was his entrance in the second act), saying
in modest trepidation, " I beg your pardon, but I thought I met
a Petticoat on the stairs."

Mr. Hill and Mr. Hawtrey, who were on the stage, collapsed
at this unrehearsed witticism—and I thought the audience would
never cease their laughter. From that night onwards *The
Private Secretary* was the talk of the town, and there were no
more vacant stalls for me.

By consenting to remain in the cast, Herbert could have
had riches and fame of a sort then and there. But his ambition
was made of sterner stuff. He resigned the part and his " gags "
to Mr. Penley, a brilliant successor, and himself repaired to the
Prince of Wales's Theatre to " create " Macari in *Called Back*.
This was a triumph—the first of his great parts.

The play ran on and on, while I kept house in Cheyne Walk,
drove or walked with him to the theatre every morning, filled
in my day till his return to five-o'clock dinner, sometimes drove
with him back to his work, waited—often out-of-doors—for his
return. There was not a sweeter place on earth, as summer
grew, than Cheyne Walk. He loved then, as always, to bring
someone home to supper with him—Godwin, A. K. Moore, Brookfield, Edward Bell, Hamilton Synge, Comyns Carr, Stuart Ogilvie
and Hugh Conway. These months were a time of marvellous
peace and joy to me—and I think he was as happy as I. His
success as Macari, following upon *The Private Secretary*, was
enormous ; the seeds of his future greatness were showing
their blades. I think this was before the Chelsea of Chelsea
Art, but the Oscar Wildes lived in Tite Street, and we often
saw them. Mr. Haweis gave parties at Rossetti's old house,
and Mr. Godwin lived in Westminster, not too far away. These
were the early days of Frank Schuster's lovely parties ; Hamilton

Aïdé was our beloved friend; W. S. Gilbert we were just beginning to know; I cannot remember anything but happiness, anticipation and heaps of friends. Money always worried us a little; but only because it concerned us too lightly—sufficient unto the day was the sovereign thereof.

In July came Viola: a never-ending joy. Herbert chose her name—hovering between Viola and Rosalind—and decided at once that she should "grow up laughing." Ramsgate—a lodging in the Royal Crescent—was chosen for me and the baby in August, while Herbert was still acting in *Called Back*. I chafed under our second separation, and soon we were back at Cheyne Walk; and I can remember little beyond the gradual coming of Viola's teeth.

When *Called Back* had come to an end, Herbert was rehearsing *The School for Scandal* with Mrs. Langtry. For some inexplicable reason Joseph Surface did not suit Herbert, though one would have imagined him ideal in the part. He was hampered, I believe, by his intense admiration of John Clayton's Joseph—a most perfect performance; polished, unctuous, elegant, persuasive, stealthy—his very fatness disarmed suspicion. Herbert's personality was slim; and though no one could be so fat as he in manner, gesture and speech when made up to be fat (*vide* Demetrius in *The Red Lamp*, Falstaff, Beethoven, Isidore Izard in *Business is Business*), he could not convey unctuousness while retaining his slim personality; or, at all events, he did not in Joseph Surface. He should have approached the character from another point of view—but, as I have said, the perfection of John Clayton's Joseph spoilt his vision. It was the same, to my mind, when Herbert came to play Iago, which one would have imagined written for him. Here, again, he had seen Maurel in Verdi's *Otello*—easy, jocose, a braggadocio, instinct with the bouncing lissomeness of *embonpoint*—again a perfect performance, whose very perfection led Herbert astray. He tried to make Iago into a Ralph Royster Doyster instead of into a Shakespearean Macari. Had he but imitated himself instead of Maurel he would have been the greatest of all Iagos. Since I am allowing myself to criticize his acting, I will allude to another part wherein he seemed to me to fail. This was Benedick (not because he had seen an ideal Benedick, **for** we never did see one). Had he but made of Benedick an Italian Duke of Guisebury he would have been without rival.

If his Joseph Surface was disappointing, how marvellous was his next part with Mrs. Langtry! His impersonation of Sir Woodbine Grafton, the dyspeptic old Anglo-Indian in *Peril*, became a feature of the play, and set all London laughing.

By this time we had left Cheyne Walk, and we flitted from a pleasant but probably too expensive house in North Audley Street to a flat over the Prince of Wales's Theatre, leased to us by Edgar Bruce. I liked it because of the colour of its walls and its carpets; Herbert, because the large sitting-room was round and full of windows. But it was no place for Argus the dog and Viola the baby, and in tropical June weather we once more repaired to Ramsgate, Herbert having a brief holiday. Unluckily for us, we fell in, while there, with our friend, Mr. Kyrle Bellew, who learnt that we were leaving for London on the morrow. "Then you and Herbert must come in my yacht!" he cried, with the boisterous *bonhomie* that was characteristic of him. "Do we like yachting?" we asked doubtfully. But he, radiant in white suit *de rigueur*, would take no denial, and towards evening, just when June—as too frequently happens— had suddenly turned to November, we were rowed in a small boat to the still smaller yacht, and were promised all the delights of a summer night's journey and the glories of dawn at our London landing. Alas! a thing called a ground-swell kept us prisoners outside Ramsgate harbour, sick, cold, starving, perishing of every evil that a rocking though stationary boat is heir to, with bales of cord for pillows and drizzling rain for coverlets. The long night, with Ramsgate's mocking lights dancing before our bloodshot eyes—what never-to-be-forgotten misery of discomfort! Kyrle Bellew was a charming friend; we spent some of our happiest hours with him—but the yachting hours must not count.

Back in London, and still at Prince's Chambers we seem to have been blithe and gay, but I remember little. I remember Lady Elcho (now Lady Wemyss) giving a Sunday dinner for us, because there, for the first time, we met Margot and Laura

Tennant and Alfred Lyttelton, to whom Laura was engaged. "You must come to my wedding," she said impulsively—radiant, joyous creature that she was, making intimate friends of us on the spot.

Herbert, with his quick eye for contrast and dramatic effect, always recalled the grand figure of Gladstone at this wedding. During the ceremony, he stood wrapt; his leonine head and large, lucent eyes lifted towards the sunshine that filtered through the stained-glass windows. Then he joined, with all the anxious correctness of a young chorister, in the hymns; but ever he kept his calm gaze fixed far away aloft. Meanwhile, as he sang, he stroked the golden hair of a child who stood in front of him. This was at a time when half England was clamouring that he should be hanged on the nearest tree.

Where was our holiday that summer? Did Herbert have a holiday? We must have taken Viola somewhere—Viola, who is a year old by now. I cannot remember—but in the autumn the Gilberts took me with them to Egypt, and Herbert was left at home (lodgings in Wilton Street this time) to look after our little girl. I was away for six weeks, while he was acting at the Haymarket in *Dark Days*, a second play by Hugh Conway, but not so good a play as *Called Back*; nor was Sir Meryvn Ferrand, though fascinating and exquisite, so sensational and unforgettable a success as Macari.

Early in 1886 we had no London home, but took a little house near Ascot—a dreary spot in March, in the tardiest of springs. Herbert had no engagement, and used to go up and down to London to watch events. Once, on his return to our not very luxurious cottage, I remember one of the very, very rare occasions—I think it was the only occasion—when I saw him utterly cast down, disappointed and discouraged. As a rule, misfortune seemed to elate him and give him new energy. It was when the Haymarket management had decided to put on *Jim the Penman*. Herbert, having enacted various villains, all with conspicuous success, in three successive plays at this theatre, naturally expected to be cast for Jim—a part which seemed written for him, and which he would have acted to perfection. But that day he had heard that Arthur Dacre was to be Jim, and that to Herbert was allotted a wretched part, which seemed to him unworthy and beneath his dignity to accept. Yet, for our sakes, he must submit—and something like despair sat upon him. " My soul is dark," he said. I did my best to pet and cheer him—as though drying the tears of a child, so like a child was he in grief or joy. And I was right to bid him take courage, for when the play was produced, lo ! the part of Jim the Penman mattered little, though the play had a great success and a long run ; but Herbert's part, the small part of the German Baron Harzfeld, became the outstanding feature of the play, and people remember it to this day.

Fortune smiled again. Now at last we take a *real* house, rather a nice house, smart and new, in Rosary Gardens ; and I begin the first of my adventures in furnishing—a form of idle activity that more and more obsessed me as the years rolled on. Herbert thought my taste (crude enough in reality) perfect, and my judgment infallible. He also thought I had the gift of hospitality, a quality he adored ; and, indeed, from the days of Rosary Gardens and its presiding kitchen genius, Mrs. Jones, we always had an excellent cook. We were now close friends of the W. S. Gilberts, who found our house for us, and made it easy for us to acquire it. It was at this time that Viola gave utterance to her first memorable remark. She refused the friendly overtures of Mr. Gilbert, nicknamed Gillie. Herbert said reprovingly, " Oh ! kiss Gillie, darling—Daddy loves Gillie." " Then Daddy kiss Gillie," she answered. This seemed to him the most miraculous philosophy ever uttered by a child of two. I think it was from that day that Herbert's idolizing love and admiration for his daughter began.

In the summer of 1886 we combined work and play by installing ourselves and Viola in a lodging among the pinewoods of Bournemouth and acting in *Othello, The Merchant of Venice* and *The School for Scandal* with the Frank Bensons. This was a happy little adventure, especially for me, who plunged into the parts of Portia and Lady Teazle " with all the airy complacency of ineptitude," as a critic once wrote of me, though happily not on the Bournemouth occasion.

Frank Benson was already making himself felt as a lover

of Shakespeare and as a Shakespearean producer ; though he must, in 1886, have but lately left Oxford. Among Herbert's treasures I find his letter inviting us to act with him :

> " DEAR MR. TREE,
>
>   " I enclose book of *Othello*. How would week at Bournemouth suit you for experiments ? Would Mrs. Tree play Portia that week and Lady Teazle, you playing Joseph ? Provincial business is very small, so I can't offer you much remuneration, but I presume that is not so much your object as an artistic experiment. How would half my profits suit you, £10 guaranteed ? That seems to me a fair thing, but we could discuss that on Tuesday. Could you see me on Tuesday, any time after 1.30 ? We might run through our dialogue together. The Bournemouth week begins August 16th. My wife (I shall be married by that time) could show Mrs. Tree some of the stock business of Lady Teazle if she does not know it and cares to talk it over with her.
>
>   " I have not heard from my friend Iago yet, but anticipate no objection on his part.
>
>   " Yours sincerely,
>   " FRANK R. BENSON.
>
>   " P.S.—I can make this off. definite. I shall want to know about Bournemouth by Tuesday at latest. It is a nice little theatre and a nice place, and I think it will be the best place for it."

The spring of 1887 (we are still at Rosary Gardens ; I am acting with the Hares and Kendals) witnesses an exciting departure. Aided and abetted by Mr. Stuart Ogilvie, who financed the venture, and by Mr. Comyns Carr, who was the *fidus Achates*, Herbert shook himself free of the shackles of other people's authority, and took a theatre of his own. Yes, he actually became Lessee and Manager of the Comedy Theatre ! This was much more of an adventure in those days, when actor-managers were rare ; later, of course, the world bristled with them. And to us it was an amazing and delightful task—a game, a gamble, a gambol ! The days of rehearsal were fraught with excitement and joyous expectation, nor was there any disappointment in store for us. To me was entrusted the care of seeing that the extra ladies (such lovely extra ladies) should be dressed in a manner befitting a ball at " The Princess Morakoff's Palace in St. Petersburg." A grave responsibility—but I revelled in the *carte blanche* allowed me at Lewis and Allenby's. The cast included Lady Monckton, Marion Terry, Rosina Filippi, Beatrice Lamb ; Robert Pateman, Charles Sugden, Laurence Cautley, Sant Matthews, Frederick Harrison, Charles Brookfield, Edmund Maurice, etc., etc., etc.—and, last and first, Herbert, as the head of the Secret Police. The play was produced April 20th, 1887, with great success—a success that grew and grew, so that Herbert and Comyns Carr used to hide in the Box Office, rejoicing like happy children over the ever-increasing demand for seats.

What was sport to them was death to our home life for the time being. I remember terribly lonely hours at Rosary Gardens while those Three Musketeers, Stuart Ogilvie, Comyns Carr and Herbert, kept the *Red Lamp* burning between the Comedy Theatre and the Garrick Club. My halcyon days, when I took part and was allotted all the leading parts in Herbert's productions, were yet to come. But days were half halcyon even then, for I shared in the joyful excitement of the success, I was happy in my engagement at the St. James's, and I was often summoned by the Three to a Café Royal lunch—and there was always the joy of fetching Herbert at his theatre after my theatre, and of the coming home together.

The Red Lamp became the fashion, and Herbert's catchword " I wonder ! " a colloquialism. The phrases of the play lent fun to our daily life. We did not ask for the bell to be rung—we cried, " One touch to the communicator, and oh ! how hideous a ruin ! " Questions as to time were answered, " It is the dawn, mad woman—it is the dawn ! " We must sometimes have astonished our own and other people's servants. " Ay, the dawn of blood ! " is no sort of answer to the meek question, " Will you call in the morning, ma'am ? "

By the way, Herbert always professed an indescribable dread and awe of butlers. " They make me feel apologetic," he said ; and of one or two of his acquaintances he used to complain,

" They frighten me, just as butlers frighten me." Yet all servants adored him, and loved to serve him—his manner to dependents, the happy mean between grand-seigneury and simplicity, was perfect.

But for his salary as actor, I think Herbert was not enriched by the success of *The Red Lamp*. A mysterious prophecy was often whispered, but never, I think, fulfilled : " Next week we shall touch profits."

Our life brimmed with laughter, for we were constantly in the company of that King of Mirth, Comyns Carr, of W. S. Gilbert (who could not speak without uttering a witticism), F. C. Burnand, George Grossmith, Oscar Wilde, John Toole, the Hares, the Kendals, the Bancrofts, the Peruginis—all the joy of the London world. Herbert, steeped in humour himself, not only adored it in others, but was the cause of it ; putting light to the flame and keeping it alive with his reciprocity and joyousness.

Lady Bancroft was one of these flames, and, with Herbert as audience-in-chief, she used, at famous Sunday dinner-parties in Berkeley Square, to keep the table in a roar. Can one ever forget her story of finding a fierce soldier confabulating with her cook in the kitchen ? Upon summary dismissal, the intruding warrior ascended the area steps with terrifying dignity, fierce protest and loud and awesome threats of vengeance by gun, sword and War Office. As the gate closed against him, he leaned over the railings and called, in a small, meek voice, " Emerly, give me my 'at." She told this the same night that George Grossmith kept us in shrieks by his account of two ladies who met and made friends on the Margate boat. Tea and shrimps called forth the best and the worst in them. For, having ascertained one another's name and made many appointments to meet, at parting : " Pardon me, Mrs. Smith, but your bonnet's a one-side." " Favour for favour, Mrs. Jones, there's a smut on your nose." They separated, deadly enemies.

It was at a brilliant party at the Burnands' that I gave utterance to my notorious *bêtise*. In great jealousy I said to my companion, " Oh, look ! Herbert is going in to supper with such a lovely woman. I wish he had taken *you* in ! " Luckily my unlucky remark was made to one of the most beautiful women in London—Mrs. John Hare ; but when it appeared in *Punch*, I think.du Maurier did not let me off so easily.

Delightful friends we had, and kept, though some of them, alas ! are gone now. First and foremost, Hamilton Aïdé ; through him, dear, adorable Mary Clarke—so brilliant, so wise, so witty ! The gifted wife of Colonel Stanley Clarke, her constant affection and friendship were of the proudest privileges ever bestowed upon Herbert and me. He loved her, admired her, and looked up to her as she deserved ; and her understanding and appreciation of him was as unbounded. A beloved friend, whose loss to her world is ever to be deplored. Then there were the Pineros, the Jeunes, the Charles Lawrences, the Manners, the d'Oyly Cartes, Arthur Sullivan, the Boughtons, the Tennants, the Lionel Tennysons, Frederick Locker, Whistler. If it was a coterie, what a coterie ! Surely of many colours !

Our Summer holiday was our first at Cromer and its adjoining " Poppyland." I remember that it was the Alexanders who told us of its advantages ; therefore thither we repaired—with much preamble and perambulator (I expect I went first, for such arrangements were left to me until they broke down ; then, all our life together, Herbert, once appealed to, could instantly repair disasters). Cromer, in those days, a huge church, two tiny streets and a sea ! At first the hotel—half cliff, half inn, with many stages and no particular recommendations—then a lodging search, which bequeathed us the landlady joke, " You'll get a loverly view of the railway-station." The town having failed us, we repaired to the ruined church, the broken, poppied cliff, and one cottage, which constituted Overstrand. We took the cottage, dreamed in the ruined church, drowsed on the cliffs. Viola was an amazing child with waves and sand ; Herbert as amazing a Poseidon. The sea seemed to belong to him and her.

CHAPTER II

WHEN Herbert began his Great Adventure—the taking of the Haymarket Theatre, in the autumn—he transferred the now famous *Red Lamp* from the Comedy Theatre, and preceded it by that lovely little play—sacred, I hope, to himself—*The Ballad-Monger*. Here Herbert found a part, in Gringoire, exactly to his taste, and exactly suited to his personality and his powers. A dreamer, a reformer, a lover, a poet, a philosopher, a scorner of oppression, a saviour of the people—here were all things that were in his own nature ; and what passion, what tenderness, what beauty, what nobility he projected into the character !

I consider that Gringoire was one of Herbert's finest parts, and there can be no question that the whole evening's performance was among his greatest achievements, for to follow the sweet starveling, the graceful, ragged poet, with his tender, wistful pleading, or his ringing and passionate denunciation, by the fat, sleek, cat-footed, slumberous, dangerous Demetrius was a feat the very ease of which spelt genius.

To my astonishment, I was given the part of the Princess in *The Red Lamp*, while Marion Terry retained her part as Olga, and was Loyse in *The Ballad-Monger*. And what an unforgettable Loyse—how sweet and perfect the play, with its haunting music ! Did Maude Valerie White compose anything more lovely and compelling than " The Devout Lover " ? Had Ben Jonson inspired Walter Pollock to the words ?

The Devout Lover.

[*By permission of Messrs. Ricordi & Co.*

From the sublime of the Willett-built respectability of South Kensington we migrated to the ridiculous of the " House of the Seven Stables," as Herbert loved to recall my calling it. This was the upper part of a house in New Cavendish Street, whose lower part was the haunt of horses and carriages let out for hire. As a dwelling, when one had grown accustomed to a perpetual champ of bit and stamp of hoof, it was pleasant enough ; and pleasant and eager were the days that we spent there. Indeed, the three years at the Seven Stables were altogether happy—the happiest, the most unclouded, perhaps, of all our married life. We were at one in everything—in our work, in our leisure, in our friends ; and there was Viola, an ever-growing joy. It was a sweet time of mutual love and trust and the labour we delighted in—there was no pain to physic. And what happened in those three years ? Oh, mighty things ! There were laid the founda-tions—nay, more : there began to rise the walls of Herbert's future and greatness. When at last the run of *The Red Lamp* and *The Ballad-Monger* came to an end, *Partners*, an adaptation by Robert Buchanan of " Fromont Jeune et Risler Aîné " (immortal book !) was put on. Shall I record our first memorable quarrel ? Why not, since this is called " Herbert and I " ? Spoilt by my un-deserved uplifting to a leading part, I considered it my right to claim *all* leading parts (alas ! we wives of actors, how many of us fall not into this foolish mistake !). But Marion Terry was rightly and naturally chosen by all concerned for the wife in *Partners*. One night at supper (Herbert and I were alone) I put forward my grievance. " *Why* Marion Terry ? *Why* not me ? " Her-bert answered, with the utmost gentleness and consideration, that there could not be a question as to Marion's superior suit-ability, personality and appearance ; and I accepted this rebuke meekly enough. (I know she will not mind my confessing all this.) But, unluckily, Herbert still went on to say : " You see, the part needs extraordinary *sympathy* "—and this gentle implica-tion filled me with a sudden ungovernable rage. I am ashamed to say what absurd form my fury took : suffice it that Herbert got up from the table where we had been supping so happily, and left the house without a word. Domestic Drama, how well you know the situation ! The dismay—the doubting certainty that he will come back—the long hours of heart-broken sobbing, huddled in a window where watch can be kept for the longed-for return—the endless, remorseless moments until the almost despaired-of scrape of the latchkey—the piteous appeal for pardon ;—then, comfort, kindness, understanding, sweet reconciliation ! " Oh, blessing on the falling-out that all the more endears ! "

Partners should have been a success, it had all the necessary elements, but nothing very important came of it, and, as was his wont, Herbert quickly gathered himself together for his next venture. This was Sydney Grundy's version, called *The Pompadour*, of a French play, *Narcisse ;* and who but I was chosen for the heroine ? But I must explain how this came to be ; for though I had lovely clothes, and won a certain amount of praise, I was not temperamentally suited to the part. Because of my unforeseen success in the somewhat exacting part of the Princess in *The Red Lamp*, I had been promised an extraordinarily important rôle at a leading London theatre. I could not believe my senses ; and it was just as well I could not, for, when the play came to be cast, the joint authors would not hear of my being engaged ; and an actress of established renown was chosen in my place.

I was terribly disappointed and grieved—a state of things which Herbert's divine heart could not allow. He dried my tears, saying, " *You* shall be the Pompadour." The author was nothing loath ; and that is how I came to have so wonderful a chance—for no young actress ever had a greater. It was the most ambitious production that Herbert had as yet undertaken— and strenuous were the rehearsals, with that splendid and gifted North-country man, Sydney Grundy, presiding. In the last act, when Narcisse denounces the Pompadour, the " business " arranged was that he was to fling me, from my agonized clinging round his neck, down the steps of the market-cross. These steps were elaborately and solidly built, and in vain I tried to learn to be flung without hurting myself. " Act ! act ! " Herbert used to cry in frenzy—" You can't be hurt if you will only *act !* " This, however, I could not learn to do, and Herbert had to content himself with flinging me from the lowest step—a dreadful disappointment, and the cause, I believe he secretly thought, of the not too overwhelming success of the play.

However, *The Pompadour* did have a certain measure of favour—it ran for at least a hundred nights, and the beauty of the production won golden opinions. What a pretty scene that must have been—when Narcisse discovers in the Pompadour, through her singing of a long-ago song, the peasant-girl whom he had loved and lost ! The song, too, how lovely !—the words by Sydney Grundy ; the haunting music, with its spinning-wheel accompaniment, by George Henschel.

[*By permission of Messrs. Chappell & Co.*

In the summer, while *The Pompadour* was still being played, *Captain Swift* glided into being. This was the beginning of our long friendship with its author, Mr. Haddon Chambers, a delightful companion, whose merry, whimsical temperament was absolutely after Herbert's own heart. Herbert produced the play at a matinée in June, and it was an instant success ; though I remember his rage and chagrin when the important critic of an important paper began his article of otherwise glowing praise with the exclamation, " That fatal last act ! How many a play," etc., etc. We, Herbert, the author and I, determined

HERBERT TREE
ABOUT 1885.

it should not prove fatal in the long run—and a long run, indeed, was in store. As Captain Swift, the bushranger, whose fortunes flung him into the bosom of an ordinary English family, where he learns love and the loveliness of duty, the sweetness of home, the calm and balm of goodness, Herbert was superb—handsome, graceful, winsome, dangerous, poetic; there never was a finer study—though " study " is the wrong word, for Herbert did not give the part an instant's thought. It appealed to him, and he could not help acting it exactly as he did.

Between the trial matinée and the production in September, Herbert and I went to the Engadine for our summer holiday. Herbert had an instinctive dislike of dizzy heights and dangerous descents (he could never bear to see from a window painters and cleaners at their rocking elevation of the ladder's top). Therefore the twelve-hours' drive in an Einspänner from Coire to St. Moritz—a skip from chasm to chasm, a flitting on the very verge of precipitate death, was half-delight, half-terror. We felt that only the sure-footed good-nature of the ponies intervened between us and eternity. We got used to the uncertainty after a time, and were able to feel that amid those rushing glacier streams, amid those everlasting hills of snow, we two did not matter extraordinarily. This reminds me of a story he used to love and quote. Tennyson, looking at the stars through a telescope, turns round and says, after a long, silent gazing, " I don't think very much of our County Families ! "

Our hearts sank when we read in Baedeker that " at this point in the Engadine, all vegetation ceases ; " and we began to be home-sick for a beech-wood. But the great mountains, the glaciers, the meadows carpeted with wild flowers, soon dispelled our depression. At evening we arrived at the Kulm, and rubbed our eyes at emerging from the mystery and awe of the twilight hills and valleys to the glare of a smart hotel, with large numbers of diamond-laden ladies streaming into the *table d'hôte*.

After less than a week of winter sports by day and midsummer madness by night—such was the " note " of St. Moritz—we migrated to the simpler life of Pontresina. Simpler though it was, I must own that we hated it at first. The bare hotel,

along whose carpetless corridors ardent Alpo-maniacs " spudded "
incessantly ;   the " spudders " themselves (Herbert had, or
professed, a great contempt and loathing for these " spudders,"
as he christened them), with their conceited top-of-the-mountain
aspect and equipment ; the Spartan spirit of the commissariat ;
the desolate winter prevailing while the newspapers lied " July "
—all this seemed to us not in the happy holiday mood we were
seeking. However, Herbert, as always, soon acclimatized himself,
made friends, coined phrases, cracked jokes, organized expeditions, even climbed mountains—climbed *a* mountain, perhaps I
had better say, for he accomplished but one of those detestable,
never-to-be-forgiven feats. Having been at last induced to
take up our spuds and walk, I vaguely remember the starting
in the bitter summer darkness before dawn, after day-before
preparations of endless magnitude ; the long walk through dark-
ling valleys, the party in a long string, very happy and cheerful
for the first few hours—but gradually sobering down, for our
spirits fell into the abysses that our bodies escaped. I remember
the difficulty of picking one's way over the ploughed fields of
moraine-scattered glacier (not a glacier made of glittering white
ice, as one had supposed, but Regent Street, with the road
up, in muddy November), the gradual mounting in the gathering
day, but always in the shadow of some giant crag, so that life
and light were extinct ; the arrival at last—about midday
—at *very nearly* the top of the particular peak to be assailed.
Further than very nearly the top Herbert refused to let me
go. I have said he shrank from dizzy heights ; and though
he steeled himself to endure to the end, he could not bear it for
me—and I was left with all but the bravest spirits of our party
to sit upon a shuddering ledge and wait for the enthusiasts' return.
As they limped back, the proper spirit prevailed of something-
attempted-something-done ; but when a glowing German
Professor commiserated me on having forgone such glory,
" Glorious it was, yes," said Herbert ; " I wouldn't have
missed it for a thousand pounds. And I wouldn't do it again
for a million."

Lovely drives we used to have—drives that, with two hours
for lunch, took us all day—drives to Silvaplana, to Samaden,
to the Maloya Pass, which was nothing but an hotel on a

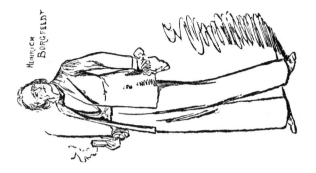

HENRICH BORGFELDT

[*Alfred Bryan.*]

BEERBOHM TREE

Hamlet.

MR TREE AS CAPTAIN SWIFT

By permission of "*The Illustrated Sporting and Dramatic News.*"]

glacier,* from whose terrace we looked down the slopes into Italy. That Pisgah sight made us feel homesick for summer. Herbert made friends and found friends everywhere ; and I think my unsociability grieved him ; but I had ever an absolute terror of being bored ; whereas he, a student of men, hardly knew the meaning of the word. Games bored him, certainly—golf, and cards, and cricket ; but swimming, riding, rowing and skating he revelled in ; and, though he did not care for it in a ballroom sense, his dancing was delicious—naturally spontaneous and gay.

On our way home from the Engadine we lingered for a few nights . seeing beautiful Nürnberg and stately Heidelberg ; then we made our way to our home and to *Captain Swift.*

As a quotation or motto for the play, my sister Bertha, she of poetic fancy and fine literary taste, suggested to Herbert the lovely words : " There is some soul of goodness in things evil," and they were delightedly adopted in all ensuing programmes and advertisements. Herbert's new reading of the last act put a seal on the success, and we never undertook a happier or more congenial enterprise. Those mysterious profits, too, began to be " touched," and I started the Early Victorian Era, as we called it—a little carriage, too obviously a hired one for fashionable feats, but a pleasant means of taking the air. Herbert, too, used to ride every day—he rode extremely well ; and it was very easy for us, with Mr. Brown, of horse and carriage fame, flourishing beneath the floor of our drawing-room, to satisfy our equine aspirations. Indeed, so easy and pleasant were the months of winter and spring that I remember nothing about them save contentment and prosperity. Ambition and enterprise were left to Herbert (and many plans were formulating in his busy brain) ; I lived but to act and to enjoy. I revelled in pretty clothes, and Herbert delighted to see me well-dressed, never scolding me, as he should have done, for my extravagance. We had a great many standing gaieties, such as Sunday luncheons and dinners, with such historic hosts as Lady Waterford, Lady Dorothy Nevill, the Wharncliffes, the Blumenthals—delightful parties at the Grosvenor Gallery ; many

---

* As a matter of dull fact, it is not on a glacier.—M.T.

and many a tiny supper or luncheon party at the theatre or at home.

Herbert had a kind of hero-worship for his father. Nothing gave him so much pleasure as when " The Sire," as I always called him, came to us to be entertained. Of course he was always a great figure at our more important feasts : but Herbert took childish delight in his father's dignified delight over good wines, choice food and a luxurious cigar at our own house : and I caught from Herbert a tender pride in trying to elicit approbation from this Spartan *bon viveur*.

Mr. Beerbohm (the name Beerbohm was originally Dutch, by the bye, and was spelt Beerboom) was born in 1810, the youngest son of parents who lived to an extreme old age, and of a family of immense strength and splendid physique, so that it was said " Nothing kills a Beerbohm but an axe." The home for generations was a small estate near Memel, on the Russian border. Herbert's sisters describe this as a rambling house, long and low and wide, with many outbuildings and stables and with a beautiful garden, a riot of syringa and honeysuckle. Distinguished guests, such as an Emperor of Russia and a King of Prussia, seem to have been welcomed in what must evidently have been this picturesque and romantic home of the Beerbohms on the Baltic Sea. But these august visitations must have occurred either before or after the time of Herbert's father, for he did not personally encounter them. At eighteen he left Germany altogether, and took up his abode in France, loving all his life French people and everything that was French. He was somewhat of a dandy in those days, and his great height and good looks gained him a nickname among his Parisian friends. They called him, not Monsieur Beerbohm, but " Monsieur Su-perbe Homme." After ten years he migrated to England, where, lodging in St. James's Square, he led a bachelor existence, full of gay and simple *joie-de-vivre*. He did not marry till he was forty, and then he chose the charming and radiant Constantia Beerbohm, who died, alas ! before her thirtieth year.

He was a man of beautiful, courtly manners ; of divine humour, of wide intelligence, of vivid industry, tempered by vivid absent-mindedness. (It is told of him that he once journeyed by omnibus and walked into his office with his bed-room slippers under his arm instead of his newspaper.) He could not bear to be bored. I remember that once, when fun was flagging, I saw him get up gropingly. " What are you looking for, Sire ? " I asked. " The door," he answered grimly. But he joined with the greatest glee in the laugh against himself when I rallied him. He had great culture and an astounding memory, and an astounding capacity for learning, without being what is called a scholar. Already master of seven European languages, he was learning an eighth, Anglo-Saxon, when he died.—When he died !—I cannot bear to remember Herbert's grief.

Then there was " The Lady." (I called them The Sire and The Lady because they were the best examples of gentle-people that I ever met.) The Lady (Herbert's stepmother) was a pattern of distinction and humour : of beautiful manners, of witty converse—the most delightful companion in the world. She had extraordinary energy and vitality—and an extraordinary activity of mind and body. To the day of her death, though the frail body became weak and the large mind became clouded, she continued to welcome, to dismiss and to appraise with persistent and unassailable humour. Her love for her husband and children and step-children was an engulfing one : she would have died every day to save them. She loved me, too, and our children ; we ought always to be grateful for so much love.

In the spring Herbert essayed his first Shakespearean produc-tion—the forerunner of his famous category. The rich humour of Falstaff, in *The Merry Wives*, had always attracted him ; while the fairy fantasy of the last act touched a chord in him which was ever vibrant. And to me, to be allowed to sing and skip at will, as Anne Page, was unalloyed delight. Rose Leclercq, that sweetest of women, that fine actress, was of course a Merry Wife. She had a heart as light as mine. She and I used rarely to address one another except in song ; the merest morning greeting meant a joyous little dance. She was with us for many years ; and I never entered the theatre without a high-pitched kind of bugle-call—" O, my dear lady, lady, lady, lady ; Oho, my dear lady ! "

She used to answer me in her clear voice, and it became as mechanical in the theatre as " Beginners, please."

Mr. Kemble's Dr. Caius, Mr. Kemble's strange, rich, mellow personality, Mr. Kemble's unique, if somewhat sardonic, humour —what a joy they were to Herbert! Mr. Brookfield's Slender, Robson's Sir Hugh Evans:—indeed every performance of *The Merry Wives* was fraught with enjoyment to that splendid Falstaff, whose light feet twinkled to the gay and tender tunes of Nicolai and Sullivan. (Strange! it may have been fancy, engendered by his " make-up," but I always thought he danced, as Falstaff, with the peculiar grace and buoyancy that only fat men have, if they dance at all : like a bobbing cork on the water, as distinguished from a straw.)

Herbert had already begun what was probably the first inception of a Repertory Theatre : *The Merry Wives* was pro-

duced at a series of matinées, while *Captain Swift* was running at night ; and *Masks and Faces* he gave, also at matinées— he as Triplet (lovely performance), Mrs. Bernard Beere as Peg Woffington, I as Mabel Vane ; a delightful experience for us ; a tremendous success with our audiences. I shall be corrected, I daresay, if I affirm that Herbert initiated Wednesday as well as Saturday matinées—but it is my impression that it was he who made this important innovation.

In June, while we were acting *The Merry Wives*, we took a furnished house on Hampstead Heath, with a garden full of roses, and with pleasant Victorian rooms. It was delicious for Viola, who made her first acquaintance with the Hampstead donkeys ; but, because of our work and the gaieties of the London season, in which we took our full share, we were there but little except on Sundays. The little carriage used to fetch us early in the day, and bring us home, often in the small hours of the morning. I remember one occasion when it waited for us at the stage-door of the Lyceum Theatre until, in the reproachful splendour of the morn, we emerged after a supper-party given by Sir Henry Irving for the Prince of Wales (King Edward). This was a wonderful entertainment of music and roses, and a huge round table on the stage at which sat not a great many guests, but a small gathering of interesting and distinguished people. I recall this because the record of it is among a very few entries in a Diary for 1889.

One annual festivity which gave us never-failing joy was the New Year's Eve party at the George Lewis' wide, warm, warm-hearted house in Portland Place. Regularly as December itself, we were invited and royally entertained from the first year that we knew them, until the death of the kind and princely host and our well-beloved friend, Sir George Lewis. To attempt a list of the light-hearted, laughter-loving guests who pulled crackers and set plum-puddings afire on those gleeful occasions would be vain—a mere Who's Whoism—but if I close my eyes I see and hear—motley as to the shape of the paper caps on their heads and pandemonium as to tin whistles in their mouths—Sargent, Tadema, Galsworthy, Pinero, Ellen Terry, Barrie, Ray Lankester, Mason, Anthony Hope, Benson, Burne-Jones, Sylvia du Maurier (to whom *Who is Sylvia?* always seemed to me to have been written), Henry James and Harry and Laurence Irving, with Herbert always the gayest of the gay.

It was at the Lewis' hospitable house that we first met Sir Ernest Cassel, at whose generous hands we received many and costly kindnesses. Dinners—they were banquets; suppers —they were—well, what best the Blue Hungarian Band loved to accompany; long week-ends and lovely Christmas presents; what peerless hosts he and his lovable sister—and as godfather to Iris, what a princely pearl-finder and gift-bringer! He was everything to all of us that a good friend could be, and an unfailing source of the excitements and joys that lay so largely in his power to give.

There were a regular set of non-theatrical Sunday dinner-givers—the Seymour Trowers, the George Boughtons, the Carl Meyers, the Morel Mackenzies, the de la Rues and the Heilbuts—by all of whom it was a privilege to be asked and a joy to be entertained. (Herbert had known the Heilbuts all their married life, and knew Mr. Heilbut well enough to call him " Sam." I remember " Sam " Heilbut once entertained Viola,

King John.

[From "The Pall Mall Budget."

MR BEERBOHM TREE.

A Village Priest.

MR BEERBOHM TREE IN TWO CHARACTERS.

MR TREE AS FALSTAFF (AND A CUP OF SACK)

Laroque-Luversan.

[By permission of "The Illustrated Sporting and Dramatic News"

Herbert and me the whole way from Calais to Paris by showing us card tricks, being, *en amateur*, a master of sleight-of-hand.)

Then there were wonderful dream-like parties in the great studios of Tadema, Leighton, Millais, Watts, Poynter, Burne-Jones and Alfred Gilbert. Here, in grand and mystic setting, one listened to the divine discourse of music, one nestled in the very heart of culture and learning and beauty.

Regularly as a dog licence, each succeeding January brought me a smart new Diary. But I must have been loath to sully those fair, polished pages, for scarcely ever are they marred by mark of pen or pencil. The bright blue one for this year, however, has red-letter days, for in it a miracle occurs. Towards the end of July there are records by Herbert himself :

July 24.   Little Viola went out to Dinard with Marie to stay with the old folks from home. We went to *Otello* (opera). Tamagno and Maurel sang and acted splendidly as Othello and Iago.

July 25.   We started on our Continental tour, leaving Hampstead at 9.30 a.m. Uneventful day—not even sea-sickness (thank Heaven !), although the sea was rough. Dined at the " Filet de Sole " Restaurant in Brussels—capital dinner —started again at 11 p.m.

July 26.   All day in train—read Amélie Rives' play, *Andrea Vertoni*—much struck with its passionate force—wonder whether she will do great things—determined to ask her to adapt for the stage Rossetti's " Last Confession." Arrived at eight o'clock at Munich—went to " Vier Jahreszeiten " Hotel.

Then, alas ! no more Diary ; but how vividly even those few scribblings recall that holiday—those holy days—wonderful and ever-to-be-grateful-for !

"GRINGOIRE."

"THE DUKE OF GUISEBURY."

"FAGIN."
A pastel by Charles Buchel.

"PAUL DEMETRIUS."

Though the recording impulse in Herbert gave out, in me it lingered for a few more days. I find that on July 29th we arrived at Salzburg ; that the next day we drove to Aigen—" long walk to top of green wooded hill "—that on July 30th we spent the morning exploring the salt-mine at Berchtesgaden, and afterwards drove to the beautiful Königsee—" a lovely dream of a lake surrounded by mountains, getting there at six o'clock, just when the light was loveliest : dined on the banks of the lake, drove home in the dark—Happy day ! "

We lingered in Ausee, in Ischl, in Munich, to find ourselves, at last, listening, enraptured, to *Tristan and Isolde* at Bayreuth. Our stay in the same house as the Henschels at Bayreuth, and Bayreuth's operas were an intoxicating delight to Herbert ; he revelled in every hour, inasmuch as for Wagner, not only as a maker of music but as a maker of plays, he had the most profound reverence and admiration. The joy and humour of the *Meistersingers ;* the love and wonder and tragedy of *Tristan ;* the sacred beauty of *Parsifal* (for Herbert was, in the depths of him, a religious man) made calls upon his heart, his imagination, his sense of beauty, such as nothing else in the world. The time spent in Bayreuth, both within and without that Temple of Art, was, to him, one of utter enchantment and bliss. I remember that there were faults in the production of *Parsifal ;* details that marred emotion and came short of perfection ; but the Good Friday morning meadows seemed to convey to him something of the divine. " I cannot bear it," he would say : " it is too beautiful "—his blue eyes full of yearning tears, and his hand seeking one's hand for sympathy.

Immediately upon our return, we must have plunged into hard work ; the long and difficult rehearsals of *A Man's Shadow*, Mr. Sydney Grundy's version of *Roger la Honte*. In this, Herbert accomplished one of the many of his amazing *tours de force*—doubling the parts of Luversan and Laroque. The play was produced on September 12th, and was an immense success. Herbert's double performance was startling in its perfection ; whether as the bewildered and tortured hero (Oh, how exactly like himself was Herbert in his tender, agonized appeal to his little child, who unconsciously condemned him ! The tears

of blood in his eyes and in his voice !) ; or as the debauched,
absinthe-sodden villain, with his harsh, satiric singing :

Minnie Terry, a child of eight, was the exquisite little exponent of Suzanne, with the historic phrase, " I saw nothing—
I heard nothing." That daughter of the gods, divinely fair,
brilliant Julia Neilson, was the " wicked woman," and what
a wonder of beauty she was ! Gifted to an inordinate degree,
and born with the dramatic sense, she, an amateur, had nothing
to learn. Indeed, her fault in those days, if she had a fault,
was that her acting was too technical for her years.

An isolated entry in the aforesaid blue diary tells me :

December 16.   Hundredth performance of *A Man's Shadow*
—Herbert has man's supper-party—
Irving makes touching speech in honour
of Herbert's father.

This was one of many a Haymarket Theatre supper-party
—a form of entertainment that Herbert revelled in, and
welcomed any excuse for giving. Unless the party were a very
large one, as on the 200th or 300th night of *Captain Swift*,
when the stage was requisitioned, he used to give these little
feasts in the only room available at the Haymarket—the first-

floor room of the little Georgian house in Suffolk Street which served as an annexe to the theatre. This was used as an office by Herbert and Mr. Comyns Carr, and I used to subject it to much " charring " on supper nights, for it was always left to me to grapple with flowers, lights, luxuries and Gunter.

How Herbert loved hospitality! What a crime it was in his eyes not to give, if one gave at all, the very best of things!

Our home-life at New Cavendish Street was, as I have said, very even and entirely happy—the days almost unvarying. He used to leave for the theatre at eleven, often borrowing Viola for the drive in his hansom, and come back to dine towards five o'clock, seldom without bringing someone to eat with us —or someone unwilling to eat at that hour, but willing to watch *us* do so. This early dinner-hour was Viola's *bonne-bouche* hour. It was then that she learnt the taste for asparagus in March and strawberries in May (for it was my delight to please Herbert by springing on him culinary surprises, as it was my custom to provide for and welcome any chance guest he chose to bring home with him). One of our most frequent visitors was Charles Allan : combined actor, secretary, *gourmet*, butt and wit, and an unfailing source of humour—at Allan's smiling expense —to Herbert. Of him Herbert invented the story (after a repast of which, as hostess, I had been particularly proud, and for which I had hoped for thanks and praise) : " I am afraid it hasn't been a very good dinner, Mr. Allan ? "—" Oh, thank you, Mrs. Tree ; it does one good to underfeed sometimes." And again, when we had filled and refilled his glass with our nearest approach to Château Lafitte : " Talking of cheap claret, Mrs. Tree, I know a man who "—etc.

These are two of the hundreds of Allanania which made laughter for us during the years that that good and gentle friend was with us. He was content with the tiniest parts, and was what is called a "safe " actor. Once—it was in *The Village Priest*—he had only one appearance to make, as a *gendarme* in the last act, and only two words to say : " *Allons ! Marche !* " Sir Henry Irving came to see the play, to our intense excitement ; and at the end, when the great guest came on to the stage, Herbert and I waited for his praise, which indeed we deserved, for the production was exquisite, and Herbert's own part—the gentle old Abbé—one of his masterpieces. Irving came, and uttered but these words : " Good night ! Allan excellent ! God bless you ! "

The Village Priest followed *A Man's Shadow,* which was attended on its last night (in April) by Mr. and Mrs. Gladstone.

Mr. Gladstone came on to the stage after the play, and asked as to the political opinions of the theatrical world. Herbert answered, " Conservative, on the whole ; but," he added hastily, as he saw a darkening in his distinguished visitor's face, " the scene-shifters are Radical almost to a man." They parted firm friends.

The part of the Abbé du Bois, in *A Village Priest,* was one after Herbert's heart ; and sweet and lovely was his performance. After all these years, one remembers the gentle, humorous, absent-minded old man ; browbeaten by his shrew-tongued housekeeper, as he sat beneath his blossoming apple-tree ; the friend of his flowers, and adored of his flock, diffusing an atmosphere that hung between earth and Heaven, but always nearer Heaven. The Abbé's garden was an enchanting scene, with its old high wall, its all-but growing flowers, and its all-but real fruit-tree in blossom. We owed that apple-tree to the genius of Alfred Parsons, who made us a most wonderful water-colour sketch of what an apple-tree in full blossom should be— a lovely little picture which he gave us, which Herbert treasured and which Comyns Carr envied him. Between them, I, who had set my heart on it, lost control of its destiny, and alas ! I have it not. But somewhere there exists an Alfred Parsons gem which belongs to Herbert and me. In dwelling upon that peaceful garden and the picture's blossoming loveliness, which we did our best to reproduce, I bear in mind that it was thirty years ago : but I do not know that anything of to-day in the way of stage-setting has put that sunny scene-plot into the shade.

The story of *A Village Priest* (an adaptation by Sydney Grundy of *Le Secret de la Terreuse*) led to interesting and exciting controversies. The subject of the dispute was put forward by a well-known critic, an ardent Roman Catholic, who bitterly resented it being allowed that the violation of

Mr. and Mrs. Gladstone at the Haymarket Theatre.

the Confessional should be presented as possible, even as an episode in a stage-play. In the course of the discussion, Herbert read and wrote many scorching letters in the Press. Several of his passionate ebullitions were, by my advice, torn up as soon as written : but the public discussions did no sort of harm (they seldom do) to the popularity of the play. " We acquit the dramatist at once of any intention to attack the Roman Catholic priesthood. He has erred in ignorance and his error is also false in art. A noble drama could have been made of the subject if the Abbé had been kept faithful under all trials to his duty." (*Catholic Times*, 25th April, 1890.)

One day in May (Marion Terry and Fred Terry and the Ogilvies had been lunching with us), we hired one of the many carriages that, so to speak, grew beneath our feet, and drove to Hampstead, with no more fixed intention than a post-prandial air-taking. As luck—or ill-luck—would have it, we chanced upon a large house standing on the summit of the Heath, surrounded by three acres of garden, and by large meadows, bearing the irresistible legend, " To Let Unfurnished." Before evening it was ours, and in a few weeks we said good-bye to our Seven Stables, and were ensconced, pic-nic fashion, at The Grange. By dint of distemper and riotous rummaging in old-furniture shops, we made it very pretty and charming, and we both loved it. It was a paradise for Viola, who looks back with love and regret to the many delights of Heath and garden. Could we but have foreseen the coming of the Tube and the Taxi we might never have known any other home : for a sweeter could not be conceived. As it was, when the perfect days of our first summer and autumn there had hardened into the grimmest winter on record, we all three lived—for we just did live— to regret our warm little house in New Cavendish Street.

But many and momentous things happened in our theatre-world before then. *A Village Priest* ran its triumphant course from April to mid-July, shortened a little after the first month or two, to make room for W. S. Gilbert's *Comedy and Tragedy*, which was played as a first piece by Julia Neilson and Fred Terry and proved a great attraction. In May, June and July there were many gaieties, some of which are recorded as engagements in my ill-kept diary. The Grossmiths, the Arthur Lewis, the George Lewis, the de la Rues, the Morel Mackenzies gave dances; the Manners, the du Mauriers, the Bancrofts, the Kendals, the Luke Fildes were our hosts and our guests, and often we went to political parties, brilliant and interesting, at Lady Salisbury's house in Arlington Street. We lunched one Sunday with the Sémons, to meet Hans Richter, and Herbert made a note in a scribbling-book of mine: " Hans Richter said of Verdi, on being reminded of the great influence that Wagner had exercised on his later works: ' Ah, yes, he has improved greatly to his disadvantage.' "

There were two parties, late in July, the remembrance of which has never been effaced: one, at Lady Ardilaun's, I remember because it was the most perfect thing that a party could be. A radiant summer night, wherein we left the lovely, stately house for the lighted garden—the first coming of the Hungarian Band, with its wild and haunting mystery of music; the gloss of satin and glimmer of pearls, the brilliant assembly—unforgettable delight to us both. The gipsy-music thrilled Herbert's gipsy heart to the very core; and there was one thing he begged them to play again and again (from *Der Vogel Händler*, I think): it was as ecstasy to him, and he christened it " Nothing Matters." That, of course, became a household word with us, and he used it as the title of his second book. But his own faith was not so cynical, for his final conclusion at the end of one of his stories was: " Nothing Matters? The pity of it. Everything matters."

Another memorable evening was our first at the Foreign Office. It was in the magnificent days, and the splendour of the scene made Herbert thirst to reproduce on the stage such a glittering effect of colour, music and grandeur; of all the wealth and dignity and worth of the world. He spoke of it to one of the greatest of our statesmen. Mr. —— answered, " I have written a play; and the third act could be the staircase of the Foreign Office." The play came to us in due course, and I have it still. I do not know to this day why it was never produced: I think because the great man, its author, would not allow his authorship to leak out, much less to be attached to it. Herbert, I suppose, did not think the play, without the *réclame* of its famous writer's name, would justify an enormously expensive production. Also he may not have liked the part destined for him. At all events, the excitement flourished, languished, and presently died. But I am grateful for an episode that brought us into familiar touch with one of the greatest brains, one of the most powerful personalities of our time.

Herbert had always ridden ; and Viola learnt from him both to swim and to ride while yet in infancy ; but I must candidly confess that even now I do not know upon which side of a horse one had better attempt to get up. Whichever it is, it never seems to be the side that one generally falls off. While we were at Hampstead, Herbert's lawyer, Mr. Webb, who lived near us, thought that I ought to be taught to accompany Herbert and him upon the many riding expeditions that they took together. So he brought a beautiful horse (I suppose experts would call it a mare)—Princess—from his own stable, and all through the sweet summer weather we used to go forth early, we three (I vainly pretending not to hold on by the mane). I found it (except galloping, which terrified me, and trotting, which I could not learn) extraordinarily pleasant and exhilarating, and a divine way of seeing " how greenly wave the chestnut leaves when the earth is full of joy." We first knew dear Mr. Webb during one of our financial crises, when we were at Cheyne Walk, and from that day to this he has been our good and faithful friend. Herbert and I used to amuse ourselves by trying to find the thing that Mr. Webb did not know, the subject he had not studied, the science he was not master of. We never succeeded. His inveterate habit of knowledge always spoilt the game. In trying to teach me to ride he would lightly scour the world of literature and art ; natural history and botany ; the stars, the earth, the sea, and the story of mankind—though often my battle with that terrible and elusive weapon, the stirrup, would interrupt the flow of his wisdom. I might have ended as a circus rider, but that those genial lessons did not outlive our sojourn at Hampstead.

Our summer holiday was spent among the roses in our own

garden, with busy mornings at the theatre, preparing for Herbert's first provincial tour. This began on August 3rd, at Brighton, whence we went to the then new and now all-familiar towns : Dublin, Edinburgh, Glasgow, Liverpool, Birmingham, Manchester. How we both enjoyed it ! And what success, what friends, what glad experience were gained by Herbert wherever he went ! What influence was spread ! The utmost luxury and indulgence were mine ; my only grievance was that I was homesick for Viola, for I had to leave her behind after Brighton. Herbert's gentle heart, loving nothing better than to spring a glad surprise, conceived the plan of bringing her back with him " as a present " when he had to travel from Liverpool to London for Sunday. I remember the fun and joyousness of his putting a rug over her and pretending she was luggage when I met him at the Birmingham station. Above all things, Herbert welcomed fun ; and he liked birthdays, anniversaries, present-giving and present-receiving ; the hidden Easter egg, the secret Christmas stocking ; the gift expected and traditional, or the gift unexpected and whimsical—how often has he not entered into their joys !

On September 27th, I find in my diary : " Last day of tour. The dear Company present Herbert with beautiful silver present. Mr. Fernandez makes charming speech, and makes both Herbert and me cry. How dear of him ! And how sweet to feel how they love and respect Herbert, and how proud they are of what he has done."

The theatre reopened with *A Village Priest* and *Comedy and Tragedy*. But Repertory schemes were surging in Herbert's brain ; he could not content himself with quiet, long runs to moderate profits ; though those about him questioned the wisdom of his unrest. Indeed, in obstinately inaugurating his " Special Monday Nights " Herbert defied the better judgment of all those who thought they knew anything about theatrical enterprise. Perhaps they were right, but only because Herbert was many years in advance of his time, and, alas ! many thousands in advance of his banking-account. He tried to do in 1890 what was looked upon as a new idea in the next century. But perhaps an actual quotation of Herbert's speech on the first night of *Beau Austin* (with which the " Haymarket Mondays " began) will tell its own tale :

" LADIES AND GENTLEMEN,

"Mr. Henley is in Edinburgh—and Mr. Stevenson is, alas ! in the Antipodes in search of health. But I am sure that both gentlemen will be gratified to hear of the brilliant manner in which their joint work has been received by you. I cannot help adding my own thanks for the auspicious manner in which we have been able to inaugurate the Monday nights, which I hope may prove a regular institution at this theatre. I hope we have at least succeeded in catching something of that old-world bloom which Mr. Henley refers to in his Prologue. I will take this opportunity of removing a slight misapprehension which has arisen about our Monday nights. I have seen it stated that we intend to present a new play every Monday ; but admirable as this plan sounds in the abstract, it labours under the disadvantage of being physically impossible. Nothing less than a strike of the Haymarket Company would be the outcome of such an attempt to encompass the unattainable. But, ladies and gentlemen, it will be my endeavour to present to you this winter season as frequently as may be the works of past and contemporary authors. Of course we shall be in a measure guided by popular support in this endeavour, but we shall not, however, consider the commercial aspect of the case of the first importance. Quite the reverse : although such a resolve may be regarded with some ridicule, that is what we mean to do. Mr. Whistler once remarked, ' There is something in a painter's art which even a photographer does not always attain to.' Ladies and gentlemen, allow me to thank you on behalf of Messrs. Henley and Stevenson and of my Company for the kindly way in which you have received our efforts."

Beau Austin ! What a jewel of a play ! Herbert's performance of the Exquisite—how exquisite ! I am proud indeed to have been included in that cast, to have been concerned in so memorable, so historic an event as a play by Stevenson and Henley.

Prologue to *Beau Austin*, by W. E. Henley

" ' To all and singular,' as Dryden says,
  We bring a fancy of those Georgian days,
  Whose style still breathed a faint and fine perfume
  Of old-world courtliness and old-world bloom ;
  When speech was elegant and talk was fit,
  For slang had not been canonized as wit ;
  When manners reigned, when breeding had the wall,
  And women—yes !—were ladies first of all ;
  When Grace was conscious of its gracefulness,
  And man—though Man !—was not ashamed to dress.
  A brave formality, a measured ease
  Were his and hers—whose effort was to please,
  And to excel in pleasing was to reign,
  And, if you sighed, never to sigh in vain.

*   *   *   *   *   *   *

" But then as now, maybe something more—
  Woman and man were human to the core.
  The hearts that throbbed behind that quaint attire
  Burned with a plenitude of essential fire.
  They too could risk, they also could rebel,
  They could love wisely—they could love too well.
  In that great duel of sex, that ancient strife
  Which is the very central fact of life,
  They could—and did—engage it breath for breath ;
  They could—and did—get wounded unto death,
  As at all times since time for us began
  Woman was truly woman—Man was man ;
  And joy and sorrow were as much at home
  In trifling Tunbridge as in mighty Rome.

" Dead—dead and done with ! Swift from shine to shade
  The roaring generations flit and fade.
  To this one—fading, flitting, like the rest,
  We come to proffer, be it worst or best,
  A sketch, a shadow of the brave old time ;
  A hint of what it might have held sublime ;
  A dream, an idyll—call it what you will,
  Of man, still Man, and woman—Woman still ! "

It was some years later that Herbert put on the stage,
Stevenson and Henley's *Robert Macaire*, but he must have been

thinking of it before 1887 (when Stevenson left Bournemouth), as this letter to him from the great author proves :

> " Bonallie Tower,
>> " Branksome Park,
>>> " Bournemouth,
>>>> " January 2nd.

" DEAR SIR,
 " Mr. Henley may have perhaps sent you on a note, but it was in his discretion ; very likely he has not ; and if so, why all the better, as fresh study of the problem has changed my views, and I write now to say that I am in love with the idea of recasting Robert ; keeping the murder, and in fact the lines of the whole second act, and simply making a new and entirely. comic first act. I believe we have some ideas that will do well ; your proposal was, I think, inspired ; a better subject cannot be imagined ; and if the thing be done as it deserve, an actor should get effects of laughter and of occasional strength out of it, quite *à la* Robson, that should bring the house down.

 " In all matters of arrangement, of course, continue to deal with Mr. Henley ; but may I say that I am persuaded, and so, I think, is he, that three weeks should be enough to run the thing together.

> " Yours truly,
>> " ROBERT LOUIS STEVENSON.

" H. Beerbohm Tree, Esq."

I am proud to have it thus writ down that Stevenson thanks Herbert for an " inspired proposal " ! As to Mr. Henley, he often came to see us, and we delighted to honour him. Once, at Sloane Street, he and Mrs. Henley brought with them to our five o'clock dinner their little girl, well called by them " the golden child," for she was like a ray of light, a being of ineffable loveliness and charm, whose death, when she was but a baby of four, must literally have broken her father's heart.

Many rehearsals and the growing importance of Herbert's managerial work made the top of Hampstead Heath seem a very

long way from the Haymarket ; and hansoms hastily fetched
by the gardener from Finchley Road were our only means of
reaching London. Sometimes, starting late, we used to tear
on foot down those long hills that lay between us and the cab-
stand, anxious, foaming and panting at the delay ; and often,
as the winter came on, we had to quit our hansom at night and
walk up Fitzjohn's Avenue, rendered impossible for horses by
the frost.   Then came heavy snowfall and drifts, through which
we had to cut our way at the stern bidding of our work, or in
order to reach the light and warmth and comfort of The Grange
on our return.   It is not to be wondered at that in the New
Year I was stricken with rheumatic fever, and that Herbert
actually stayed " out of the bill " for one night with acute
bronchitis ! This was almost the first week of his triumphantly
successful production of *The Dancing Girl*, by Henry Arthur
Jones—and nothing would induce Herbert to give way to his
illness, or to surrender his part, in which he made one of the
greatest successes of his life. So he was taken away from The
Grange in a brougham, wrapped in blankets, and accompanied
by nurse and doctor, I weepingly watching him from the window
of my sick-room, and having my tears turned to laughter when
he insisted on putting on his top-hat over the rug that enveloped his head. He was put in hospital at the hotel next
door to the theatre, nursed all day, and permitted (because he
insisted) to act every night. This was the only actual illness
he ever had. Mine was a much longer one—and it was many
weeks before I could leave my room—so that I did not see *The
Dancing Girl* until it had been filling the theatre for about two
months, though I had been at all the rehearsals, and had seen
beautiful Julia Neilson grow into her wonderful performance,
Fred Terry into his, Lionel Brough, Rose Leclercq and Rose
Norreys into theirs. But I had not guessed what an enchanting
personality was to be given to the Duke of Guisebury by Herbert.

" Mr. Beerbohm Tree achieves by touches fine, as well as
touches broad, a marvellously lifelike portrait of the genial,
generous, courageous rake, cynically bent upon his own destruction. He is a delightful creature, this ducal defier of *les con-
venances*, as he chats to his dog, Bully-boy, as he dissembles on
the eve of his intended suicide, and as he prepares to wind up

his life as a game that he has played and lost." So wrote one of the most important of London critics—while the Hazlitt of those days pronounced: " Mr. Tree's performance is perfect ; " and added : " The third act places Mr. Tree (where he has not hitherto stood) on a level with our very best stage-managers. No social picture on so large a scale has ever been so successfully presented. It is a Du Maurier in action."

Herbert, the dare-devil Duke, fascinating, lovable, became the idol of the matinée girl ; Bully-boy, the goal of the dog-stealer ; beautiful Julia Neilson the very byword for the stealer of hearts ; and Rose Leclercq as the aunt of the " wicked Duke," the pattern for all time of the theatrical Great Lady. I remember the roar of laughter and applause that greeted her exit in the third act, when the Duke, having determined to take his life, tells her, as he bids her an affectionate adieu, that he is on the eve of a long journey : " I don't know where you're going, my dear ; but wherever you go, you'll shock them." Bully-boy was the most charming bulldog the world has ever known ; the adored of all who knew him, and the applauded of thousands, who hummed with excitement when the time came for his stately waddle on to the stage. He was lent us, for both home and theatre, by the Outram Tristrams, and he made much joy for us at The Grange, where Argus and he never had an instant's dispute, although, collie and bulldog, " by their nature they did not agree." Bully-boy, of course, had his song, which he listened to with proud complacency :

> " 'E's the pride of Piccadilly :
> 'E's the Pink of Pall Mall "—

And :

> " Oh, 'e's a beauty.
> What's 'is duty ?—
> Only let 'im know, 'e says,
> Then 'e'll be glad to go, 'e says "

(to the tune of a Strauss valse).

All this spring (1891) we had rooms at Garlant's Hotel, next door to the theatre, and we divided our time between hotel and home. As to me, a sojourn at Bath with my dear Lady

　　　CARICATURE BY "SPY."

Stanley Clarke had completely restored my health ; but Herbert, who had no " cure," no rest, no change, was sensitive to the after-effects of bronchitis until the early summer had come— and I tormented myself and him with anxiety about his health. There used to be many " scenes," because he would not take enough care, and, to anyone less tolerant than he, I should have been the Princess of bores. (I remember, as I write, that Herbert, as the Duke of Guisebury, gave as the reason of his undying love for the Dancing Girl, " she never bores me ; " a sentence repeated over and over again in answer to a screed of protest from his lawyer. I think Herbert must have written that thought himself. What a good thing for good women to add to their prayers for others : " Give me the strength, common sense and sympathy to keep me from being a bore ! ")

May and buttercup-time bring him restored health, and bring us back to what is by now our lovely home. (" Our lovely home," recalls that so-often distorted story of Herbert and the cabman : " Home !." he shouted through the hansom's roof. " Where, sir ? " asked the driver. " Do you think I'm going to tell a person like you where my beautiful home is ? " It was Comyns Carr who once said to a strange Jehu, " Drive on ; " and to the " Where ? " he answered, " The place whither they brought her warrior dead." Without another word the cab-man took him to his home.)

It was on the sunny terrace of the Hampstead house that " Spy " made his " Vanity Fair " caricature, and it was walking up and down that terrace that perhaps the most momentous episode in my stage career took place. Herbert had made up his mind to satisfy his deep longing to act Hamlet —and he was steeping himself in the beauty of it. My reign as leading-lady having now come to an end, I somewhat timidly approached the subject of Ophelia, and learnt to my grief and mortification that he had set his heart, not on Julia Neilson —which would have seemed inevitable and not to be fought against—but upon another actress, already famous, who seemed to him his ideal. I recognized the soundness of his judgment and the force of his arguments ; but I must have pleaded so pitifully, and have protested so meekly (an attitude always sym-pathetic to him), that at last he promised me I should at least essay Ophelia in Manchester, and my playing it in London should depend on the measure of my success. I always remember and bless that June day, that sunny terrace, that (for me) triumphant hour.

Meanwhile, though I was not sharing in the acting honours of *The Dancing Girl*, I shared in all the luxuries of its financial triumph ; and among many things, the best Broadwood that money could buy arrived at The Grange as a profitic present, a long-anticipated and well-rehearsed " surprise." This Tinkling Symbol of success has been a lasting delight such as no jewel could have given me. Among many famous musicians, fingers no less hallowed than Paderewski's have touched its dulcet keys.

Alas ! for the Repertory Theatre and the " Haymarket Mondays " ! These would have broken the brilliant run of the most popular play in London, and with silent acquiescence on both sides of the curtain they were dropped. As Herbert so pungently remarked in later years : " When is a Repertory not a Repertory ? "—" When it's a success."

With summer, while *The Dancing Girl* danced victoriously on to its crowded houses, there were many gaieties of the usual kind, some of them unusual and consequently remembered. Our first Derby, for instance : in Frank Lawson's box. Mary Lawson (once Mary Fortey, my college friend, afterwards Lady Benedict) was both admirer and admiree of Herbert. He found her finely humorous and intelligent. " She glints," he said : a golden opinion which she was proud to win. Herbert was amused by the Derby crowds—by Beauty at its worst, and Beasts at their best—but he took scant interest in the actual racing, though his eyes shone with delighted sympathy when any of our party won ten shillings, and he was laughingly tolerant of my first (and last) encounters with the book-making world. And hard upon this excursion into the racing sphere came another : our first Ascot. Herbert and I attended a *cause célèbre*, invited by Sir Edward Clarke, a lifelong friend ; during its course, Lord Coventry (then Master of the Buckhounds) leaned over to us and said, " Come to Ascot ? " And so we went ; to my inexpressible delight (I attended religiously on

MR BEERBOHM-TREE & MR HARE
IN COURT

MRS
FAUDELL
PHILLIPS

'SIR EDWARD CLARKE
ADDRESSING THE JURY.

The Baccarat Case.

all four days, and religiously every summer), and to Herbert's
somewhat jaded amusement (one day sufficed for him).

And with the end of June came the end of our Hampstead
home—so short-lived ; so often regretted. Now, after long
years, I wish with all my heart that we had never given it up.
But we left it almost without a sigh, so much did we dread the
thought of a second winter of our discontent, with all its attendant ills. Our pretty " furniture and effects " were warehoused
—thereby out-Harroding Harrod—while we light-heartedly
packed our trunks and set out for Scotland. There was not
time for the Engadine again—and Braemar was suggested as
the nearest approach to Switzerland's revivifying qualities.
So to Braemar we journeyed—Herbert, Viola, her governess
and I. It is recorded of poor little Viola that " she spoilt
Mother and Daddy's holiday "—a terrible indictment ! But,
in truth, she developed an extraordinary capacity for naughti-
ness, unsuspected, unprecedented and unrepeated. And, indeed,
during a fortnight of incessant rain, how could one expect a
little child, to whom butterflies and birds'-eggs were life (and
many a death), to enjoy long tramps by silver stream-paths
between purple mountains, amid angry skies, albeit sublime
with shifting light and colour ? Our stay was not prolonged
beyond the prescribed fortnight—and the rest of our July was
spent in Norfolk—at North Repps, a poppied two miles from
the sea. We had a lovely little house, covered with honeysuckle, and a garden full of lilies and pansies. Both here and
in Scotland, Herbert was hard at work—and how he revelled
in it !—studying *Hamlet.* I had learnt to love the play in my
girlhood, so that it was a joy and never a *gêne* (as with many
another part he had to learn !) to hear him his words. Herbert
admired Irving's Hamlet enormously ; had no criticisms
against it ; and boasted that he had seen it twenty times (this
was before he and I had met). His familiarity with Irving's
methods did but make his own enthusiasm the greater ; but
again I say that Herbert (perhaps it was a proof of genius,
perhaps it was a fault) concerned himself only with learning the
words of a part, however great. Master—or assistant-master
—of those, he acted them in spite of himself. In all his life

I have never known him " study " in the general acceptance of the word. So, sitting on the sands, lying on the cliffs, smoking in the clematis arbour, his Hamlet took form—and little Viola soon began to suck in the honey of the music words, as she heard them declaimed to sea and sky.

Relegating her to a little house we took at Sittingbourne— an Elizabethan cottage in the heart of a nut-wood, called Queen-Down Warren—we started on our tour, beginning on August 1st at Dublin. The now-famous *Dancing Girl* was, of course, the *pièce de résistance*, with Julia Neilson, Fred Terry, Lionel Brough and Fred Kerr, as in London ; while I was given the part of Sybil Creyke, the lame girl, which had been created and made momentous by Rose Norreys. It did not suit me in the least ; but I was delighted to be included in so brilliant an entertainment, which was received with ovations wherever we went. Sybil Creyke, of course, has to clamber down the great staircase, in spite of her lameness, just at the moment when the Duke, bent on suicide, raises the poison to his lips. I accomplished this feat perhaps a hundred times, but never without an agony of dread, lest I should not get there in time to place my restraining hand upon his. What would have happened had I, one night, failed to reach the Duke who, but for me, was a dead man ? No doubt Herbert would have invented some way of saving himself ; but it is the kind of terror that makes one " scream suddenly in the night." Apropos of this, Herbert used to tell an actor's story of a villain whom it was necessary to dispatch by a shot through the bars of the window that he was forcing. No shot was forthcoming, however, and yet he had to die—and rather than fail the situation, he cried, " My God ! I have swallowed the file ! " fell dead, and saved the play.

But *The Dancing Girl* paled its ineffectual fire before the glowing adventure of *Hamlet*. On this our thoughts and hearts were fixed ; and it came into being during the second week of our fortnight in Manchester. Although October, it was summer weather ; and, stifled in the hotel, we took a furnished house with a garden on the outskirts of the town. We sent for our own servants, and, of course, for Viola. Mr. Henschel came to stay with us—Mr. Henschel, who wrote the lovely overture and incidental music for Herbert's *Hamlet*.   It was a divine time—that time of getting ready—for, however long the rehearsals, one could never tire ; with such words to repeat ; such material to manipulate ; such enthusiasm as Herbert's to lead one on.   Sheer love of my task enabled me to glide into Ophelia with no other guide than that love.   I had never known such joy in acting.   September 9th was the date of the production.   I find only one entry in my Diary for all that autumn : " A great day in our lives— Herbert plays Hamlet for the first time and with enormous success."   Would that I had recorded more !   But I remember it as a dream of happiness—of congratulation—of that sensation of walking-on-air, which comes of joy and security after agonies of apprehension.

There can never have been a Hamlet and Ophelia who so reverently, so almost religiously, gloried in their parts.   For many and many a night, both in the Manchester trial-run and afterwards in London, it was my delight to sit in the wings and watch Herbert's Hamlet—which was so far more beautiful, more scholarly, more " Royal Dane " than was allowed him, even by the most enthusiastic of his critics.   It was indeed a thing of beauty and the remembrance of it a joy for ever.   With what passionate delight he merged his individuality (not so unlike Hamlet's own) into that of the sweet Prince !—A sweeter never was sung by flights of angels to his rest.

[*By permission of Messrs. Novello & Co.*

I have said that Herbert did not " study " Hamlet in the actor's sense, but he made profound study of the character of Hamlet : ever striving actually to get inside the mind of Shakespeare (Shakespeare, as we know, was Herbert's Angel) : for he believed, and probably rightly, that in painting Hamlet the Poet drew himself.

In October, 1891, this, Herbert's second provincial tour, reached its end, intensely to my regret, for it had been full of excitement, adventure and success. Herbert must have loved it too, for he spent some of his happiest hours with the lifelong friends that he made. Of these, the distinguished society of Dr. Mahaffy and Mr. Edward Dowden were necessarily of supreme interest to him, and many delightful hours were spent over the absorbing topic of Shakespeare—the idol of all three.

In Manchester, the late Mr. Broadfield was our constant friend. He had the simplest and sweetest of natures, combined with a very powerful intellect ; every moment spent in his company was of value and enjoyment, and he remained our honoured friend until he died.

This tour was made iridescent with the weavings of romance. Fred Terry and Julia Neilson had loved one another since they had met as lover and heroine in *Comedy and Tragedy*, but it was not until this autumn that, either breaking down or defying opposition, they married. By this time, having begun with no such tender tendencies towards her, I had learnt to love and admire Julia, had learnt to know the large and lovely amiability of her disposition, her steadfastness and loyalty. Her spirit was as lovely as her face ; she was grand of heart as of person. Her marriage was more or less of an elopement, and I was more or less in their confidence. Does she remember, I wonder, bringing to my dressing-room a little ruby heart, as a token of gratitude for sympathy ? Well, Fred Terry and Julia Neilson married, and in October Herbert reopened the Haymarket Theatre with *The Dancing Girl*. It had all the old success because of the happy-ever-after love affair, for Julia and Fred were already adored of their audiences.

Except for Queen-Down Warren we were homeless this autumn : lodgings in Cadogan Place, a flat in Mount Street :— but wherever I lived I trod on air, for I had nothing in the world to grieve or vex me. All Herbert's friends were my friends ; the theatre, whether or no I acted, seemed mine as much as his. I sang my existence away ; sang, house-hunted, devised clothes, collected furniture, read a little, laughed incessantly— had a silly habit of pirouetting through life. I write of what I

did, or rather did not do, on purpose to acquit myself of any
claim to all that Herbert was quietly achieving. " You take
things so lightly," was his gentle comment, his severest reproof.
But he marvelled at the unconquerable rebound of what I called
my india-rubber ball of a heart.

CHAPTER III

In the winter of 1891 we lighted upon a little house—77, Sloane Street—which was destined to be our home for ten years. It was supposed to be a fairly cheap undertaking, because of the misleading words, " Rent without premium." This advantage soon disappeared under the iron hand and itching palm of the builder and decorator. Electric light was still somewhat of a departure (I find the Haymarket programme of this date making this alluring feature: " Theatre lighted by electricity!"), but 77, Sloane Street, soon saw it expensively installed, while I ransacked old shops for fittings, and found, indeed, some lovely ones—one pretty little old chandelier is in the Royal Room at His Majesty's to this day. Then our dining-room of white wood, our green drawing-room, and our blue drawing-room, our rooms, Viola's rooms—all were sweet and dainty ; but your bill, Mr. A——, whose taste was so unerring and exacting, hung long and heavy on our hands, though I fear that its burden weighed more seriously on your mind than on ours ! Herbert liked the little house, and was proud of its prettiness. Five-o'clock dinner, and always enough supper for three or four after the theatre : these were ministered to us by charming servants. Are we not both for ever grateful to you, Sarah Sisterson (Dinah Morris in face, form and disposition), Ellen Weeks and dear, incomparable Mrs. Browning ?

Sir Charles Dilke was our landlord and our next-door neighbour, but though we used to hear regularly at nine every morning the awe-striking clash of swords as he practised his invariable fencing, we did not know him. It was Viola who eventually began our friendship with him and Lady Dilke—a friendship we treasured to remember. A high wall separated our gardens, and one day Viola clambered up in search of some ball, kite or animal that had escaped her. Her vaulting ambition o'erleapt itself, for

67

she was found (he always declared) hanging by her stocking from a nail on Sir Charles Dilke's side of the wall. He rescued her, and she was promptly invited to learn fencing. So, later on, was I, but, " I am no fighter, sir," and the glinting rapiers frightened me out of my wits. Herbert used to ride with Sir Charles, and we used to go to delightful parties at their house —interesting, political, with stories of Napoleon, Bismarck and Parnell (did we meet—could we have met Parnell there ?). At one luncheon-party there was Colonel Saunderson. He went in terror of his life at that time, because of Fenian ill-feeling against him. He lived in Sloane Street, a few doors from our house (this is the story of another of Viola's escapades). He described at luncheon how the treacherous enemy had lately contrived a deadly plot against him by the devilish introduction through his study window of certain death in the form of a poisonous adder. As his story proceeded, Herbert and I looked at one another, half in dismay, half in merriment, and it easily transpired that " the poisonous adder " was a grass-snake, one of Viola's pets, which had escaped from our window, been searched for and mourned, and which we now learned had come to an undeserved and tragic end. " One more injustice to Ireland," was Herbert's comment.

While I burrowed in a groove of painters, glaziers and candle-stick makers, Herbert was intent on larger ideas—" widening the skirts of light "—every day growing in influence and authority.

He was becoming more and more popular as actor, man and manager, and his sayings and doings were much recorded and commented upon. I find one letter of his on the question of Music Halls *versus* Theatres which, in the light of these latter days, may not be without interest. Sir Henry Irving wrote as follows :

" To the Editor of the *Daily Telegraph*.

" SIR,

" Regarding your remarkable leader of to-day, I trust that it is not out of place to ask whether in any legislation for the consolidation of laws relating to places of amusement it is necessary to change the conditions under which theatres have hitherto received their licences, and further, whether it is necessary that, even if for structural purposes theatres and music-halls have to be considered together, they should be held in the eye of the law as having a common aim and object. Surely, whatever powers the London County Council may be granted, should there not be from first to last a distinct position reserved to theatres, which are the necessary homes of what we hold to be Art ? I do not mean for a moment to speak with disrespect of music-halls or music-hall artistes, but I must claim for theatres and actors a distinct purpose and place for them in the civic and State economy.

"In the Parliamentary Commission of 1866 it was shown that the great difference between theatres and music-halls was that in the former the play was the chief attraction, the refreshment saloons being merely for the convenience of the public attending the play. But if music-halls be allowed to play pieces of forty minutes long, a deteriorating change will probably take place with regard to many theatres. The plays thus limited will, by a very natural process, be lengthened, as, for instance, in the olden days plays were frequently divided by songs, recitations and dances between the acts. If managers of such places have the privilege of theatres without sacrificing their liberty of smoking during the performance, or of serving drink in the auditorium, a good many theatre managers will ultimately, under temptation of gain and strain of competition, find it to their monetary advantage to turn their theatres into houses for the performance of plays where smoking and drinking will be encouraged—an evil system of which the theatre proper is at present the antidote.

" I speak in this matter without any personal concern whatever, for to me and certain other managers any such change in the law will make no difference. We shall continue to conduct our theatres as we have done, with the purpose and the hope of sustaining and advancing the art of acting and all that surrounds it—a purpose and hope in which the public has ever encouraged us. It is for the future that I speak when I ask the public to pause till they settle the question. Is the suggested change a wise one, leading to a good end ?

" I am, sir, your obedient servant,

" Lyceum Theatre, February 23rd. HENRY IRVING."

Upon the same subject, but in far more fiery a strain, follows Herbert's letter—and how he escaped with his life after its publication baffles conjecture.

" To the Editor of the *Daily Telegraph.*

" SIR,

" ' Any attempt to turn the public-house into a theatre would end in turning the theatre into a public-house.' These words were spoken by a manager of great shrewdness and enterprise. ' And,' he added, ' I, for one, shall—if the new County Council Bill passes—give a theatrical entertainment during the winter, and turn my theatre into a music-hall during the rest of the year.'

" The County Council, having become discredited, and dreading perhaps the united influence of the Licensed Victuallers (a society perfectly organized and wielding practically unlimited powers), has thrown to that body a sop by giving the music-halls *carte blanche* in matters of entertainment. All distinctions between theatres and music-halls are, we are told, to be removed. As Mr. Irving and Mr. Hare have pointed out, the theatres have, by their own efforts, unaided by the State, gained for themselves a not unenviable position, and it is now proposed to remove by one stroke the work built up by many years of earnest striving. Of course, there are among us those who will refuse to howl with the wolves and bleat with the lambs. There are managers who will decline to conduct their theatres on the lines of music-halls ; but these theatres must inevitably go to the wall, as they could not in the long run compete with those rivals who derived their chief income from the sale of intoxicating drinks. The character of the entertainment would, of necessity, deteriorate, and the rising generation would practically be excluded from the education which a well-conducted theatre may claim to supply. Thus, both the ethics and the æsthetics of our Art would be outraged. The County Council being largely composed of persons who are not only not in sympathy with, but are absolutely opposed to, the claims of Art, are disqualified from exercising over us those unlimited powers which they would now usurp.

" The Lord Chamberlain has practically the power to veto

any performance and to close any theatre at any moment. To this autocracy no manager can object, for the Lord Chamberlain's office is administered by persons of culture, refinement and responsibility. But were these powers transferred to the tender mercies of the County Council, a condition of things would arise which would be at once intolerable to managers and irritating to the public.

"As an instance of the tactics pursued by the County Council towards theatres, I may mention that, some time ago, I received repeated complaints that the bolts on the doors of the Haymarket Theatre did not meet the requirements of the County Council. The bolts were, however, made on the very pattern of the bolts approved by the County Council at five new theatres. But still the County Council continued to persecute me with requisitions, and put me to much trouble and expense. They finally threatened legal proceedings. Being by this time exasperated, I determined to ignore their communications, and to allow them to proceed. I put the case before my solicitors, and was advised to let the matter go into court. It was planned that we should subpœna the entire body of County Councillors in order to demonstrate in open court and before the public the ignorance and unfitness of those entrusted with the supervision of theatres. At the last moment, however, the Council declined to prosecute. The bolts remain ; but I have received as yet no apology for the treatment to which I was subjected. If in structural matters these arbiters of the theatre are not all that could be desired, the mind shrinks from the contemplation of their sway in the more abstract regions of Art and taste.

"If we have not the advantage of State aid, let us at least be exempt from a State suppression. The County Council may have reckoned with its publican, but without its public.

"I remain, sir, your obedient servant,

"HERBERT BEERBOHM TREE.
"London, February 26th."

One wonders how these two eager and consistent upholders of their Art—Irving and Tree—would have met the suggestion of Trades-Unionism with regard to it—at least, one does not wonder, one is absolutely sure.

A lecture he delivered in December at the Playgoers' Club (Sir Squire Bancroft in the chair) caused no little stir. It is amusing to note that Maeterlinck, in a contemporary paper, is spoken of as " a young Flemish writer," etc., etc. " Some Fallacies of the Modern Stage " was afterwards embodied in Herbert's book, " Thoughts and Afterthoughts." I remember his composing it on one or two evenings after supper, for midnight oil always soothed the troubled waters of his imagination.

So punctuated with fun and pungent humour was Herbert's lecture that one hardly knows whether he was admiring or condemning the Maeterlinck and Ibsen whom he alternately crowned and jumped on ; but his passionate admiration for *The Doll's House, The Enemy of the People* (Dr. Stockmann almost his favourite part) and *The Master Builder* is well known ; and it was his fixed intention to produce *Peer Gynt.* As to Maeterlinck, he loved every moment of *L'Intruse,* and one of the disappointments of his life was that *The Blue Bird* did not come his way for production. Although Herbert's judgment remained always sane and evenly balanced, his expression was often bewildering, because of the will-o'-the-wisp quality of his humour and the unconquerable whimsicality of his wit.

Soon after the lecture, we gave an isolated performance of *L'Intruse* at the Lyceum. It was an intense pleasure to us to act and to perform, but it fell upon the unheeding ears of a fashionable Charity Matinée audience, and made no great effect.

On January 15th, 1892, *The Dancing Girl* reached its birthday, and though by no means had the sands of its popularity run out, it was withdrawn. This was because Herbert's longing to give London a taste of his Hamlet could no longer be stilled, and, accordingly, on January 21st, it was produced. It evoked volumes of criticism, oceans of praise, as it deserved, while, apart from the Press, the public flocked with eagerness and unbounded admiration to the new Hamlet.

The three months that followed were surely the happiest of

my life, for I had more than my share of praise and applause. I seem to have lived only " to strut and fret my hour upon the stage," and that hour as Ophelia was Heaven. The only duty

Playgoers' Club.

[By permission of " The Daily Graphic."

I set myself, as far as I can remember, was to take care that the flowers I used in the Mad Scene were duly chosen and delivered day by day—for nothing but real flowers would content me, and the more beautiful they were, the more it pleased me to toss them and tear them. This was not from cruelty to the

flowers, which I loved, but from an idea I had that the mad
would play with beauty and then destroy it.   I wonder if our
good friends Sir Henry and Lady Lucy remember sending me
columbines from their sweet garden at Hythe?   "There's rue
for you, and columbines."

Herbert, too, was happy the whole time that he was acting
Hamlet.   He approached his task each night with love and
reverence, and his impersonation grew and grew in strength and
beauty.   There was a girl, Ethel Webling, who came every
single night of the more than a hundred nights to draw him
while he was acting.   She stood in the wings, one side or
another, with the result that there grew a wonderful book, the
text, as Herbert gave it, annotated by pen-and-ink sketches.
It is an exquisite piece of work, and it was, to the end of his
life, a delight to Herbert.   We did not possess the original
one that Miss Webling made (would that we had!), but one
she copied from it for us, with, I think, rather fewer of her
marvellous drawings in it.   Nevertheless, it is a thing of beauty
and a great treasure.

We were a delightful company of players: Rose Leclercq,
Henry Kemble (Polonius), James Fernandez (the Ghost), Fred
Terry (Laertes) and Arthur Dacre (Horatio).   It was a beautiful production, too—praised even by the severe *Times*—and
there was the continual delight of Henschel's music.   I was so
intensely happy in the theatre that I wanted to make others
happy; so every evening I used to assemble all the children
who appeared in the play, and hold a little court, half Bible
class, half literary society, in which I think we all revelled.
One of the little girls, Nellie Reid, adored us both, and long
afterwards wrote me letters of love and devotion.   Alas! she
perished in the Chicago Theatre fire—I believe through going
back in search of a comrade.   (I forget the object of so many
children in Herbert's production of *Hamlet*, but there they
undoubtedly were.)

Hamlet ran its hundred happy nights, and then came to an
end, and *Peril* was put on, with Julia Neilson as the heroine,
and Herbert, of course, in a repetition of his famous Sir Wood-

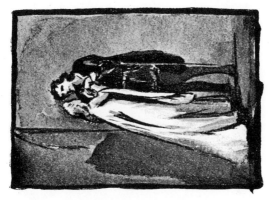

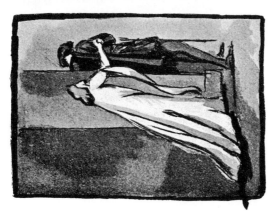

"HAMLET AND OPHELIA."
Drawings by Ethel Webling.

bine Grafton success. A translation of *Le Passant* by Cotsford
Dick gave us a delicious little prelude to *Peril* in *The Waif*,
and I revelled and greatly admired myself in the part of Zanetto,
while flatterers—among them Sir Charles Wyndham—whispered
to me of Rosalind and Viola—dreams, never, alas! to be
realized.

This programme seems to have filled up the summer season,
though at its very end *Hamlet* was revived, and I can quite
understand that Herbert did not want to close so eventful and
brilliant a year by appearing in the small, albeit inimitable presentment of the irascible Anglo-Indian Colonel. I remember
Herbert's speech on the last night, for in it he made special
mention of me as Ophelia—thereby with his own hands, as it
were, working up for me an ovation. Well did I call myself
that night, " Too happy, happy Tree."

This year Marienbad is chosen for our holiday, and thither
we repair, taking Viola and her nurse with us. Of the journey
all I remember is that at a certain hour in the early morning
Viola was to waken to see the castled Rhine, upon whose legends
she had been reared. When the time came, she utterly refused
to open her eyes or lift her head from the pillow, and so she saw
nothing. Herbert made a little teasing song, which recurred
at intervals during the whole of our holiday : " She never
saw the Rhine, she never saw the Rhine, she never, never,"
etc., etc.

Herbert adored the life at Marienbad—so much so that for
ever afterwards it seemed to him the only indispensable and
immovable feast of the year. He entered into its régime, its
routine with infinite zest—was first in the early morning at
the Pump Room, or whatever it was called ; came back to
fetch lazy me for the walk through the woods to Waldmühle
or Egerlande, where we breakfasted—sedulously took baths,
drank waters, drove, walked, dreamed in the pine-forest, wrote,
studied, made friends, lived and laughed and sang away in-
dustriously idle days. I never put on the proper spirit of
Marienbad ; those never do who are not up and out and drinking
waters when the morning hymn is sung. But I had an easy

and luxurious life ; read a thousand novels, basked in the woods, watched Viola dance among the honey-scented pines, and closed my eyes to her scientific destruction of lovely butterfly-life.   I went sometimes to the play or the opera (but Herbert liked to go every night), slept much, and tried to learn German of the multitudinous American visitors.   But that first year of our going there was long before Marienbad was sought after. It was a little place, and the Grünes Kreuz had the most delight-ful rooms wherein to lodge—while the arbour of the Hotel Weimar was a place wherein one dreamed away the eating hours.

On our return, after a very happy three weeks, we stayed a night at Frankfort.   At Cologne (mainly through Herbert's perfect German, which for some extraordinary reason no German official could understand), we missed all trains, all connections, lost our luggage, stormed and raved, and finally altered our homeward route.   I recall this only because Viola and I delighted to tease Herbert about his German which we alleged was too good to be true.

Before we started on our autumn tour, all the plans were put in being for Mr. Stuart Ogilvie's adaptation of *Hypatia*, which was to be Herbert's winter production at the Haymarket. Also Oscar Wilde brought us the scenario of *A Woman of No Importance*, destined to prove such an amazing success.

In the autumn our provincial tour began no further afield than Islington ; which reminds me of one of the few songs (although as a boy he had a lovely chorister's voice) that Herbert ever consented to sing in private life—this was " The Bailiff's Daughter of Islington " in French :

> " Il y avait un garçon,
> Très aimable et très bon," etc., etc.

He sang it delightfully to the old tune which I, as a child of four, had been stood upon a table to warble, gaining great applause and many a prophecy by my pathetic rendering of " She died, sir, long ago."

From Islington we went the usual round of towns ; finding ourselves in the North, as I see by an isolated entry in my diary : " My birthday in Glasgow.   Herbert gives me lovely fur coat, girls give me silver arrow.   Supper-party."   " The

girls " were lovely, beloved Lily Hanbury and her sister Hilda.
Lily, one of the sweetest souls to grace the earth and leave
it all too soon, was the beautiful cousin of beautiful Julia
Neilson ; she came on tour with us to act the " Dancing Girl " in
Julia's stead. She was scarcely " out of her 'teens "—radiantly
handsome and gay, brimming with sympathy and affection, brimming with talent and reciprocity. Herbert and I loved her
as she deserved loving.

It was in Glasgow that Oscar Wilde came to stay with us,
bringing us the completed manuscript of *A Woman of No Importance*. This occupied three days of delighted listening,
planning, and—inevitable in his society—laughter, badinage,
partridges, oysters, champagne ; feasts of no particular reason,
flow of no memorable soul.

Once the play accepted, settled and practically cast, the
glamour of him as a guest palled a little, and I remember how
glad we were, Herbert and I, when some smart invitation recalled
him, and we were enabled to pursue the even tenor of our tour
—a tour which ended, as it began, in the environs of London.
" Stratford-atte-Bow " at the end of November, recalls dim
recollections of long journeys along the Whitechapel Road
in hansoms, and of turtle-soup at some famous eating-house
in the heart of the City on matinée days.

Thenceforward Herbert was engrossed in the rehearsals of
Hypatia and in the preparations for its beautiful production.
These brought us in close touch with Alma Tadema, who lent
us his genius, and with Sir Hubert Parry, who made the lovely
music for the play. It was many years later that Herbert's
production of *Julius Cæsar* excited the wonder and admiration
of the play-going world, but I doubt if that of *Hypatia* was less
astoundingly beautiful and complete. At all events, the same
master hand, that of Alma Tadema, was in a great measure
responsible for both.

Strenuous as were the rehearsals of *Hypatia* and manifold
the details of the production, Herbert yet found time to say and
do things outside the theatre. I venture to allude to one speech
he made, because it gives a clue to the intention which he realized
ten years later—his foundation of the now-flourishing Academy

of Dramatic Art in Gower Street. A society was formed, not
by Herbert himself, and short-lived, I am afraid, which seemed
to Herbert a foretaste of the good things he had in his mind.
Extracts from his speech at the inaugural meeting will show that
he was already advising in 1892 what he achieved on his own
account in 1904.

My idea is that an important department of this
Society might be a school—shall I call it a conservatoire ?
—in which the young actor and actress could acquire those
implements of their art, the want of which the playgoers
of to-day cannot but sometimes deplore in watching the
performances presented in our theatres. I mean a school
of fencing, dancing, and elocution. As for acting, that is
an affair of the imagination, and cannot be taught, but if
it cannot be taught it can be practised. It would be a
fallacy, I think, to maintain that acting is so precise a
science as are the arts of music and painting. Witness the
fact that most children are natural actors, and often as-
tonish one with the appropriateness of their gestures, the
genius of their exuberance. They are, in fact, untrammelled
by self-consciousness. We start from the garden of childish
confidence before we emerge into the promised land of
artistic maturity. Nowadays there is practically no recruiting ground for the young actor, save that provided by
amateur clubs, and of those the full-fledged actor cannot
avail himself. The system of long runs which prevails
in our theatres renders it out of the question that young
actors and actresses can obtain in the theatres to which they
are attached that practice which is absolutely essential
to their artistic development. Such performances as the
projectors of the present scheme have in view would, of
course, afford those opportunities of which the rising generation stands sorely in need—those opportunities which in
former days were afforded by stock companies throughout
the kingdom.

But to return to the question of a conservatoire, or dramatic academy. Efforts have been made before now to
establish such an institution ; those efforts, however, have

" HAMLET "
Drawings by Ethel Webling.

hitherto not been successful. But many things are possible to-day which were not possible ten years ago. I am confident that there is a larger contingent of our young actors and young actresses who would avail themselves of the opportunity of acquiring, as it were, the tools of their craft, if they could be purchased at a reasonable rate. There are, of course, many teachers of elocution, there are many fencing masters, there are numberless dancing academies, but it would be a considerable boon if a recognized school, at which the various teachable branches of theatrical art were taught, could be established.

Hypatia ran its hundred nights, a lovely play exquisitely acted by a company headed by Herbert, Julia Neilson, Fred Terry, Henry Kemble, Olga Brandon, Lewis Waller and James Fernandez. By the way, there is no Issachar the Jew in Kingsley's novel ; Mr. Ogilvie introduced the character, probably foreseeing the great character-study in which Herbert's impersonation resulted. There was naturally no part for me in *Hypatia*, although I pleaded with tears for that of Ruth. It would not have suited me, and Olga Brandon acted it to perfection. But it used to please me to make my moan by emerging from my disused dressing-room, which was kept sacred to me, and by sitting on a certain bridge connecting the Suffolk Street house with the stage. There I used to exult in my grief by watching the lovely play, and by greeting (with careful traces of recent weeping) Herbert, always genial, always sympathetic, as he returned between the acts. How kind he was ! How indulgent to my grievances ! How eager to atone when in reality I had nothing whatever to grumble about !

The year, 1893, was a year of marvellous summer ; I remember it well, because I journeyed with Viola to Lyme Regis in the middle of March, and the train-guard said : " We have had eight hours of sunshine on this line for a week." It seems to me that eight hours of sunshine grew to fourteen and lasted from March to October—a " white muslin year " I called it, and such as I had not known since childhood. Herbert came to Lyme Regis while the theatre was closed the week before Easter, and we all loved the little place. We had lodgings actually on the beach, and between glinting wave and " rathe primrose " we met Spring halfway in her triumphant march.

Soon after our return there were the rehearsals of *A Woman of No Importance*. In this a delicious part was assigned to me ; so there was no more wailing and gnashing of teeth. They were delightful, those rehearsals. Every day we used to break off and repair to the Continental Hotel, which was then a famous place for lunch, and exactly the reverse, I believe, for supper. Oscar Wilde, Comyns Carr, Herbert and I, and anyone whom we happened to bring with us made a merry table—intellectual, too, wit-sharpening and full of interest. I remember Oscar Wilde telling us the plots of three short plays he had in his mind —*Salomé, The Florentine Tragedy* and *La Sainte Courtisane,* almost writing them on the tablecloth as he glowed over his themes.

The " Continental " was one of a long chapter of restaurants resorted to almost daily according to the fancy of the man of the moment or the play of the moment that most influenced Herbert. Blanchard's in New Burlington Street (on rich days) had an early vogue—and we commandeered the pleasant bow-window table that looked down upon the happy *va et vient* of Regent Street (of course, over the *hors d'œuvres* I was the Lady of Shalott). On poor days, we descended to Blanchard's in Beak Street, where a " cut from the joint " took the place of *Canard à la presse.* (I remember Herbert's delight when I stigmatized a glaringly untruthful newspaper poster as a " *Canard à la Press.*") Herbert liked the chariots of lamb and salmon that were victoriously driven up to one's plate at Simpson's. Here humour took the place of allure, and Herbert must, even in eating, be allured or amused, or his capricious appetite failed him. At one time we used to go to Verrey's every single day for many weeks, when old Mr. Verrey himself used to wait upon us at sleepy, unwaiterous hours. This was during Mr. Godwin's production of Dr. Todhunter's *Oenone* at Hengler's Circus in Argyle Street. Mr. Godwin chose " this wooden O " for his lovely production, so that one could catch the real spirit of the Greek drama—its wreathed spectators, its moving chorus. Herbert did not act in it, but he taught me to act *Oenone,* and he lived in every moment of this emanation of Godwin's genius for the art of the stage.

A Woman of No Importance, with Mrs. Bernard Beere as the heroine, was, as it deserved to be, an amazing success. Produced at the end of April, it ran all through the summer, and only came to an end in September because a date had been fixed for the production of Mr. Henry Arthur Jones's play.

Meanwhile Herbert was swimming triumphantly on the top of a victorious wave : had become a Man of Great Importance : was sought after, fêted and quoted. As a contemporary says :

" IMAGINATION AND THE PLAY

" Mr. Beerbohm Tree, the famous actor-manager of the Haymarket Theatre, has been the recipient of an honour which we believe is unique—that is to say, has never been offered to any other player. The Royal Institution authorities have invited him to appear at the noted Albemarle Street Hall ; not in his function of performer, but in that of essayist. Mr. Tree is to read a paper on ' The Imaginative Faculty in its Relation to the Drama.' He is a scholar of some attainments and a thinker of some originality as well as a splendid actor, and those who have the good fortune to hear him will have a rich intellectual treat. The honour done to Mr. Tree by the invitation is a striking testimony to the rapidity of the growth of interest in England in the finer questions affecting the drama, as well as to the increasing recognition of the culture and versatility of the leading players on the British stage."

I had no holiday, being too happy in my part to care to give it up ; but Herbert went with Viola to Westgate, of all places in the world. There there was a little coterie of Mrs. Patrick Campbell, Haddon Chambers and his wife, and, I think, the Comyns Carrs, making music and laughter to their hearts' content. I remember coming one Sunday and feeling rather glum, as one always does in a world that has gone beyond one. Haddon Chambers was writing his play *John-o'-Dreams,* which Herbert was to produce with Mrs. Patrick Campbell as its heroine, and the air was full of plans and visions shut out from me, a mere Peri at the gate of Paradise. But I forgot to be disconsolate when in one dreamy July midnight we put out in a wide sailing-boat upon a still and silver sea. There Mr. Haddon Chambers, who, to many varied accomplishments, added the pretty trick of manning a schooner, sang with the sailors snatches of old chanties—rhythmical sea-songs with incoherent choruses: " Blow, blow, blow the man down, Give me a penny to blow the man down." I hear their voices now, echoing over a waste of waters. Westgate vanished, the Beach Hotel was the Doge's Palace glimmering across the dark lagoon. Indeed, Tosti's Venetian Boat-Song formed an appropriate part of the concert contributed to by us all.

Herbert loved Tosti—Tosti of keen wit, of infinite mirth and humour. He thought him the best company in the world : so he was ! And his music ! Shall one ever forget hearing him accompany Melba in " Good-bye " ? Shall one ever forget an evening party at Mrs. Alfred Darby's (sister of Sir George Arthur, that charming friend of all our married life). Princess Mary (Duchess of Teck), that royal lady of historic brilliance and goodness and wit and charm, was there—always a great friend of Herbert, who delighted her because he made her laugh ; and " Mattinata " was sung for the first time, Tosti accompanying it. Enchanting memory—I shall always think " Mattinata " the loveliest ballad ever written.

During the whole of August, Herbert was hard at work over the ambitious production of *The Tempter*, a romance of the days of Henry IV. Chaucer and Goethe would seem to have combined to supply Henry Arthur Jones with his theme, " Faust " and " The Canterbury Tales " struggled for mastery in the plot's unfolding. The Woes had it. Herbert's part, practically Mephistopheles, appealed to him strongly ; it was glamorous, daring, lurid, with an immense amount of red fire, blue limelight, and phosphorescent effects ; but I doubt if his performance, though clever and fantastic, was memorable. The play, written partly in prose, partly in poetry, if it did not add to the great reputation of the famous author of *Judah, The Middleman, The Dancing Girl* and *The Liars* (exquisite comedy

I AM THE REVOLUTION!

MR. BEERBOHM TREE AS THE REVOLUTION.

HAZELDEN

Col. Newcome.
By permission of " Punch."]

Narcisse.
[*By permission of ",The Illustrated Sporting and Dramatic News.*"

of which Sheridan might have been proud), yet had a considerable run and was a sensational success. As the unhappy lovers—" two halcyons tempest-tossed "—Julia Neilson and Fred Terry gave really fine and lovely effects. I remember how wonderfully beautiful was their death-scene, both in writing and interpretation—a scene I used to watch every night, and always it moved me to tears.

The little waiting-maid, by the bye, was acted by Irene Vanbrugh (her first part, I think), who, scarcely more than a child, instantly won all hearts and has kept them forever.

The year closed somewhat gloomily : for *The Tempter*, in spite of its success, was too expensive and over-peopled a production to spell money-making. It ended, and a short revival of *Captain Swift* filled in the few weeks while Herbert was rehearsing *The Charlatan* by Robert Buchanan. This, a pretty enough play, gave Herbert a part, eerie, poetic, half-villain, half-hero, such as only an Irving or a Tree could enact. It recalled several of his brilliant successes : Macari, the Duke of Guisebury, Captain Swift and Hamlet ; being compounded of, and yet distinctive from them all ; the kind of performance which in a highly-successful play would have become historic. I was given the wonderful part of the heroine, and was allowed to sing " Der Asra " of Rubinstein to Lily Hanbury's accompaniment (how did I dare ?). It was appropriate to the situation and to the characters. Isabel (my part) was the Princess, Philip Woodville (Herbert's) the slave—who daily grew pale and more pale for love of her. There were the elements but not the accomplishment of a fine drama in *The Charlatan*.

After two or three months' run, this play gave place to *Once Upon a Time*. This was Herbert's happy title of a poetic comedy by Louis Parker, founded on Hans Andersen's " The Emperor's New Clothes." It was an exquisite piece of work, owing its complete failure to two mistakes. First and foremost, *Once Upon a Time* was in advance of its day ; had it been produced fifteen years later, and had Herbert cast himself for the part of Omar, the magician, instead of that of the vainglorious King, a different fate would have awaited it. As it was, a disastrous run of about three weeks plunged me into despair (since mine was one of the most charming parts I had ever been given, and my success in it abnormal), while bitter disappointment and chagrin (for he loved the play) did but nerve Herbert to new effort, new venture. It was then that I and those who watched and loved him christened him the Splendid Loser : a fine reputation nobly earned and lived up to. On perhaps the third night of the play, when he and I had struggled through our parts to an all-but-empty house, we came home to Sloane Street to a supper which certainly should have consisted of bitter herbs. Not at all : I can see Herbert now, as he paused over his meal and leaned his head upon his hand—" I wonder if Grundy has anything," he mused. Nowadays we should have " rung him up " : that night we hailed a hansom, past midnight though it was, and drove to Sydney Grundy's house in Kensington. A light in his study window assured us he was up and working, and we were scarcely admitted before he showed us a comedy, by miracle ready and admirably suited to Herbert's need. *A Bunch of Violets* was read to us then and there, and instantly accepted, Herbert and the author casting the play as the pages were turned. The part of the hero was as though written for Herbert ; that of the wife as though written for Lily Hanbury ; Lionel Brough, Holman Clark (already acting in poor, doomed *Once Upon a Time*) sprang to our imaginations as the only actors for various parts. But there was one brilliantly-written character of an adventuress which gave Herbert pause. " Whom on earth," he asked ruefully, with a lack-lustre eye, " can we get for Mrs. Murgatroyd ? " " There sits the only actress who can play it," said Mr. Grundy, pointing his pipe at me—at amazed and incredulous me.

We left the pleasant, book-lined room in Addison Road in the small hours of a March morning, having lighted upon one of the greatest of Herbert's successes ; while I had been accorded one of the three great chances of my theatrical career. The play was put into rehearsal the very next day, and was produced less than a fortnight after Herbert's happy inspiration. Never did there fall from the sky greater good-luck. The play was an instant success, both artistically and financially. Herbert's part, Sir Philip Marchant, was a new departure : a man of iron —cold, hard, cynical—with yet one stream of passionate warmth and love deep down in his nature : his adoration of his only daughter. The character gave splendid scope and opportunity, and the result was one of his finest performances. He was very proud of my almost sensational success as the dreadful Mrs. Murgatroyd, especially as it followed with startling contrast the part of Rita, the peasant child in *Once Upon a Time*, in which Herbert was pleased to call my acting " perfect." I must be forgiven for speaking of a pronouncement so dear to my remembrance.

May, June and July were filled up with a great many gaieties for me, and such as his work allowed him for Herbert. A supper-club called " The Amphitryon " came into being, and many a party was given for us or by us there. The Grosvenor Gallery parties occurring every week, I think, were a delightful rendez-vous ; and we were entertained every Sunday either at dinner or for the week-end. Delightful week-ends they were, too—at Wilton, at Panshanger, at Taplow Court, at Ashridge, and, most memorable of all, at Hatfield. There, with royal fellow-visitors, we spent an adorable Saturday to Monday in July. Dear, great Lord Salisbury—for whom one had with the rest of the world a deep hero-worship—you spent an hour alone with Herbert and me, showing us the house and its manifold, luminous, illumining treasures : and you, Lady Salisbury, witty, wise, of divine manners ; you, who had an affectionate admiration of Herbert's humour and genius—you showered your great and simple friendship of hospitality on us. Sweet and ever-to-be-remembered two days of memorable hours !

One visit to Taplow Court tells its own story, in this little letter from Lady Desborough, which came in answer to one of mine asking her the date of her " coming-out " ball. For it was at this, when she was Miss Ethel Fane, and engaged to Mr. Willie Grenfell, that we first saw her ; and Herbert, without even speaking to her, fell down straight at her feet. He thought her the loveliest thing he had ever seen : and later on, when he came to know her, he learnt to think her the wittiest and rarest being he had ever met :

> " Taplow Court,
> " Taplow, Bucks.
> " April 17th, 1919

" MY DEAR LADY TREE,

"It was such a great and true pleasure to get your dear letter—it called up so many happy days. And very, very well I remember the first time that you and Sir Herbert came here, in the early summer of 1891. Oscar Wilde was here, and I remember him stepping in mid-river from my punt to the one you were in with Willie—with heavy oscillations—and your delicious greeting to him, ' Welcome, little stranger ! ' Do you remember ?—and a good game that we played in the evening, invented, I think, by my uncle Francis :—an imaginary letter from a woman thanking a man for flowers when she wasn't *quite* certain whether he'd sent them or not ! Yours began, ' Roses, roses everywhere.'

"There was a ball at St. James's Square in 1889, and one in 1891—but my ' coming-out ' ball was, alas ! in 1885 (we were married in 1887).

" I was so deeply touched by what you said about Sir Herbert, and so intensely pleased.

" It is strange how increasingly vivid the early years become as the milestones grow ever quicker—it is one of the great joys. I often think of the Browning words : ' If I hold the past so firm and fast, Shall I doubt if the future hold I can ? '

> " Yours with love,
> " ETTIE DESBOROUGH."

This year our summer holiday began at Spa, where Viola and I were left while Herbert went on to his beloved Marienbad. As long as he stayed with us we were entrancingly amused : Julius and Evelyn Beerbohm were there, and Clara Butt—a grand creature of eighteen splendid summers. At the feet of this goddess both Herbert and Julius fell prone, and a deadly rivalry raged merrily between the two brothers. One day, in an evil hour, one overheard the other promising to send " the divine Clara " an armful of roses. But when the time came for the fulfilment of this fragrant purpose, lo ! the town had been ransacked at dawn and every single flower had been bought up and already presented by the rival brother. Not a single blossom remained for the discomfited Julius (or Herbert, I forget which ; but I rather think Herbert, who substituted some witty symbol for the lost posy).

There were picnics and *batailles-de-fleurs*, and the insidious allure (to me, not to Herbert) of the gaming-tables. Julius, who happened to be rich at that moment, was the gaming-table king ; and I remember how Herbert used to watch him, in horror and amazement mingled with fascinated admiration, as he held the bank while onlookers held their breath.

Julius and Evelyn's only son, " young Evelyn," was about Viola's age, and here at Spa, as in the long Sloane Street gardens, as in the Kentish nut woods, these two intrepid cousins were inseparable over the tops and tadpoles of their happy youth. Later on Evelyn became the wonder and the hero of those young-eyed cherubim, Felicity and Iris, and the fascination of Herbert, who rejoiced in his incessant and ebullient humour.

Alternately as he was Fortune's favourite or Fortune's fool, Evelyn rode to hounds, drove four-in-hand, joined a smart Hussar regiment, or pursued a precarious existence upon the stage. But whatever he undertook he did magnificently and in a magnificent way. So he died magnificently commanding his Battery at Polygon Wood. The outbreak of war had given him the career he had always longed for. At first his commission was in his boyhood's regiment, the 3rd Hussars, then a Captaincy in the 12th Lancers, a Majority in the Royal Field Artillery, a Staff appointment in German East Africa, home again for the " big push " of 1917, and then his death, two months after that of his Uncle Herbert whom he had so looked up to and so loved.

On our return from Spa, there was the usual provincial tour, easily recalled this year because, while we were in Edinburgh, we were " commanded " to give a performance at Balmoral. I rejoice to think that Herbert had audience and speech with great Queen Victoria, who embodied—shall we say concealed ?—in her gentle touch, her sweet voice, her simple personality, the power, wisdom and might of England.

In December our second daughter arrived, and we called her

VIOLA AND FELICITY.

Felicity. That word, in Arabic, was graven on an amulet I found for Herbert at Juliano's pretty shop, declaring that while he wore it happiness would stay with him. Great happiness came to us, at all events, with the new baby's advent, and Herbert gave me her lovely name wrought in diamonds for my Christmas present. But when she was but five weeks old we had to absent us from Felicity awhile, leaving her and Viola with a crowd of devoted aunts, nurses and well-wishers, as we started forth on our first American tour.

CHAPTER IV

WE left for New York in January, 1895. It was a blessed voyage. The greater part of Herbert's company had travelled a week sooner than we ; therefore our party comprised only ourselves, Max Beerbohm and Lionel Brough. The latter twain, while yet the ship was lying at anchor outside Queenstown harbour, disappeared from view and were never seen again until they were landed upon the quay at New York. Thus, for the first time for many years, I had Herbert completely to myself. To me this was a return of the golden age, and I appreciated and loved every hour of that eight days' journey. Herbert in no way succumbed to the horrors of a sea voyage ; but the dread of something after each heave and roll of the liner kept him chastened and subdued ; wistfully inclined to be waited upon and looked after, so that it made Heaven for her who had fretted under his more mercurial and elusive moods. How I adored and looked back upon the long-drawn days of that week ! Days that never came again, though something very near them was the last fortnight of his life. I reminded him then how, remembering my "μηδένα νομίζετ᾽ εὐτύχειν πρὶν ἂν θάνῃ," I had tried to put into Greek, " Call no wife happy until she has her husband safe under a linseed poultice." This passion to monopolize, " this fever of the mind, this jealousie," does it most resemble love or hatred in its egotism ?

The ship we travelled by was fuller of luxuries than of passengers, and it seemed to belong entirely to us—to Herbert and me. Ah ! the hours slipped by too quickly. Nothing happened except endless relays of food and long, lazy afternoons on fur-bedizened deck-chairs : a shoal of porpoises, a shadow on the horizon that called itself an iceberg, and at last one morning something gleaming in the early sunlight—the Statue of Liberty at the entrance to New York harbour. These were the excitements and the finale of that dream-week. Eheu ! Immediately a crowd of reporters, who arrived in a galley and clambered up the ship's side, surrounded Herbert, elbowed me out of existence and blotted out my pageant. I was discovered in our state-room weeping among our boxes, because my happy, cherished hours were over. Herbert dried my tears and promised me that everything should come again ; but it never did.

Herbert was, as it were, borne off upon the shoulders of the press-gang, and I saw him no more until we were established in our hotel—the best that New York boasted in those days, breathing Versailles, the Winter Palace and the Vatican : replete with more civilized warfare against time, space and eternity than could be compassed in a miser's dream. One felt curiously like Marie Antoinette in her glorious days—it was the hotel made one feel it—but like Marie Antoinette in a hurry. One was striving day and night to recapture lost time, lost trains, lost opportunities, lost empires : lost everything that one could lose, if one did not make haste—breathless, frantic haste. One was never late, never early, yet one was always rushing, always seeking, with one's mind racked, one's senses on tiptoe—one's very dreams a whirlwind.

We found our rooms rioting in flowers, and we revelled in the great bunches of Parma violets, the great sheaves of American Beauty roses, the giant cyclamens, the forests of lilies-of-the-valley. Among the first to greet us with posy-laden hands were Mr. and Mrs. Kendal, then at the zenith of their enormous popularity in America. Mrs. Kendal and Herbert had kindred wits, and, once together, they lighted one another's humour into a blaze. We were much fêted, the Four Hundred as well as the Four Thousand opening its doors to us for lunches, dinners, suppers and balls. On the very night of our arrival we were taken to the Opera (*Lohengrin*, with Jean de Reszke). It was the height of the New York season, and the beauty, the clothes, and the tiaras glittering on every graceful head seemed to make Covent Garden pale its ineffectual fire. After about ten days of ceaseless gaieties, we began our acting, Herbert wisely choosing *The Ballad-Monger* and *The Red Lamp* for his first night. The contrast of the starveling poet Gringoire and the

cat-footed, dropsical Demetrius, and the impossibility of finding
the man Tree in either part, caused New York, in its critics' parlance, to sit up—to stand and deliver an ovation; and when
A Bunch of Violets, *Hamlet* and Falstaff followed one another
in nightly succession, one cannot wonder that Herbert's acting
became the rage.   I, too, was praised, and I will not say unduly,
for I, too, in the Princess Morakoff, Mrs. Murgatroyd, Ophelia
and Mrs. Ford, had parts which at all events proved my
versatility.

When we had been acting about a week, there happened a
great Charity Matinée at Washington, and it was arranged
that Herbert and I and a few of his company should travel to
the capital during the night, appear in a scene from *Hamlet*
at noon, and return to New York in time for our evening performance.   This is what man proposed; but the weather was
indisposed.   The midnight ferry that took us across the Hudson
had to plough through blocks of ice, the river having frozen
(an unusual event, I think), and this was only the beginning of
that long journey's happenings.   We entered the train, lingered
long over supper, then went to our beds.   We slept as though
we should never wake; and when at last we did open our eyes
we wondered that it was not yet morning—we wondered, too,
why the train no longer moved, and why darkness enveloped
the outlook.   Looking at the time, we found that it was ten
o'clock, and we soon learnt that we had been embedded for
many hours in a snow-drift half-way between New York and
Washington; and that the dull thuds that had been beating on
our ears were the efforts made to dig us out of our white-walled
prison.   There we remained, however, hour after hour, and
it was in vain to storm and rage, as Herbert undoubtedly did,
marching like a caged lion up and down the aisles of the
train.

We reached our destination during the afternoon, and were
all the more enthusiastically received because of our adventures.
Of course the theatre in New York (where we arrived in the
grey of the next morning) had to be closed that night.   But
the " bills " posted all over the town did us no harm, for what
was lost in a " house " was made up for by unlooked-for and
gratuitous advertisement.

Our stay in New York lasted six weeks—six weeks of success, gaiety, interest, excitement. We were charmed with the atmosphere of crowded, high-spirited life—charmed with the kindness, the exuberance and festivity of our many friends, charmed with the wealth and taste and comfort of the homes we saw. Of the parties to which we were invited, above all I remember one. It was at a lovely old house in unfashionable but beautiful Washington Square. There Melba sang, and Maurel, and after supper the leader of a light-hearted frolic was the beautiful Nancy Astor (it was before her marriage), gay and lightsome as a fairy-child, who seized Bret Harte by the hands and insisted upon his dancing up and down the room with her. Unforgettable picture : the lovely, laughing girl, and the white-headed man, treading with unerring grace and rhythm a fantastic, unpremeditated tarantelle !

All that there was in New York of gay, memorable and remarkable was ours to share, to see, to know : music parties in dim, rich rooms where Ethelbert Nevin would croon his sweet songs ; a cotillon brilliant with costly favours within the historically rich portals of Mrs. Paran Stevens ; the Assembly Ball ; special festivities on Washington's birthday ; tearing drives on Sundays out to some twenty-miles-distant Country Club ; many and many a joyous, impromptu gathering, where we would entertain or be entertained by Dixie, the famous American actor, Clyde Fitch, the author, the Abbeys, that prince of romanticists, Joseph Leiter, and all the glad Bohemian spirits of the hour.

After a great farewell ovation, we left for our second destination, Chicago, leaving our hearts in New York, where we had been so fêted and so happy.

An interminable journey of a night and a day brought us at last to the busiest city in the world. It had been painted for us in very sinister colours by Chicagophobes of New York ; so that it was a relief to find the huge place not quite so black as we had feared. We made good friends there, had wonderful success, and gradually—for we stayed a fortnight—acquired a fondness for its ruthless work, its ruthless play, its whirling, grinding wheels of never-resting life. In its homes there was endless wealth, of course ; and wealth was bringing with it all that it can buy of beauty and culture. Chicago was crying out, in a loud, hoarse voice, for the Best ; and to get the Best was a large part of its daily, its almost blood-stained toil. This is how it seemed to us, Chicago with its million factories, its unending noise, its lawlessness (sand-bagging the stranger in the streets at night was a fashion prevailing at the time), its great, immeasurable Lake, its great, immeasurable industry, its somewhat elephantine gaiety, its breathless hurry, its fevered incompleteness. But I speak of twenty years ago. No doubt Chicago has achieved a beautiful, classic calm in the meanwhile.

In quaint and pretty Philadelphia, with its avenues of trees, its old houses, its sense of Penn and a mighty Peace, we fell in with two sweet friends of whom, though I never saw them again after leaving America, we cherished loving memories. These were Mr. and Mrs. Lippincott. They were devoted to Herbert and me, and they devoted themselves to us. At parting she gave me a golden twenty-dollar piece, saying : " Keep this, and you will always have money." How often have I longed for the £5 it represented ! But I have never parted with it, because of her kind prophecy. It was on our way either to Philadelphia or to Baltimore that Herbert, as was his genial custom, invited the whole company to dine with us on our Sunday arrival. In due course we were assembled, and Herbert ordered the usual magnums wherewith to slake our thirst. To our dismay, to his rage, we were told that no wine could be served in that town on Sundays. Furious at this thwarting of his hospitable intent, alternately speechless with wrath and voluble with invective, Herbert denounced the whole American race, predicted its speedy downfall, declared that the matter should have world-wide publicity, and was only stemmed in his torrents by someone suggesting that some such keepsake as Mrs. Lippincott had bestowed upon me might soften the heart and open the cellar. The dinner proceeded, and a hilarious evening ended amid a sea of champagne and liqueurs. Herbert said on that occasion, as on many and many another, " I can always get what I want." It was true.

Boston—beautiful city on its beautiful river—is memorable because of our visit to Harvard, where Herbert delivered a lecture to the students. It was a great occasion, and one of lively

emotion. Wonderful it was for him, for us both, to see, to address, to hear the plaudits of Young America : so fresh, so eager,
so warm in their welcome, so tumultuous in their delight.   I
remember their enthusiastic appreciation of his point about the
proverb, " Whom the gods love die young."   To Herbert this
had always meant, and he told them so, " Whom the gods love
never grow old "—good tidings to their yearning, aspiring youth !
Then it was, in the course of this speech at Harvard, that Herbert
first gave that wonderful " stunt " of his—delivering " To be
or not to be " in the voice and manner of Falstaff : delivering
Falstaff's " Honour " speech from *Henry IV.* in the voice and
manner of Hamlet—for Herbert declared the philosophy of both
speeches was exactly the same.   Harvard rose to him.

In Boston, too, we went to see the Girton of America, which,
to my mind, tremendously out-Girtoned our own Women's University ; but I daresay I was prejudiced by the charm and
quickness and reciprocity of our girl-graduate hostesses, who
surrounded themselves with all that was most beautiful in modern
thought.   Their shelves teemed with poets, their walls glittered
with reproductions of Old Masters and the gems of Watts and
Burne-Jones : they seemed athirst for beauty and culture.   Immediately on our arrival at Washington we were entertained by
the Henry Whites, they of the beautiful bearing and exquisite
manners, who, for some reason or other, were absent for the
moment from their diplomatic duties in London.   This plunged
us *in medias res* of political life : Sir Julian and Lady Pauncefote
entertained us at the Embassy, and their daughter drove me
about and around, sight-seeing.   Washington, the white city,
whose stately streets are as rays emanating from the Capitol
environs !   " Whither the tribes go up, the tribes of the Lord,"
sprang to my lips the moment I saw those gleaming streets
converging and mounting in the winter sunlight : and I never
think of Washington without those words coming into my
head.

Presentation to the President (who had attended our opening
night) was, of course, part of our happy experience, and we have
often since contrasted that ceremonial with the far simpler one
of our presentation to Queen Victoria.   To gain access to Mr.
Cleveland was through tortuous mazes of police, soldiers, servants,

secretaries; through endless succession of chambers, ante-rooms, corridors, staircases; arms presented, pistols levelled (as it seemed to us), until, at last, suddenly, just when we had given up all hope, we came to a massive writing-table, from behind whose piled documents there rose—for all the world as though it might be Whiteley—a massive man, who gave us courteous greeting. Once in his actual presence, the awe and difficulty of our penetration thither were at an end. He was delightful: simple, affable, amusing, so that really one forgot to tremble in the orbit of the vast powers bestowed upon him.

In Washington it was that Herbert and I had the privilege of meeting two of her distinguished writers, Thomas Nelson Page and Colonel John Hay. Delightful company themselves, they bequeathed us delightful company, in the shape of their books, treasures still jealously guarded. They came to supper with us, and our other guest was Rudyard Kipling, who charmed us with stories of his farm in Vermont, " and all its wild life tamed by love "—surely the cradle of his " Jungle Book " and " Just-So " fancies ?

The Leiters' house, whose white *salon* was dreamy with exquisite, priceless Boucher panels, was memorable to us because of its three daughters, each one more radiant than the last. The eldest, Mary, with her angel-face, had just become engaged to Mr. George Curzon, who was already a shining light in the English political world. It is impossible to imagine a more exquisite two—destined as they were to a great future. I have already spoken of Joseph Leiter, the son of the house. His stories of adventure and hair-breadth 'scapes were told with such conviction, such childish faith in their truth, that one found oneself accepting them with breathless belief. One of the simplest of his escapades had been the rescue of a convoy from destruction by his having held back by the weight of his own unaided body an express train travelling at full speed ! Pale with wonder, we were wont to listen; and only afterwards, when Herbert, less sceptical by nature than I, would go over the story in horror-stricken corroboration, did he begin to have his doubts.

We were loth to leave stately Washington of vivid impressions; still more loth to leave America, as we did a week or two later. It was arranged that we should all see Niagara before our departure ; but at the last moment we sent the Company without us, as there was much to be done. Fortunate, indeed, was it for Herbert that we stayed behind, for on the very last night of our sojourn in New York we saw acted *Trilby*. After the second act Herbert left our box, completed the purchase then and there, and sailed the next day with the MS. in his pocket. Many friends came to see us off, and the vessel seemed in danger of shipwreck from the wealth of flowers and fruit laid at our feet. Glad as we were to be going to our children, yet the bright gold of the Statue of Liberty was dimmed by our tears as we passed it in farewell. Sweet, sweet memories did we retain of fine, eager, great-hearted America.

We reached home laden with trucks of toys, " notions " and books for Viola and Felicity, and our home in Sloane Street, graced by the children's greetings, seemed very fair and good to us.

CHAPTER V

HERBERT lost not a day in getting into Haymarket harness. He had, I think, already decided on his scheme for the building of a new theatre on the site of the old Her Majesty's Opera House, and the air was all a-flutter with his plans. After a stop-gap or two, Herbert revived *Fédora*, with Mrs. Patrick Campbell as Fédora, himself as Loris Ipanoff, and—glad tidings when it became known—Lady Bancroft as the Princess.

This proved for a time an unparalleled success, for Mrs. Patrick Campbell had immense vogue, and the part of Fédora suited her mysterious beauty, her passionate wistfulness, her shadowy grace, to a miracle. The return of Lady Bancroft to the stage was also a great attraction, and this revival should have been a sensational " money-maker "—but unfortunately, after a few weeks of the fever-heat of popularity, Mrs. Campbell lost her voice and was unable to appear ; the excitement faded, the houses dwindled, the fireworks fizzled out. I say this to my shame : for it was I who played Fédora in Mrs. Campbell's stead, learning the part in one night and acting it the next—to perfection, as I fondly believed. Whatever the rest of the cast in Sardou's drama, it is only Fédora herself who counts, and in my failure there could not have been a better example of the triumph of a puissant personality over mere talent.

The Summer months are busy with plans for the new theatre, whose building cannot actually begin until the old Her Majesty's is demolished, and also busy with the more immediate plans of finding a Trilby. To this end—to the discovery of a Trilby who should embody, literally from head to foot, *La Grande Trilby* of the novel, Herbert, du Maurier himself, and many a lover of the book devoted themselves.

Photo by]

MISS DOROTHEA BAIRD AS "TRILBY."

[T. C. Turner.

It seemed an impossible task. Great height, a perfect head, a perfect foot, joyous youth and health, brown hair, blue eyes, the figure of a Venus of Milo, and last, but above all, an actress— how could such a combination even exist, much less be ready to hand ? Yet it was found : exact in every detail, in Dorothea Baird, a divine girl of eighteen, who would seem to have fallen from Heaven in answer to the prayers of author and manager. She had had only a year's experience, but that had been of the best kind—Viola, Beatrice and Hermione in Mr. Ben Greet's Shakespearean productions. Mr. du Maurier used to tell me that when Herbert and he broke in upon her, they found her lying all her lovely length upon a sofa, surrounded by books, and engaged in studying Desdemona. They asked her if she would like to act Trilby, and in their hearts decided then and there that none other should. By the end of the week she was rehearsing, and her success is, of course, historic.

" On the stage the resemblance to du Maurier's heroine had been perfect. Form and features alike suggested the ministering angel of ' Les trois Angliches at the Place St. Anatole des Arts,' but would the resemblance hold good in real life ? Trilby herself came downstairs to meet me, with parted lips and outstretched hands, ' wistful and sweet.' This was Trilby in the flesh. With a difference, though. The singularly level brows were not thick and dark, but finely pencilled, as if drawn with a camel's-hair brush in a tone that exactly matched her beautiful golden-brown hair, which hung down far below her waist and clung in delicious little curves round her broad, low brow."

Trilby was first produced at Manchester in the course of our autumn tour. The success was beyond our wildest dreams. It took Manchester, as it was destined to take London, by storm. There can never have been a more radiant cast of a radiant play. First, that ideal Trilby, " whom to look at was to love," who won every heart before her opening " *Salut, mes enfants*," had left her mouth ; then the three, the perfectly-looked and acted three, Taffy, the Laird, and Little Billee (Lionel Brough, Edmund Maurice and H. V. Esmond), Madame Vinard, embodiment of jollity and good heart (Annie Hughes, succeeded in London by Rosina Filippi), those darling spirits of mirth, Zou-zou and Dodor

(Gerald du Maurier and Herbert Ross), that pathetic figure of Gecko, the delicious low-comedy (I grieve to record this, for I believe that low-comedy as regards these parts was not the author's intention) of Little Billee's father and mother ; the wild, glad dancing of *really* gay *grisettes*, the happy choice of tuneful melodies—how the audiences revelled in and rose to all these ! And Svengali ! In the language of a London critic : " Svengali, marvellous Svengali—a weird, spectral, Satanic figure—he literally took away our breath." Yes, it was a creation that took away one's breath with the sheer force of its genius, with its wealth, its unfathomable depths of fantastic, unpremeditated art. The creation was so rich, so rare, so subtle, that it was beyond estimation, and thus beyond praise.

Needless to say that when the Haymarket reopened in October with *Trilby* it proved the greatest success that Herbert had ever had. It was " the rage," as it deserved to be. We were rich and very happy. When it had been running for many months, I remember someone looking askance at my un-tiara'd brows, and asking, " What jewel did your husband give you out of his success in *Trilby* ? " I answered : " Her Majesty's Theatre, but I am not wearing it to-night." Indeed, that was the precious stone he gave me—its foundation-stone. This, in June, it was my honour to declare well and truly laid, in breaking a bottle of champagne over it, even as Shakespeare slaughtered his sheep " with a fine, tragic air."

From that time it was Herbert's joy and mine to watch the gradual growth of his theatre's walls. Herbert grew tired less quickly of acting Svengali than he did of most parts : I daresay because he was never two nights alike in it, and because he enjoyed the riotous fun of it. But his ambition could not be satisfied with simply raking in guineas and golden opinions. " Such inaction was abhorrent to your soul," as Mr. William Archer wrote of him at the time. So in the spring of 1896 we find him producing *Henry IV.* (First Part) for a series of matinées. It was done upon a very elaborate scale, as befitted the rich and lovely play, and it was finely acted. It had been Herbert's intention to alternate the parts of Falstaff and Hotspur, a *tour de force* which he actually accomplished later, but in London his own success as

Svengali.

By permission of " Punch."]

Mr. H. Beerbohm Tree.

John-o'-Dreams.

[By permission of "The Illustrated Sporting and
Dramatic News."

the fat knight and Mr. Lewis Waller's success as Hotspur made it inadvisable to change a perfect cast. The matinées were as popular as was every performance of the rival *Trilby*, which had by now reached its two-hundredth night.

And when the summer came, we gave our last performance at the Haymarket, which had become very dear to us, and which was haunted by many a happy memory. We had had our failures as well as our successes, but, as I have said, to Herbert failure never meant defeat, and some of our most exhilarating recollections came of his persistent refusal to cry " Hold, enough ! " " If you can meet with triumph and disaster, And treat those two impostors just the same," must surely have been written of Herbert ; indeed, there are many things in Kipling's fiery Sermon that stamp Herbert " a man, my son ! " He could wait and not be tired ; he could be hated and not hate ; a dreamer, he could awake to action ; a loser, he could start again from his beginnings ; at work he could indeed hold on till there was nothing in him except the Will which cried to him " Hold on ! " Yes, above all his great qualities there shines that splendid, that unconquerable Will.

In the autumn of 1896, while yet Her Majesty's Theatre was a seething mass of scaffold poles, Herbert left for his second tour in America. Reasons of health forbade my going with him, and I was left disconsolate in Sloane Street. To give me hope and occupation in his absence (for I was heart-broken at his going, so closely had our lives been knit since our journey to America together), he put me upon a sort of Committee that met every week for the consideration of the new theatre's progress. It pleased me to imagine myself useful and important, and I find that Herbert kept all the letters I wrote him, letters full of little things—complaints, musings, repinings, rejoicings—Oh ! how sweet, how bitter in widowhood to re-read !

Herbert was absent from October until the end of January, and our third little daughter, Iris, was a week old when he returned. It had been quite settled and determined beforehand that the new baby should be the boy of the family, for both Herbert and I longed for a son ; but the frost of our disappointment was soon melted away by the calm and inextinguishable sunshine of the new-comer. " Shall I compare thee to a summer's day ? " became an invariable morning question, and her blue eyes smilingly answered, " I am more lovely and more temperate."

The American tour had not been too successful, and there was rather an anxious time ahead, for the new theatre was a monster whose devouring jaws opened wider and wider every day, demanding the bullion and specie which had somehow to be found. While Herbert was waiting for the completion of its building, we went together on a little tour, though autumn and not spring was the accepted time for touring. No great good came of it. It served, however, as " a prelude to the swelling act of the Imperial theme," and brought the proud hour nearer when Her Majesty's Theatre should open its doors.

The day came at last, and a great day it was. To the very last moment details were being added, our friend Mr. Romaine Walker, to whom we owed the internal decoration, and Mr. Phipps the architect, presiding and insisting that the proper Louis Quinze spirit should prevail. Well do I remember looking in as late as six o'clock, and finding to our horror and dismay that some kind firm of pottery-makers had sent in hundreds of huge vessels, crude, shiny, in shades of yellow, peacock blue and crushed strawberry—the very worst products of an ugly age. By dint of frantic endeavour, these abominations were removed in time to prevent their marring the beautiful symmetry and simplicity of Mr. Phipps' and Mr. Romaine Walker's design, but they had given us a terrible shock, and had nearly driven from my head the Poet Laureate's inaugural address which it was my privilege to speak.

Thus trivially, and probably with a hundred other such pin-pricks, was ushered in so great an hour in Herbert's life—how great he may have guessed, but I had little idea. It is easy, looking back, to gauge the courage, the foresight, the leadership that urged him to embark upon so huge an enterprise, but at the time one accepted it as no more than the launching of a new play. Except to him, who always went breast-forward, never doubted, the undertaking gave rise to a hundred head-shakes. Many a wiseacre foretold a debtor's prison if not a felon's death for the brave builder of the House Beautiful (or, happier still, of the

House Full, as it so often proved). The opening night was a delirium for both of us of pride, terror, joy, anxiety, hair-breadth 'scapes (as, for instance, when the Prince of Wales entered the theatre the electric current failed, leaving the Heir-Apparent in all too apparent darkness)—too fast each one of these did tread upon one another's heels. Time has not spread a greater mist over that first night than did the fevers of the night itself. In a dream I nerved myself to part the crimson velvet curtains and confront the dazzling, kindly, sweetly-welcoming audience. In a dream Herbert and I heard the noble voice of Clara Butt ring out " God save the Queen "—in a dream we heard the thunder of congratulating applause that greeted him, as for the first time he made his bow to one of the enthusiastic thousands who were destined to throng his theatre in triumphant years to come.

" Very well met, and welcome," were the first words spoken to an audience in Herbert's theatre, and it was to me that Herbert accorded the honour of speaking them. Sweet and sacred it is for me to recall this grace, as it is sweet and sacred to remember that he chose me to bless its first stone.

" This is a great moment in my little life," said Herbert in his speech at the close of this memorable evening. " I feel very proud as I stand here facing this theatre and this audience to-night. There is so much I should like to say, so little that I can, yet I must express my thanks to those to whom I owe this beautiful theatre ; I hope you are satisfied with it ? I am ! Fate is blind, but I have one great power behind me in that I have your goodwill and that of the Public. And this at least I can promise, in the words my wife spoke to-night, we shall do nothing to shame the name we are honoured in being allowed to use. I hope you are pleased with the play, and that it may be given to me to cater for you for many years to come, as I have been proud and happy to do in the past."

It was with Sir Gilbert Parker's *The Seats of the Mighty* that Herbert's career at Her Majesty's began. This was a vivid and picturesque drama by the playwright from his novel of the name, and it served as an admirable send-off to Herbert's enterprise. It was followed after three or four months' run by Sydney

Grundy's adaptation of *Mademoiselle de Belle-Isle*—a delicious play to which he gave the title of *The Silver Key*. This was produced as late as July, so that it should form part of our tour programme. It proved an immense success, witty, dainty, bewitching trifle that it was. Herbert's part, le Duc de Richelieu, and mine were delightful comedy parts, and Evelyn Millard—lovely, gifted actress—was the heroine.

It was at the opening of Her Majesty's Theatre that Mr. Dana came to us in the capacity of Acting Manager—and acting manager he remained for twenty-one years. He was a slave to Herbert's interests and to his work, and absolutely devoted to his " Chief " ; so much so that he was sometimes a little hard on those who were not his Chief. But that is the perfect Lieutenant, when there is disregard of everyone and everything that interferes with single-hearted loyalty to the Head. Herbert had a great and true friend in Henry Dana, who served him for so many years. The following letter will show the affection and confidence existing between them :

" DEAR LADY TREE,
" Your request that I should give you a few recollections of my association with Sir Herbert takes me back over a period of twenty-one years, during which time our relations were of the happiest character. We went through strenuous times together, and the run of success was not by any means unbroken. At times we differed as to the policy of the theatre, when heated arguments followed, but that never made any difference to our mutual esteem, and a good understanding was soon arrived at.
" I recall one occasion when temper ran high. I left the room. He called me back, and I refused to return. Within a few minutes he followed me up to my office, and held out his hand, frankly admitting that he had been in the wrong, and, needless to say, a complete reconciliation followed. It takes a big man to do that to an employee.
" Another fine point in his character was his accessibility to the smallest member of his company or the most humble member of his staff. He treated all with equal courtesy, the

result being esteem and loyalty from all who served under his banner.

" He had the exceptional gift of bringing out any latent talent in his artists. Many of the leading actors and actresses of to-day owe their rise in their profession to the early training they received at his hands. He was an optimist and an opportunist. The former trait often led to trouble, but the latter served him well. One point in our long association was somewhat unique. During the whole period, we never exchanged even a letter of contract. We each knew that the other's word was sufficient. This was the more remarkable as we were not by any means always in agreement and we were both hot-tempered, impulsive men. But the real affection and appreciation we had for each other tided us over any temporary misunderstanding.

" It must be left to abler pens than mine to do justice to one of the most remarkable personalities that the English stage has ever known, and I can only add in conclusion that it will ever be with me a proud and happy memory to have been associated with the glorious record of His Majesty's Theatre.

" Sincerely yours,
" HENRY DANA."

Herbert had meant to open Her Majesty's with *Julius Cæsar*, but time and the particular cast on which he had set his heart were lacking ; so that it was not until the end of January, 1898, that he was ready with this, his fourth and most ambitious Shakespearean venture (one must not count *Katherine and Petruchio*, for it is but a garbled version of *The Taming of the Shrew*). Herbert hesitated long as to which part he should choose in *Julius Cæsar*—Brutus or Marc Antony. Wiseacres used to come to him and say, " *You* must be Cæsar," " You must be Cassius," and even, in spite of his slim build, " Casca is the only part for you, Chief ! " But it was only between Brutus and Marc Antony that he wavered, and, owing, I think, to my entreaties, he settled on Marc Antony. For Casca he cast Louis Calvert, that fine Shakespearean actor, who not only acted the part to perfection, but also rendered Herbert invaluable service over the production, for long experience and great theatrical forerunners had made him master of many a masterpiece of the stage.

The play was, I think, perfectly acted. Cæsar (Charles Fulton), Marc Antony (Herbert), Brutus (Lewis Waller), Cassius (Franklyn Macleay), Casca (Louis Calvert), Portia (Evelyn Millard), Calpurnia (Lily Hanbury) ; even all the little parts, such as Lucius, for which I cast myself (at the same time casting my shoes and skimming barefoot all over the stage) ; these made up an *ensemble* that can never, *should* never be forgotten. Sir Alma Tadema not only designed and with his own hands draped every dress in the play, but also with his own hands made phalerians, shields, armour and insignia. I can see him now, in the Property Room, showing exactly how the faggots borne by the red lictors should be bound ; I see him drawing the letters of the S.P.Q.R. that were lifted aloft by the Roman Guards. What happiness it was to see the gradual growth to perfection of so much beauty !

Herbert did actually *study* Marc Antony ; spurred to this unusual effort by Louis Calvert, who urged " tradition," and by me, who thought I knew every intonation that the part required. But it all ended in Herbert going his own way, and we, his would-be teachers, had to acknowledge in the end that his own way was best.

Nothing more noble and splendid can ever have been seen upon the stage than Herbert's production of *Julius Cæsar*, and it met with all the appreciation and enthusiasm that it deserved. The gorgeous pageantry of the opening scene, instinct with a life and meaning that made doubly beautiful the fateful, sonorous speeches ; the mystery and loveliness of Brutus' Orchard, with its terror of gathering storm even as gathered the storm in Brutus' tortured heart, even as gathered and muttered the storm of conspiracy ; greatest of all, the wonder and horror of the scene in the Capitol, enhancing as it did, by the mere force of its staging and grouping, the wonder and horror of the immortal words— how memorable were all these ! Night after night was one drawn to watch that glowing picture ; to watch " this our lofty scene be acted over," from the gradual, stealthy approach of the crowd of white-robed, crimson-mantled Senators towards the feet of imperious, purple-clad Cæsar until they had formed a ring of murder round about him ; on to the terrible uplifting of their dripping swords, as they cried in dreadful unison, " Peace, Freedom and Liberty ! " Then the silent, breathless, fearsome falling apart as the great figure of Marc Antony appeared, like a grim question silencing the heroics that died on guilty lips.

It is, of course, Shakespeare, and not any interpreter of him, that we must blame for the almost unbearably tragic intensity of this moment. There stands Marc Antony among the murderers, searching their eyes with his own scorching, agonized gaze, as each man renders him his bloody hand, while Casca with rude intent and purposeful cruelty smirches with a crimson stain the arm of butchered Cæsar's friend. One actually saw a new soul grow in careless, light-hearted Antony who revels late o' nights ; one saw grey purpose blotting out the gay colour of his life ; one saw doubt, fear and foreboding spread like a pall over the confronters of this new Antony, this changed man come to judge the cruel issue of these bloody men. This scene was not acted—it was *lived* by all concerned. Herbert towered above them (again Shakespeare is to be blamed) like an avenging angel : albeit an angel with no less of Lucifer than of Gabriel in his attitude.

Something too much of this, I fear ! But I must be forgiven for dwelling upon scenes so perfect, so unforgettable ; I must be forgiven that there rings in my ears for ever the wistful cry :

" O world ! thou wert the forest to this hart,
  And this, indeed, O world, the heart of thee."

Julius Cæsar aroused pæans of praise and established Herbert at once and for always as a great Shakespearean producer. I am tempted to quote from a foremost critic :

" The performance of *Julius Cæsar* on Saturday night may fairly be called a revelation : it was the most magnificent presentation of a Shakespearean play that has been seen in our time."

And again :

" The impulse which prompted Mr. Tree to revive the greatest of Shakespeare's historical dramas was a sound one ; and nobly has he executed his design. It was less a drama than an immortal page from the world's history that was last night unrolled in a series of gorgeous Tadema pictures ; and it was more than an honourable page that we then saw added to the history of our English stage.

"What Mr. Tree has accomplished in this revival of *Julius Cæsar* must give every student pause. He has lightly brushed aside the difficulties that have seemingly paralysed his managerial predecessors. He has removed from the theatre the reproach of fifty years' neglect of a great work of universal interest. With loving labour and at infinite cost he has resurrected ancient Rome in all its unimagined glory. And incidentally he has paid to the genius of our national poet a tribute unequalled in our time. . . ."

It was but natural that throughout that happy, auspicious spring and summer we should tread, Herbert and I, upon air. We both gloried in his triumph, in his justification as a Master-Builder, in his establishment of his theatre thus early in its life as an Institution, a noble and dignified one, worthy of the art that he who reared it loved.

The play and the theatre absorbed us both a great deal— absorbed Herbert, of course, almost entirely. I suppose we what is called " knew everybody and went everywhere," or rather, we were asked everywhere ; but Herbert grew less and less inclined for " social functions," and loved nothing so much as a gathering of two or three people at our own home. He had honour, love, obedience, troops of friends—ah ! and some enemies too, or one could not have pronounced him really great. Among the new friends that *Julius Cæsar* brought us was Lord Rose-bery, whose own adoring knowledge of Shakespeare made him grateful to Herbert for his. After one of his visits to the theatre (a visit, I remember, succeeded by a charming supper at his house, where either our host or Herbert invented a Shakespeare guessing-game, in which, much to their father's delight, the daughters of the house distinguished themselves)—after one of these visits Lord Rosebery made a speech at a County Council meeting in St. James's Hall (can it have been the initial meeting of this body ?), and in the course of it he gave Herbert historic praise. " The Roman," he said, " was proud of Rome. He should be prouder still of London. Why, gentlemen, within a stone's-throw of this Hall you can see put upon the stage with all the splendour and

all the art that taste and expenditure can afford, the sublime
tragedy of Julius Cæsar." These little sentences were treasured
by Herbert as among his proudest tributes.

In our home-life it was still my delight to collect pretty
things, and to have the little house as dainty and comfortable as
it could be, while it was Herbert's unconscious pride to bring his
friends to it. The children—Iris, a baby, Felicity a lovely three-
year-old, and little Viola, an incipient Royal Academician, of
literary, sporting and dramatic tastes—the children were a daily
delight to Herbert, who, short as was the time he could give them,
was happiest of all in their company.

He used to ride every morning, and the children loved to
waylay him in the Park, or to follow him in perambulating
procession as he ambled up Sloane Street. His horse—ah !
thereby hangs a tale (not unnaturally). One winter—1896,
perhaps—I had gone without Herbert on a little visit to Lady
Wantage at Lockinge. There on the Berkshire Downs I saw a
lovely horse which was for sale. In my mind's-eye I put Herbert
upon its back, and the picture pleased me. I returned to London
the secret possessor, for the sum of £60, of what the groom
described as "a very nice little bit of horseflesh." On one
another's birthdays we were wont to spring little surprises—a
bicycle pretending to be a bonnet, a watch inside a breakfast roll,
and so forth. On this particular birthday of Herbert's I first
brought him up "Bingo," our accustomed poodle, with a new bow
tied among his ringlets, and a declaration that he was this year's
lovely present. Herbert laughed at the joke, but grew wistful
at the disappointment ; whereupon I told him I had a piece of
furniture in the hall, but could not bring it up. This roused him
to scant enthusiasm, for he knew my modern antiques too well.
When he came down, however, crying, "Where's this boasted
present ? " the front door was opened, and there on the doorstep
stood Viola, holding the horse's head—the horse on the pavement,
its front hoofs on the mat ! Nothing I ever gave him—though
how he loved and cherished his watch and the chain woven of all
our initials !—nothing gave him so much pleasure as the horse,
which he rode for so many years that some unkind wag declared
that it turned from a roan into a chestnut. This (kept at an

A SNAPSHOT, 1896.

adjoining livery-stable), the poodle, an exquisite greyhound given us by David Murray, and the perfection of a white Persian cat, completed our sum of household pets ; for Viola's snake-craze had died an unnatural death with the demise of the Saundersonian reptile.

In the autumn of 1898, after an unusually triumphant tour, which, of course, included *Julius Cæsar*, Herbert produced *The Musketeers*—an adaptation of the immortal Dumas romance by Sydney Grundy. This brilliant piece of work had an enormous success. Mrs. Brown-Potter was still in the zenith of her beauty and grace, though no longer the girlish wonder who had pulverized London ten years before, and her Miladi, Herbert's D'Artagnan, Mabel Love's Gabrielle, and the delightful Porthos, Athos and Aramis of Louis Calvert, Gerald du Maurier and Henry Mills, together with a perfect production, made up an evening of unalloyed joy and high spirits. As the Queen, I had lovely dresses and jewels, and I sang " *Enfant, si j'étais roi* " to a delicious setting ; otherwise I did not matter much ; though every performance in that great theatre, full to overflowing, was as full of joy, amid constant happenings and excitements.

From November to April, 1899, " Mr. Tree's superb production of *The Musketeers* dazzled and delighted London," as a leading critic put it, and it was taken off, alas ! in the heyday of its success, because Herbert was under contract to produce another play, a modern drama, *Carnac Sahib*, by Henry Arthur Jones.

In the autumn Herbert produced his splendid, his beautiful *King John*. It was superbly given, superbly acted ; who that saw it will ever forget the Constance of Julia Neilson, the Hubert of Fernandez, the Arthur of Arthur Colmore, that strange, tragic, panther-like King John, the King John of Herbert Tree ? And the exquisite stage-pictures—who should describe their utter beauty ?

The play of *King John* is less human, less appealing to a public than *Julius Cæsar ;* but Herbert's courage, perception of beauty and genius of stage-management were manifest no less in one than in the other ; one was no less a tribute of love and reverence to Shakespeare than the other.

To quote from a contemporary critic : " Meanwhile, let us

be grateful for *King John*, and go to see it all we can, for it is a page of English History set in glorious motion, of which we may be proud and never tired."

But while the mimic battles were waging without the walls of Angiers at Her Majesty's, there fell upon England the mutterings of real war. Strange days began of elation and triumph, fading to gradual apprehension, mourning and dismay.

The early days of it were hectic and hectoring. London, such of you as stayed at home, you swaggered and banged a great deal ; and you were never " tired of killing Kruger with your mouth." Apropos of Kipling's poem, I had a great adventure of my own in connection with it—an adventure of which Herbert at first disapproved, but of which later he learnt to be a little proud. I had been asked to recite for some important charity, and I saw that Rudyard Kipling's new poem was announced to appear on the same day that my concert was to take place. With unusual courage I telegraphed to the Editor of *The Daily Mail*, asking if I might be allowed an advance copy of the promised poem, so that I might learn it and recite it at St. James's Hall on the very day of its appearance in his paper. Very courteously my request was granted, sanctioned by the author, and I received (I have it now) the proof, typewritten and corrected by Kipling's own hand. It reached me, I think, on Friday evening, after Herbert had left for the theatre (there was no part for me in *King John*). I read it and had the judgment to see in it one of the greatest human appeals ever made. Without a word to Herbert, who would most certainly have forbidden it, I took hansom for the Palace Theatre, then the most prominent of music halls ; nor would I rest until I was in the presence of Mr. Charles Morton—dear, good Mr. Charles Morton—to whom I unfolded my plan. I would learn and recite " The Absent-Minded Beggar " every night at the Palace Theatre for a king's ransom of a salary—half of which I would give to war charities. In a few minutes the whole affair was settled. I was to appear on the following Monday. There remained but to confess to Herbert ! I hardly dared to, for in those days a feud, with Herbert as commander-in-chief, was raging between theatres and music halls. In great trepidation I waited for him to come trailing his golden robes from the stage to the wings, and I saw his greeting smile die upon his lips as I made my avowal. He was angry and horrified, but the mischief was done and beyond repair. Reluctantly he gave his consent, though only on condition that I used none of my salary myself, but devoted the whole of it to the war. " Give all—give all," he cried. " Half is half-hearted." So it came about, and for ten triumphant weeks, for the first and only time in my life, I, without aid from anyone but my author (aid enough, in all conscience !), drew the town. On the second night at the Palace the audience rose and showered gold and silver on to the stage—an impulse which was unfortunately checked, lest the hurling of the coins should hurt me. I would willingly have run the risk of " two lovely black eyes " for such a golden result—but Mr. Morton came on to the stage, making a speech in which he miscalled the feverish generosity of the audience " an outrage," and in which he entreated them to desist. Alas ! notices were placed all over the theatre begging that enthusiasm money should be placed in boxes provided for the purpose ! Of course this meant a loss of thousands of pounds : there is all the difference in the world between the act of soberly and after reflection dropping a cold coin into a casket and the joyous abandon of flinging in a fine frenzy every valuable one has—even the brooch from one's breast —in answer to a passionate appeal, with outstretched hands, to " Pay, pay, pay ! "

My example of reciting the poem and of giving everything I earned was imitated all over the kingdom, and I believe I was responsible directly and indirectly for mints and mints of money ; but then, as I have said, " The Absent-Minded Beggar " made irresistible appeal. Of all the praise I had—and I had much—I liked best that of brilliant, all-conquering Harry Cust—that passionate Imperialist—who came, after hearing me, and said, with tears in his eyes, " You seemed like a bit of England."

All this is about me ; and not about Herbert and me ; but yet it did concern our shared lives, for it taught him a new pride and reliance in me. And my adventure concerned him, also, in after-time, for it was this utterly unprecedented departure of mine that helped in the end to break down the barrier between theatre and music hall. This is a fact, however, for which Herbert was by no means disposed to forgive me—or not for many years.

I had to forgo my triumphs at the Palace after ten weeks, and long before the tumult and the shouting had died, because Herbert wanted me for Titania in *A Midsummer Night's Dream.* I have often wondered how so unlikely a mortal as I came to be cast for that fairiest of fairy parts. I think it must have been because of my great love for the words and my sense of mystery and music. At all events, it proved not the least happy bit of casting in an extraordinarily happy cast, crowned by the Oberon of Julia Neilson. This was a noble and radiant creation, a golden King of the Fairies, instinct with poetry and dignity. With what majesty of beauty and utterance she spoke the divine speeches ! " And the imperial votaress passed on, In maiden meditation, fancy-free "—rings in my ears ; as does her lovely singing of " I know a bank whereon the wild thyme grows." By the by, it was my suggestion that she should sing this to the setting of Mendelssohn's " *Auf Flügel des Gesanges.*" It must have been an entrancing production, carried on to every available atom of Mendelssohn's entrancing sounds. Music-lovers would come over and over again to see the play, arriving at a quarter to eight that they might hear the perfectly-played and interpreted overture.

Well do I remember the final dress-rehearsal two days before the production. It was one of those fiasco rehearsals such as from time to time precede a triumph or a disaster. It lasted until the small hours of the morning. The poor, tired little fairies had all been sent home at midnight, stuffed with sandwiches and stuffed into cabs. Everyone except Herbert was cross, worn-out and correspondingly despondent. He, as always, rose to the occasion ; summoned a few of us to his room, and for an hour— probably from 4 to 5 a.m.—we discussed how failure was to be averted, how things were to be pulled together, what could be done to evolve order and beauty from chaos. And lo ! the first night brought a performance without a hitch ; such fairies, lighting and scenery as had never before been seen—a very Midsummer Night's Dream of loveliness and magic.

It ran for many happy months, being one of Herbert's greatest managerial successes. As actor, there was really no part for him in the play. Oberon is the hero, the be-all and the end-all of *A Midsummer Night's Dream.* I hated to see Herbert acting Bottom the Weaver, as I hated to see him act Caliban in *The*

Tempest—I had rather have seen him as Theseus in one and as Prospero in the other—but one's opinion could not always prevail.

On the other hand, as Herod, in Stephen Phillips' beautiful play, which succeeded *A Midsummer Night's Dream*—as Herod I considered Herbert's performance unsurpassable. This was the first of the three Stephen Phillips plays that Herbert produced ; and Herbert gave it all the love and care and beauty that it deserved.

The production of *Herod* was called " a great night for the English Drama," and Herbert was lavishly praised for " his courage, faith and enterprise as well as for his devotion to that glorious side of his art which ennobles the stage "—while the setting was called prodigious—triumphant—a wonder—a miracle —a noble undertaking. " The whole tragedy is great because Herod himself is great." Herbert's acting, too, as the king

> " Pinioned in bondage of barbaric pomp,
> A tiger soul, freezing the gentle blood,
> Steeping man's destiny in dark despair "—

was widely acclaimed as reaching in its splendour and majesty the highest point of tragedy. " The close affects us like the close of some great symphony," wrote one, of that long, poignant stillness as of death when Herod, hearing that his beloved Mariamne is no more, remains " in catalepsy bound " while the Physician in his tender prophecy ventures a hope of balm to the tortured mind. (How Herbert loved these words !)

> " Rest and a world of leaves and stealing stream,
> Or charm of human words that drip and drip
> And falling boon of the beloved hand,
> And solemn swoon of music may allure
> Homeward the ranging spirit of the King.
> These things avail, but these things are of man.
> To me indeed it seems, who with dim eyes
> Behold this Herod, motionless and mute—
> To me it seems that they who grasp the world,
> The Kingdoms and the power and the glory
> Must pay with deepest misery of spirit,
> Atoning unto God for a brief brightness
> And even ransom like this rigid King
> The outward victory with inward loss."

This brings us to the spring of 1901 : when all England—all
the world—was thrown into sorrow and mourning by the death
of Queen Victoria.   I was sorry that in going to Windsor for the
funeral, Herbert missed one of the most memorable and impressive ceremonials that ever took place.   How wonderful it was
to see a nation mourning, as through the London streets the gun-
carriage bearing that small flag-covered coffin made its sad and
solemn way ! Poignant, prophetic was the rise and fall of
the music as Chopin's March, now sorrowful, now triumphant,
echoed, like a wandering voice, through the air.   Thus was
the great Queen carried through London amid her people's tears.

So profound and universal was the grief created by the
Queen's death that it seemed as though the spirits of the populace were damped for ever—it seemed as though the gaiety of
the world had suffered eclipse.   But very soon routine reasserted
itself : work, play, life glad, life dull, the everything and the
nothing of every day were quickly resumed.   In February,
Herbert put on his beautiful, memorable *Twelfth Night*, which I
will not for one moment allow was not that play's best revival
of these days, and far, far the most successful from a monetary
point of view, for it ran more than three months, to the capacity
of the theatre, which means that about 200,000 souls saw it.
I hope I may be pardoned these sordid facts, which are put
forward rather in a spirit of truth and justice than of boastfulness.

Let there be no boastfulness in my own story of Herbert's
Twelfth Night : for in connection with it I made the mistake of
my theatrical career—perhaps of my whole life.   Remembering
the flattering prophecies of Sir Charles Wyndham, for whose
judgment one had naturally a limitless respect, I hungered for
the part of Viola.   Herbert had set his heart—and events proved,
as they generally did, how absolutely right he was—on Lily
Brayton.   She was a new-comer to our theatre—a tall and
beautiful girl, who had been playing with Sir Frank Benson
in the provinces, but who with us, as yet, had merely played
two or three times as understudy for Mariamne in *Herod*.   That
she should be Viola was settled : and I was given—actually
given and I refused it !—the heavenly part of Olivia.   (I should
have acted it beautifully, by the by !)   I took the notion into
my head that Olivia was dull—dull !—and announced my inten-

tion of playing Maria. This was because I still wanted to flit and dance about the stage ; and I wanted to sing the delightful song, " Roses, their sharp spines being gone," so sweetly set to music by Paul Rubens. (Paul Rubens, I remember, made nearly all the music for the play : evolving it on the spot, on our piano one evening after supper.) Well, Olivia was assigned to beautiful Maud Jeffries, and I chose the part of Maria. I rehearsed it several times, a little dismayed to find myself ill at ease : for as a rule I fell into my parts with confident facility. One evening Mr. Dana arrived to see me—sent by Herbert, whose tender heart dreaded to administer the blow—to beg me to give up the part. " Maria ?—Maria is a *soubrette*. If you try all your life you can never be a *soubrette*," he urged ; and with many tears I could not but acknowledge he was right. It was Winter trying to be Spring, I remember ; and Herbert took me away to Aldwick, where we had a little sea-shore house—took me away to cheer me, for I was terribly cast down, as well I need have been. I filled the rooms with daffodils in yellow jugs—and daffodils in those particular yellow jugs to this day recall my pain and disappointment. Mr. Webb and Stephen Phillips were our guests, and of course all the children were there. Stephen Phillips read us " Marpessa "—divine poem—and the outlines of " Ulysses "—and in rather a sardonic spirit I held the book of *Twelfth Night*, hearing Herbert the words of Malvolio. Strange, vivid, fervid little holiday—and a gate, too—a gate that closed behind one while one was idly examining its lock.

Everyone remembers the success of *Twelfth Night :* gay, dreamy, sweet, fantastic *Twelfth Night*. Everyone remembers Olivia's garden, with its broad grass terraces (as a matter of fact, Herbert copied this scene from a garden picture in " Country Life " : stumbling as he so often did upon something that months at the British Museum could not have given him). Everyone remembers sweet, witty Viola ; gracious Olivia ; Norman Forbes' inimitable Aguecheek ; Lionel Brough's superb Sir Toby ; Herbert's Malvolio—ah ! what a Malvolio !

Herbert's Malvolio—" fantastic, dignified, abundantly absurd, yet as undeniably pathetic "—Herbert's Malvolio seems to me one of his finest acting achievements—all the more so for its utter spontaneity. Once more he drifts instantly and mechanically into the very inside of the man : there was never the slightest hesitation as to make-up, manner, or method. From the first rehearsal Malvolio materialized—if one can speak of a conception so feather-light as materializing. Herbert loved this part—loved the whole play, and used over and over again to be found in the wings shrieking with laughter over the kitchen scene, that highest point of Shakespearean fun—or so it seemed to us as acted then. One of the greatest features of Herbert's *Twelfth Night* was the Feste of Courtice Pounds—he of the exquisite voice, he of the gay and lightsome personality, he of the dancing heart. His performance ranked with Herbert's, with Lionel Brough's, with Norman Forbes'—as absolutely perfect.

The following letter from Norman Forbes is interesting :

"MY DEAR LADY TREE,

"There are so many good things that dear old Herbert has done and said since we were practically boys, that it is impossible to give you more than one or two examples of the many stories I have told you within the limitation of a letter. In case you have forgotten the Hurstmonceux one, this is it :

"When Herbert and I were with Claude Lowther one day in the garden of the castle, a large party of trippers arrived upon the scene, on a day when the castle was not open to visitors ; one of the party, however, approached our host and raising his hat said : ' Excuse me, but are you Colonel Lowther ? ' to which Claude immediately replied, pointing to Herbert, ' No, that is the Colonel.' The visitor then addressed Herbert in these words : ' I am sorry, Colonel Lowther, to have brought my party here on the wrong day, but since we are here would you allow us just to look at your beautiful gardens before we return ? ' ' Certainly,' said Herbert, ' and pick as many peaches as you like.' This was too much for Claude, who immediately advanced and said : ' Yes, and my name is Herbert Tree of His Majesty's Theatre, and I shall be delighted to put a box or stalls at your disposal whenever you care to write.' When we were all three dining together afterwards, Claude told Herbert that some of the party had asked him if he couldn't make it for the Coliseum. None laughed more heartily at this joke of Claude's than Herbert.

" He told me he had received a beautiful machine from a gramophone company for his acceptance with the request that he would allow them to publish his letter of acknowledgment. Herbert wrote : ' Dear Sir,—I have received your instrument, which seems to me to add a new terror to life and makes death a long-felt want.'

" The provincial managers, as you know, cover the hoardings and walls of towns with huge letters of the name of a London star. I happened to be passing through one of these towns on my way to see your husband and was confronted with his name in enormous block letters. I twitted Herbert with this, and he said : ' Yes, you are quite right, and when I pass my name in in such large letters I blush, but at the same time instinctively raise my hat.'

" One of the best things he ever did for me was when we first knew each other. He took me to some pretty rooms in Orchard Street and introduced me to the lady to whom he had been engaged the night before. She sang the ' Creole Love Song ' with infinite beauty and feeling ; it rings in my ears as I write and calls up the picture of those two handsome lovers and Herbert's joy at my enthusiasm of her singing. The result of this union was three handsome daughters, Viola, Iris and Felicity, the three Graces, not only embodying beauty and the Arts, but the divine sense of humour, a rich inheritance from their distinguished Father and Mother.

" What a long letter ; I hope you will be able to get through it.

" Ever yours affectionately,

" NORMAN FORBES."

CHAPTER VI

AND here this reverie of mine—for it is nothing more—this reverie called " Herbert and I " should come to an end ; for after the production of *Twelfth Night* it would be idle to pretend that in reaching towards his high goal Herbert walked hand-in-hand with me. A little chain of us followed him : Viola, Felicity, Iris and I making up the links, for he made even those tiny babies interested in his work. According to their temperaments, Felicity when she was four was hearing him his parts, Iris when she was two was repeating them by heart, Viola from infancy was designing his scenery.

One reason why it is no longer " Herbert and I " is that our ten years in Sloane Street came to an end. That meant good-bye to our happy little suppers there : good-bye to a great deal that had made our home so sweet. When a passing doctor set his heart on our white front-door and the lattice windows of our dining-room and arrived, cash in hand, to buy us out, we were beguiled into giving up our little house. Certainly we had outgrown it, and Viola's manifold pursuits cried aloud for something of a studio ; but I am afraid we left behind us more than what a polite interviewer described as " Mr. Tree's exquisitely appointed and tastefully decorated dwelling " !

Long were we in finding a new home. We pic-nicked for a year in Westminster, where I found a tiny little Georgian house in a street which Herbert thought " slum," but which is now the abode of all the rich and most of the great. There was no room for the two little girls, who had to have lodgings with their nurse in the house opposite ; there they languished over " whooping the whoop," as Herbert called it (whether then or after " looping " I cannot remember). But by this time Herbert's beautiful " Dome " room had come into being—and he became all too independent of entertaining rooms or rooms for business transactions at home. There followed many years of entertaining joyful gatherings, happy carousals there ; but there he was the host, and though I was responsible, as at Sloane Street, for the well-being of our guests, I never conquered my feeling that I was a guest myself. However, our home life, though in abeyance for a time, was by no means over, and when we found the lovely Charles-the-Second house at Chiswick, all our household gods emerged from their warehousing, and my passion for curtain-hanging and furniture-hunting began anew. Walpole House in Chiswick Mall, which we took in June, 1904, had been rebuilt by Charles the Second for Barbara Villiers—and there could be nothing more beautiful, comely and stately than its rooms and staircases, its windows, wainscots, its terrace, its high-walled garden and orchard, its tall and graceful iron gates. Over those very gates did Becky Sharp fling the lexicon at Miss Pinkerton, for Thackeray made Walpole House the scene of Becky's school-days.

Tapping with her little heels along the broad, shallow stairs, and standing in the tall, stately windows of the great drawing-room, the ghost of Barbara Villiers was to be heard and seen— seen, wringing her hands for the loss of her beauty ! During our time there is no record of her having been encountered ; but I remember so well, before we actually took the house, meeting a lady in the garden whom I had never seen before, whom I never heard of again. She said to me very gravely, " Are you quite, quite determined on taking this place ? " " Quite," I answered with enthusiastic determination. She turned away with a sigh, murmuring, " Then I will say no more." *She* may have seen poor Barbara Villiers—but she did not unfold her tale, and I was left wondering. Certainly there came a day when a woman stood at one of those stately windows over-looking the broad silver river—stood and bewailed the loss of such good looks as she ever possessed. Perhaps my mysterious garden-lady foresaw that such a misfortune would overtake the châtelaine of that house ?

Oh, but that house !—to which I devoted all my taste and care ; and her studio and garden, to which Viola devoted her life and thought—how enchanting they were, and how Herbert loved the all too little time there that each busy day allowed him ! That was its drawback : its disenchanting distance. A motor we had by now, but more often than not our early motors, like our early chauffeurs, refused to work ; and taxi-cabs had not yet attained their proper rank. Thus Chiswick Mall seemed miles and miles away. All our interests—the theatre, the children's education, Viola's singing lessons, Viola's friends, my friends—all were seven leagues from our home—and so it came that much of its loveliness was lost on us. We saw more of the ugliness and squalor of King Street, Hammersmith, than of the peace and dignity of our King's house, our garden and our river,

"Though deep yet clear; though gentle, yet not dull."

I cannot add " without o'erflowing full," for the Thames had a curious and disconcerting habit of entering our kitchen unannounced, and we used to find the servants riding the waves on broomsticks. This only happened twice, for our good friend and landlord, Sir John Thornycroft, came to our rescue in the character of Canute, and, more effectually than his forerunner, forbade such procedure on the part of the tide.

But, remembering our dwelling-house, I am losing sight of the Play-house—and it was at his theatre that Herbert's life was centred. I must go back to 1901, when in June *Twelfth Night*, sweet, enchanting *Twelfth Night*, though it was still crowding the theatre, had to be withdrawn because Herbert had arranged the previous autumn that Sarah Bernhardt and Coquelin should have Her Majesty's for their six weeks' London season. Well, it could not have been devoted to a more brilliant purpose, and we were proud indeed of our distinguished lessees. I remember arranging at home a little supper-party, to which Madame Bernhardt, Madame Réjane, Coquelin, Paderewski and others were coming. Mr. Alfred Rothschild was invited, and—the only time that he was on his knees to me—he implored me to transfer my supper from Sloane Street to his house. He had on the *tapis* one of his historic gatherings, and my guests were among the guests he most wanted to entertain. It ended happily in one of the brilliant Stanhope Place parties, and in

A PENCIL DRAWING BY THE DUCHESS OF RUTLAND.

my little *festa* taking place another night. (Mr. Alfred Roth-schild—what a princely host! What happy week-ends—like a fairy-tale for splendour—did Herbert and I have at Halton in after-years!)

Our sweet friend, Maud Capel, writes me the following :

" DEAREST MAUD,

" You ask me to tell you what I remember of a certain supper-party at which I was present in your house, 77, Sloane Street, long ago. Indeed I remember it all very vividly, for it always stands out in my memory as a most delightful evening. The guests of honour were Madame Sarah Bernhardt, Madame Réjane, Monsieur Coquelin and Sir Alma Tadema. Sarah Bernhardt was very late, and kept us all waiting a long time, and then rushed in like a whirlwind, exclaiming : ' *En retard comme toujours !* '

" We then proceeded downstairs, and sat down to an excellent supper, served at two tables. You presided at one, with Sarah Bernhardt of your party, while I sat at the other table with Sir Herbert and was very happily placed between him and Monsieur Coquelin, while on my host's other side was Madame Réjane, and next to her Sir Alma Tadema. Sir Herbert made a perfect host, and the conversation was very entertaining, consisting a great deal of very amusing repartee bandied across the table between Coquelin and Réjane and Alma Tadema. But I, also, had some personal talk with Coquelin, which I greatly enjoyed, as his was a most attractive personality and he was a delightful talker, in his exquisite French. Altogether a delightful evening, and a very happy memory of dear Sir Herbert, who was always invariably charming and kind to me. I remember it was a lovely night, and he escorted me home to where I then lived with my mother and brother in Lowndes Street, and I can see him now, standing bareheaded as he wished me good-night on my doorstep.

" Your affectionate friend,
" MAUD CAPEL."

In the autumn, after a provincial tour which, alas! and for the first time, did not include me, Herbert produced that delicious play by Clyde Fitch, *The Last of the Dandies*, in which Herbert had the pre-eminently " Tree " part of Count D'Orsay. I shall be accused of pronouncing everything that Herbert did " perfect." It is no more than the truth that, in nine parts out of ten that he essayed, his acting *was* perfect. There are actors who in many of his many parts could have equalled—not outshone—him ; but what other actor could have lived, as he lived, them `all ?` Now, in one year, he has darted from Malvolio to Count D'Orsay—with a morning call now and then on Robert Macaire, Beau Austin, Svengali, Demetrius, Gringoire, Sir Peter Teazle and Hamlet ; now he flits to Ulysses—Ulysses in Stephen Phillips' beautiful play—and from Ulysses to Falstaff ; with a passing nod to Herod on his tour. Ah ! say what you will, Posterity, here was a great, great actor. We shall not look upon his like again ! I make no more apologies for praise.

The Last of the Dandies was a delicious play—perfectly put upon the stage. For the first act—D'Orsay's dressing-room—London was looted for priceless Empire furniture (the cheval-glass still survives), and Herbert was lent an heirloom of a silver-gilt dressing-case, historic, superb. For the second act—a boating-scene—a river of real water was let into the stage of the theatre, to Herbert's intense and almost childish appreciation. A wonderful effect ensued.

How he loved to try and bring woods and streams and founts and skies and mountains on to the stage ! And pillared palaces, and long-drawn aisles : stately castles, grim battlements, battle-fields, pine forests, beech woods, fields jewelled with daisies, and yellow sands ! Who has striven towards all these so lovingly, so persistently ? Herbert condescended to " curtains " for a brief space in the course of his career—but he hung them to prejudice, not to conviction. He knew perfectly well that the writer of plays, be he Pinero or Shakespeare, requires—nay, demands—everything that the art of the stage can do for him.

Ulysses, by Stephen Phillips, succeeded *The Last of the Dandies*, and here again I was cheated (as I chose to think) of acting in it. I had been promised Pallas Athene, a small but a divine part, and I conceived that she should *seem* divine. In my mind's-eye I clothed her in gold from head to foot, her face and her whole figure were to be shrouded in a golden veil ; and such an effect of misty golden light was to glow upon her continually that she should always appear to the audience as more than mortal. Unfortunately, so jealous was I of my idea that I did not air it in time : and meanwhile, for some inscrutable reason, perhaps not unconnected with the Coronation of King Edward, Herbert and Percy Anderson and Stephen Phillips had conceived Pallas Athene as Britannia ! Once more a timid deputation awaited me, and told me I had neither the looks nor the physique for Athene (or Britannia), and thus my dream of a golden goddess perished. It is but fair to add that beautiful Constance Collier more than justified their choice of her instead of me—indeed, the whole casting of the play was beyond praise.

I believe there are some Stephen Phillips enthusiasts who admire *Ulysses* more than any of his plays ; but I confess to preferring *Herod* and *Nero*—though who can deny its beauty ? It ran from January to June—and then Herbert had a brainwave which captured the imagination of London. He decided that in Coronation year Shakespeare should not be left uncrowned, and he gave him a crown indeed ! He had to move Heaven and Earth to secure both Mrs. Kendal and Ellen Terry as Mrs. Ford and Mrs. Page : but Heaven and Earth met him half-way ; and a historic, famous revival of *The Merry Wives of Windsor* was the result. With those two great actresses supporting him, his Falstaff was finer than ever : and there were Lionel Brough, Oscar Asche, Courtice Pounds, E. M. Robson and Henry Kemble to make up a marvellous cast. What an utterly glad time those three months were : and how happy I was that I was given my old part of Anne Page ! I do not think we ever had such uproariously overflowing audiences. It was the *comble* of Herbert's first five years at Her Majesty's, which, by the way, now became *His* Majesty's Theatre. On April 25th, 1902, the fifth anniversary of the theatre's opening, Herbert gave a supper-party on the stage. (If you turn this page you will find the names of his guests.)

Herbert had love and admiration profound for Ellen Terry— a love which, when he was little more than a boy, and when

the stage was as yet a closed book to him, had taken the form
of passionate adoration for an unknown goddess. He used to
tell how, when she was acting Portia under the Bancroft management, he, besides haunting the gallery of the theatre, used to
wait outside the stage-door every night to see her emerge : and
once, recognizing her in a four-wheeler in the Strand, courted
violent death by running after her cab for two miles ! Talking
of violent death, we very nearly dealt it to the beloved Ellen
Terry herself during the sojourn of those two perfect *Merry
Wives* with us. In August, Herbert closed the theatre on
Saturday nights—as neither Mrs. Kendal nor Ellen Terry liked
playing twice a day—and I, having bought a motor (later on
I must tell the story of that guilty acquisition), proposed that
we three, Herbert, Ellen Terry and I, should motor to our little
house by the Sussex sea. In high glee, we left London about
six, and reached Horsham, where we dined quite wisely and quite
well, and then, in the coming of a sweet August night, began to
traverse the thirty or forty miles which lay between us and
Bognor. All went swimmingly—or should I say skiddingly ?—
until we reached Bury Hill, when, half-way to its summit, the
engine stopped, and our little Panhard with its precious burden
began a precipitous career of its own backwards down a winding
precipice. Luckily, our driver, a Frenchman, who had lost chain,
brake, control—everything except his head—managed to keep
enough of that to steer us into a ditch, and so averted our destruction. This happened about ten o'clock, and all through the
wide August twilight of night we sat upon the thymy plots of
Bury Hill, the ground starred with glow-worms, the heavens
with a thousand eyes. The driver had to walk to Arundel to
get us a carriage, which after some four hours, appeared—and
we reached our cottage exactly at five o'clock in the summer
morning. Herbert and I were terribly anxious for our darling
Ellen Terry, who was accustomed to much care and petting ;
but she never for a moment lost her radiance, her good-humour,
her sweet flow of fun.

The autumn play was an ambitious one, involving tremendous
outlay, strenuous rehearsals, lavish display—*The Eternal City*,
by Hall Caine. It proved a great popular success, and this

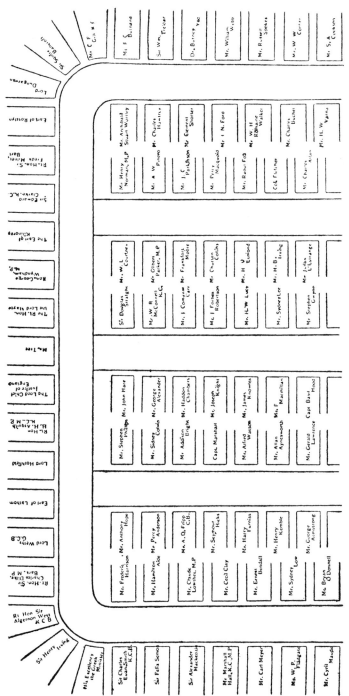

MR. BEERBOHM TREE'S SUPPER PARTY AT HER MAJESTY'S THEATRE

success I think it deserved. It ran for three months : then, in January, Herbert revived *The Merry Wives of Windsor*, with Ellen Terry again, though, alas ! not with Mrs. Kendal. Her part descended to me, and though I was proud of the distinction, I could not conquer an apologetic frame of mind—which marred both my enjoyment and my acting : one cannot be ebullient and diffident in the same breath.

At Christmas, Herbert and I had gone to Paris to see Tolstoi's *Resurrection*, and we came back determined that it should be his next production. Mr. Michael Morton adapted the French play—so divinely acted at the Odéon, and as divinely acted, while better produced, at His Majesty's. Lena Ashwell and Herbert were the hero and the heroine in that exquisite heartbreaking drama, and there never was anything finer or more poignant than their two performances. There are some who think Herbert's Dmitri Nehludof the greatest thing that he has ever done—so reverent, so tender was it ; so large and devotional ; so happy, then so full of pain ; so simple, yet so fraught with grandeur. Through the character there shone that " large lucidity of soul " that glowed in Herbert himself.

I must go back now and tell how I became possessor of a motor-car. In the spring of 1901, when Herbert and I were in Paris, we saw Hervieu's *L'Enigme*. I bought it with what I fondly called my own money (probably a gift from Herbert), and set Mr. Frank Harris and my brother-in-law Max to adapt it for me, calling it *Cæsar's Wife*. Herbert bought a *Grand Guignol*—" au Téléphone "—and took a theatre for me (Wyndham's), where I produced my two plays. Both Herbert and that good friend of ours, Russell Spokes, put money into my venture, about which I will say no more than that it cost my backers three thousand pounds, while I emerged with a triumphal sum sufficient to buy myself a motor-car ! Clever Mr. Russell Spokes, who was a kind of financial adviser to Herbert, used to try and explain this paradox to me, but perhaps I was not so eager to grasp the enigma as the ill-gotten gains.

" Financial Adviser " reminds me of one who preferred the title " Literary Adviser " to the private secretary that he was.

I append Herbert's disclaimer.

[*Referee*, 22nd Sept. 1901.]

"MR. TREE'S LITERARY ADVISER.

" To the Editor of the *Referee*.

" DEAR SIR,

" I have of late noticed in the Press frequent references to ' Mr. Tree's literary adviser.' As I have such good reason to be grateful to the valued members of my staff, I should be loth to burden any of them with the errors of judgment, of style, of grammar and of spelling inseparable from the works of an actor-manager. Will you kindly allow me to state that the only responsible ' literary adviser' attached to Her Majesty's Theatre is your faithful servant,

" HERBERT BEERBOHM TREE.

" Central Station Hotel, Glasgow.

" September 18th, 1901."

For a year we were picnicking at our Georgian cottage in Westminster. Being rather fond of it, I set on foot a scheme by which we should have had one of the sweetest houses in London ; for I found that I could acquire another, in Smith Square, at right angles to and adjoining ours. Aided by experts, I made plans for converting the two houses into one—by which means we should have had perfect rooms, ample space, every luxury, comfort, aspect and delight. Unsupported by Herbert, snubbed by the County Council, and defeated by the Bank, my project died. How often Herbert and I regretted it in after-years !

In the autumn of 1903, Herbert produced his *Richard II*. I quote from *The Times*, because its distinguished critic used many of the epithets which I should employ could I write as he does :

" This is a character (Richard II.) that suits Mr. Tree to perfection. The curious blend in the man of shrinking effeminacy and philosophic irony, the dreamy languor interrupted by crises of feverish excitement, the yearning for affection and the bouts of half-crazy speculation—all these things the actor brings out with such completeness as to make his Richard probably the most haunting figure he has yet given us. The great scene of abdication in Westminster Hall, culminating in that wonderful passage of the broken mirror, was given a quite beautiful ending of the actor's own invention, in his silent, pathetic leave-taking of his few faithful friends. His parting with the Queen, too, was unspeakably touching."

And another leading critic :

"Mr. Tree is among the very princes of producers of plays. His instinct for effect is little short of the marvellous. None but an artist by temperament could have devised such elaborate framework for a series of historical pictures ; as we were taken from scene to scene, our wonderment increased. The mounting is a dream of beauty. As one sat and pondered over each scene, and tried to realize the amount of thought it meant, the intimate knowledge it required to produce such a series of perfect *ensembles*, the more one was disposed to thank Heaven that one had a manager who was so obviously indifferent to the silver, so long as he could present what he considered a striking picture of the times. As a spectacle, Mr. Tree's production of *Richard II.* surpasses anything we have seen."

That memorable *Richard II.*, with its magnificent cast ! Oscar Asche and Lyn Harding, how gorgeously you bore yourselves ! Then there were Fisher White, Basil Gill, Lionel Brough and William Haviland—and that sweet Child-Queen, Lily Brayton. A great cast in a great production indeed ! One watched it, enchanted, night after night.

Herbert did not believe that acting could be taught. Of course, it cannot be, any more than a poet, a painter, a musician can be made. But he believed in stage training—believed in giving opportunity for the *feu sacré* to burn. So in 1904 he at last realized an old ambition ; off his own bat, as it were, he set the ball rolling of the " Academy of Dramatic Art." He took two houses in Gower Street, furnished them, and set up a school, with George Bancroft as Administrator, and Viola, when

she was old enough, as one of the pupils. Having done so much, he
then proceeded to leave it somewhat to its fate, but he had
put into the ground a sturdy plant, and it soon began to do
honour to the parent Tree.

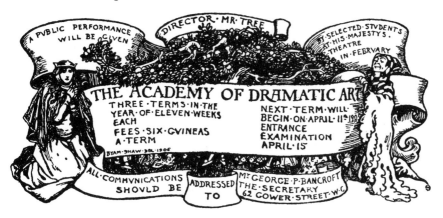

The next production is Belasco's *The Darling of the Gods*—
one of Herbert's easy leaps of a million years—from Plantagenet
to Samurai—from wistful Richard to greasy, sinister, satanic
Zakkuri. I thought it an enchanting play—melodrama though
it was. (But, oh, the joy of a fine melodrama and its amazing
superiority over a dull comedy !) *The Darling of the Gods*,
produced on New Year's Day, 1904, was a sensational success,
and it required no successor until the autumn, when *The Tempest*
took its place. By this time our little Viola had been lured on
to the stage. This departure caused a certain amount of friction between Herbert and me, though the prayers of both of
us were only for her happiness. I chose to maintain that *not*
in the life of an actress is great and lasting happiness to be found.
It is a poison, too—a drug. Once drinking deep of that divinest
anguish, it is very difficult indeed to accustom oneself to hum-
drum—or hum-dram—again. These were my arguments—as
they have been to many and many a stage aspirant. Luckily
in Viola's case I turned out to be wrong. She appeared in the
provinces at first as Viola ; and then she took her place in the
London Theatre world as Ariel—a lovelier or a more fairy-like
could not have been found.

The Tempest was immeasurably beautiful. The music and scenery—the voices from nowhere—the atmosphere of wonder and enchantment, and a poetic and glowing fancy beyond one's imagining—it was in some strange way what summer dawns and April twilight are—ineffable. Caliban, too (though I wanted Herbert to be Prospero), was strangely wistful and pathetic : his eyes were those of a beseeching dumb thing—and a picture never to be forgotten was his long, lone gaze across the water as, Ariel released, the full-sailed ship and its happy mortals faded on the sight, leaving him and his island desolate.

By this time we were installed at Walpole House, and such hours as he could spend in it Herbert adored. Its stateliness and complete loveliness charmed his sense, and all the time he could give it he gave. Sunday luncheon-parties became our fashion. At these Felicity, who had (at that age) an angel's face and the voice of an angel, used to come down at coffee time and sing to us. Viola had taught her some of her songs, and there are those who say that an experience never to be forgotten was that little child lifting up her lovely head and singing " Myrrha, oh, Myrrha ! I soon will come to thee ! "

Herbert was an unutterable joy to the little children— whether we had people or no, he was a Sunday lunch institution. Then would he keep them wide-eyed with wonder and mad with merriment over his " parlour tricks." His short-sighted man and the salt ; his tipsy man ; his absent-minded man ; his epileptic man ; himself dozing under the reading of a bad play, his head slipping off his hand, his elbow slipping off the table— what frantic delight they caused ! One Christmas morning I remember him wandering forth with the children, taking off his hat and handing it round among the infantile inhabitants of a neighbouring slum, and begging contributions " for the rich of Chiswick." But I leave it to the children themselves to say how full he was of sweet and blessed fun—the yeast of mortal bread, the wine of life !

A yearly function at Walpole House, and one that gave Herbert great joy, was our Boat-Race party. For this I used to " char " tremendously, trying to make every one of the lovely rooms of the house more lovely than ever. Because about

MAUD TREE AND HER DAUGHTERS, VIOLA, FELICITY, AND IRIS.
Pencil drawings by the Duchess of Rutland.

thirty windows commanded a perfect view of the river, one must needs arrange in addition an extensive system of platformery upon the roof : but every plank was pleasure, so much did it gladden us to make holiday when we could.

Rather stupidly, we did not often have people to dine with us at Chiswick ; we had a feeling that it was too far a quest for a quail. But I remember one party we gave, because Herbert thought it such a wonderful evening. It was June—and the music after dinner was to have been in the garden. But Winter set in in the middle of Summer, as only Winter can ; so we stayed in the house. We had about twelve people to dine, and I remember making the unpardonable mistake of hiring a *chef* from London's most fashionable restaurant to help my cook. He arrived with a battery of pots and pans, and with a battalion of strange, enraged kitchen-men, who gazed at the mullet with fishy eyes, played pitch-and-toss with ortolans, and, as I forlornly apologized afterwards, sent up everything cold except the ice. That nightmare of a dinner ! (I remember a woman saying to me, " Your dinner was a dream," and in my pale soul I wondered what *kind* of a dream.)

But it came to an end, and we had a wonderful evening, succeeded—the gods be praised—by a perfect supper. Sweet music was made in our beautiful drawing-room, where a great fire blazed on the wide hearth (there was no time of year when Herbert did not want a fire), and while a guest was playing the violin so divinely that one wept to hear, I turned out all the lights and only the fire-glow illumined the room. Herbert often and often recalled that scene.

Much Ado About Nothing succeeded *The Tempest*, and sweet Winifred Emery—she whom I had cheated of Ophelia many years before, though she never knew it—was the winsome and gracious Beatrice. Viola was Hero, Herbert, of course, Benedick, Laurence Irving, Don John, Lionel Brough, Dogberry. It was a beautiful production, full of sweet sights and sounds, and the whole play was taken in a delightfully high-spirited, generous and light-hearted vein.

And after *Much Ado About Nothing* there is *An Enemy of the People*. Herbert revived this after ten years, having always loved the part of Dr. Stockmann—and no wonder, for he was marvellous in it. It suited his temperament exactly—indeed, there was much of Dr. Stockmann in Herbert's own character. He revelled in the passionate longing to right wrongs, the passionate scorn of bigotry and sham, the passionate impulse to kill prejudice and stupidity. Herbert's wit seized instantly upon the subtlety of that combined love of fun and want of humour in the affectionate, generous, blundering Dr. Stockmann.

Says *The Times*:
" Here (in the third act) Mr. Tree gets his great opportunity, and he uses it greatly. Dr. Stockmann pouring forth his stream of denunciation of the pettiness and corruption of municipal life, now carrying the public meeting with him, now infuriating it with home truths and reducing it to sullen silence with hard sayings, until at last the forces of ignorance and reaction win the day, and the champion of the doctrine of temporary truth is almost torn to pieces by the fury of the orthodox—all this makes a scene not easily forgotten. With a fine contempt for possibilities, one might almost say the part of Dr. Stockmann in Ibsen's *Enemy of the People* was written for Mr. Tree— Mr. Tree is brilliantly successful."

The play drew golden opinions, but never, except at its first matinée—and that, I think, was an invitation one—golden houses. It was always played to a loss—a fact which made Herbert furious, so much did he love the play and love playing the part.

This year (1905) sees the inauguration of Herbert's famous Shakespeare Festival, carried out religiously every year from now onwards : a gigantic undertaking, involving greater toil, greater courage, greater sacrifice than anyone could know or guess. But it was his labour of love, and he revelled in the joy of the exploit. This year he gives (acting in them all himself) *Richard II.* (twice), *The Merry Wives of Windsor, Twelfth Night, Hamlet, Much Ado About Nothing*, and *Julius Cæsar* (twice) ; all between

Monday, April 24th, and Saturday, April 29th ! His own words will show his gladness and pride.

After the fall of the curtain on *Julius Cæsar* he said :

" Our Shakespearean Festival has come to a close, and I need hardly tell you how overjoyed we are that our efforts to do honour to Shakespeare should have met with so enthusiastic an appreciation on the part of the public. Spring is upon us once more, and in the spring the joyous note of the cuckoo is heard—so also is the croaking of the raven. It happens that I have been reading to-night a leading article in a great daily journal lamenting the decadence of the drama. Our best answer to these lamentations is that during the present week more than twelve thousand persons have witnessed the plays of Shakespeare at this theatre, and, indeed, for many years past there has taken place here a revival of the Shakespearean drama. Never was there a greater love of Shakespeare than there is to-day, and you who are lovers of him will, I am sure, be glad to hear that—God willing—we shall give another Shakespeare Festival next year—I hope on a more extended scale. However great and far-reaching the decadence of the drama may be, I am glad to know that it has not yet reached that section of the public whom I have the honour to serve, and to whom I tender my loyal thanks."

I must make brief mention of *Business is Business* (Sydney Grundy's adaptation of *Les Affaires sont les Affaires*) because of Herbert's fine blending of humour and tragedy in the part of Isidore Izard. The play was not a success, but Herbert's acting of the part of the millionaire was one of the greatest things he ever did.

In the autumn a dramatization by Comyns Carr of " Oliver Twist," gave us, besides an excellent play, three memorable performances—Constance Collier's as Nancy, Lyn Harding's as Bill Sikes, Herbert's as Fagin. Surely nothing that the stage has seen was more daring and more touching than Constance Collier's Nancy ? And Lyn Harding—I hope he will forgive me—Lyn Harding *was* Bill Sikes. As to Herbert's Fagin— " this grim, lurid Fagin, like a musty, dusty raven "—it was what one would expect : a greasy, greedy, shuffling, dangerous, humorous devil ; a merry old gentleman to the life ; a despairing, shuddering, shrieking heap of rags to the death. The most haunting and the most typical picture of him that recurs to one's memory is his sitting on Oliver's dirty pallet, patting him with tender hands to sleep, and singing with ghoulish expression a little song of Herbert's own composing, " Hush-a-bye, Oliver —Olly, hush-a-by-a-ye ; hush-a-by-bye, Mister Fagin is here ! "

At the beginning of 1906 there came Stephen Phillips' *Nero*, and in this, slightly to my astonishment, I was given the wonderful part of Agrippina. This called for great tragic acting, and naturally it was not in me to rise to the heights it demanded. If I succeeded in it at all, I owe my success to the untiring patience and kindness of Herbert and of Comyns Carr, who between them taught me a new low voice, between them watched that my gestures should be grand and few, between them imbued me with a spirit which was not altogether unlike the spirit of tragedy. Oh, the happy days of *Nero !* How noble, how beautiful the play, how gorgeous the setting, how haunting the music, how full of excitement and glory the traffic of the stage ! During the dream-like four months of its run I lived only for the theatre : everything else went by the board. The cup of my existence brimmed. The audiences brimmed, too : we never had a greater financial success—this in spite of the fact that it cost considerably over two hundred pounds a performance to (as they say) " ring up the curtain."

True to his word, when Shakespeare's birthday came, Herbert dared to interrupt the brilliant run of brilliant *Nero* for a week by his second Shakespeare Festival. These are the plays that he gave, acting in every one of them himself :

> *The Tempest.*
> *Henry IV.*
> *Hamlet.*
> *Twelfth Night.*
> *Julius Cæsar.*
> *The Merry Wives of Windsor.*

The Merry Wives of Windsor was given twice, and the second time it was made the occasion of Ellen Terry's Jubilee. Has

there ever been such a scene in any theatre ? Once more I quote
from my friend *The Times :*

" It is fifty years to-day since Miss Ellen Terry first appeared
on the stage, an eight-year-old member of Charles Kean's company at the Princess's Theatre. Such an anniversary could
not pass unnoticed. In those fifty years the theatre has undergone changes which it is very difficult for us, who did not know
the former state of things, to realize ; and, of the two manage-
ments to which the changes were principally due Miss Ellen
Terry was not unconnected with the one and was an essential
part of the other. It was so long ago as 1875 that she went to
the old Prince of Wales's Theatre—where now, through *forza
del destino,* stands the Scala—to play Portia in the Bancroft
revival of *The Merchant of Venice.* Will she ever forget how wild
the town, the whole country, went about her ? She looked
' a portrait by Veronese ; ' her acting, though, indeed, she was
not new to the public, impressed them as something they had
never dreamed of before. Three years later she joined the new
management at the Lyceum (having already acted with Henry
Irving in *Katherine and Petruchio* at the old Queen's Theatre
in Long Acre), and took the part of Ophelia in the famous revival
of *Hamlet.* ' She looks like a living model of Giovanni Bellini's,'
wrote M. Jules Claretie of her Ophelia ; but it was not Miss
Terry's appearance alone that showed the wisdom of what had
been Henry Irving's first step towards forming his company.
Ophelia, the playgoers of the time tell us, had acquired a character, a thing she had never before had on the stage ; every sentence in her ' mad-scene ' had a reference and a meaning. So
began that partnership, perhaps the most famous in all theatrical
history, which lasted till the end of the great days of the Lyceum
Theatre. Miss Terry was a loyal partner ; she did what she was
told, took parts that were not really suited to her special gifts,
and always gave a good account of them, thanks not only to her
great abilities, but to her staunch support of the master-mind
that directed the theatre. If the celebration of her jubilee is
the special festival of her own achievements as actress, it is also
an opportunity of commemorating the share she took in the great
work for the drama that was done at the Lyceum Theatre.

" To see her play Mistress Page last night in *The Merry Wives of Windsor* was to realize that time cannot wither Miss Ellen Terry's brightest gift, her sense of fun. Certain of her tragic parts will always be remembered with pleasure ; but she was never a tragedy queen. She is at her best when she has to laugh —just where most actresses are at their worst. Who can think of her Beatrice without smiling at the recollection of those delicious quips that used to come bubbling, as it seemed, into words before she knew that she had said them ? And the raillery of her Portia, how fresh, how delicate it was ! She is the perfect image of the witty woman. Always charming, always gracious, she made an apt foil to Sir Henry Irving, with his severe intellectual appeal. That gracious charm of her womanhood may be seen still unimpaired in *Captain Brassbound's Conversion ;* it is the very essence of the character. And, though she is at her best when her ebullient spirits have play, her tenderness and pathos—the pathos of Olivia and Nance Oldfield—are as genuine and as beautifully expressed as her humour. In the last act of *Charles I.* her grief and affection rose to an equal height with the majestic sorrows of the King. We look back with fond regret on these parts that Miss Terry will never, it may be, play again ; we cry ' Pereant qui ante nos juvenes fuere ! '—the men who saw Ellen Terry play Beatrice in 1864 or Portia in 1875 ; but we are not so badly off. If there was anyone present last night who had never seen Ellen Terry act before, he has only to go on to the Court Theatre this evening and he will have gained a better idea of the charm and the powers of her prime than any other actress could give who has been on the stage for fifty years.

" The enthusiasm last night ran high. Every reserved seat had been sold for many days before, and people were waiting outside pit and gallery from the early morning. Miss Terry's reception, when first she appeared, was deafening ; then the house settled down to laugh at *The Merry Wives of Windsor*, and laughed heartily. Mr. Tree was at his best as Falstaff ; Mr. Hearn made an uncommonly good Dr. Caius ; Mr. Brough and Mr. Somerset as the host and Bardolph gave their ripe humour ; and, with Miss Terry as Mistress Page and Mrs. Tree as Mistress Ford, the play ran its jolly course. The manner of its performance at His Majesty's Theatre is too fresh in the public mind to need description ; it is, at any rate, a rollicking piece of fun.

"When the crowd of fairies were tripping off, and Mistress Page was trying to slink away unseen, Falstaff cried, ' Stop, mistress, stop ! ' And then came a pretty little scene devised and written by Mr. Louis N. Parker. A rhymed address, spoken by Mr. Tree, ended with the lines :

> " ' Roll, Drums ! and flourish, Trumpets ! Let the cheers
> Many a long day re-echo in your ears !
> But, through their clamour, may my whisper move you ;
> We praise you ; we admire you ; and—we love you ! '

" Whereupon, after a tucket had sounded, Miss Terry stood ' in pretty bewilderment and confusion.' She had to say something. What ? Down from the sky flew a dove bearing in its beak Miss Terry's speech, a pretty speech, which she spoke with obvious emotion. When this scene was over, Miss Terry was presented by a deputation from the Playgoers' Club with a silver casket, which she acknowledged in a few words touched with apt references to *The Merchant of Venice* and recalling the fact that this year she and Sir Henry Irving were to have been publicly honoured together. After that ' Auld Lang Syne ' was sung by the whole house, and the ' jubilee ' was over."

(One would seem to make an absolute fetish of *The Times*. In extenuation I ought to confess that from my babyhood I had been brought up, probably fed, upon *The Times*. My godfathers and godmothers must have wrapped me up in it at my baptism —and when I came to years of discretion, though often lacking sixpence, I never lacked *The Times*. This extravagance—conservatism—republicanism—whatever it may be called—was carried on into my married life. Perhaps that is why, though often prosperous, we were always poor. Now I come to think of it, our richest time was during the years that *The Times* cost only a penny.)

At the end of May *Nero*, triumphantly resumed after the triumphant Shakespeare week, gave place to an adaptation by Michael Morton of *The Newcomes* Herbert's performance of

Colonel Newcome was just what it was certain to be—a thing of beauty. Tender, lovable, gay, gallant, infinitely dignified, infinitely touching, with all its sweet weaknesses and sweet sublimities : there is everything in Colonel Newcome that Herbert most admired and revered. This was perceptible in every instant of his acting. Strange ! having revived this play in New York in 1917, the last word that Herbert ever spoke upon the stage was " Adsum ! "

A few weeks further on, and he whose heart was as the heart of a little child was in the presence of his Maker.

Herbert did not act in *A Winter's Tale*—the more's the pity : he would have been a wonderful Leontes. But he made a beautiful production of it for Ellen Terry, whose Hermione was a noble performance. I was Paulina ; Viola was Perdita, and she seemed indeed like one of the " daffodils that come before the swallow dares and take the winds of March with beauty."

Herbert's next Shakespearean production was *Antony and Cleopatra*—put upon the stage with all his glowing sense of gorgeous pageantry. But I consider it to have been one of his rare failures. This is perhaps because I think *Antony and Cleopatra* the one play of Shakespeare's that I have seen (and I have seen this often) that is better read than acted : there are things in it that are too ineffably beautiful for stage utterance and presentment. I had been spoilt, too, for the Roman aspect of its splendid production by *Julius Cæsar* and *Nero*, and for the Eastern part of its production by *Herod*. There was for me nothing new under the sun of its splendour. I do not think Herbert himself counted it as one of his successes, though oh ! what loving pains he took—what loving pains were taken for him—what thought and care and money were lavished upon it !

The Beloved Vagabond—an adaptation by Mr. Locke of his own delicious novel—followed ; and it gave Herbert just the sort of part that he loved : dreamy, fantastic, poetic, debonair ; indeed, when I read the novel, as I did when I read " Trilby," before either play was thought of, I exclaimed, " What a part for Herbert ! " The play, with Evelyn Millard as its charming heroine, had an immense success in London and in the provinces.

I cannot resist quoting here one of the letters Mr. Locke wrote me :

" Corner Hall,
" Hemel Hempstead, Herts.
" 5th September, '17.

" DEAR LADY TREE,

" Very many thanks for your exquisite little mémento —and for your letter, which touched me deeply. When I first wrote it was difficult to say much amid the rush of feelings. One is accustomed, as it were, to death in these dreadful days —but his came with the shock of newness, as though there had not been death in the world before. It is given to few men of a generation to colour the life atmosphere of those not only immediately around him—but of the greater circle with whom he comes not too frequently into personal contact. In my own life he meant this vivifying bit of colour. At first I thought it was utterly wiped out, and I felt a curious integral loss—it is so hard to get at these very real feelings except allusively—but now I find that it is not all gone, for it was shown there in the first place in the immortal spirit of the man. And there it will always be

" I am very proud to have known and loved him.

" Again thanking you for your letter and with my truest sympathy,

" Yours very sincerely,
" W. J. LOCKE."

When this Beloved Vagabond of ours (for we who knew his lovableness and his vagabondage used to call him so)—when, in 1909, he was given his knighthood there were those wise counsellors and head-shakers who urged that he should put bounds to the sea-coast of his Bohemia ; but he would exclaim, shudderingly : " Don't ask me to become genteel." To his delight, I capped the discussion : " A verray parfitt, but not a *genteel* knight."

The event itself—the bestowal of his knighthood—brought about a time of unmitigated joy and excitement—of a million congratulations, of a sea of goodwill. When the advent of the honour was intimated to him, he thought—perhaps he only tried to think—that he was indifferent to it. But when it came, and it seemed as though the whole world were rejoicing over it, he began rejoicing too, and he ended by being as proud and glad about it as it was but fitting he should be.

As it happened, Herbert had not held his Festival this year at Shakespeare's birthday-time, having been compelled to postpone it until June. However, he made up for unpunctuality by added richness : the Festival lasted a fortnight instead of a week. In those twelve days he gave altogether twenty-one performances : certainly three of these were non-Shakespearean though highly distinguished, for Dr. Ethel Smyth produced her *The Wreckers* at our theatre, and repeated it twice during those feverish days.

So it came about that when his knighthood was given him, he was in the heart of his heart's delight, the Shakespeare Festival ; and the play, on June 25th, was *Twelfth Night*. It goes without saying that the huge audience gave him an unending ovation on his first appearing ; and when he reached the line (which his humour did not allow him to mitigate), " Some have greatness thrust upon them," the house literally rose at him. Holding Viola's hand and mine, he made a happy speech at the end : the audience forced it from him ; and it was all the prettier, like so many of his sudden speeches, for being unprepared. He said : " I have no words to thank you for the kindness you have shown me. This has been a very touching day to me, and in moments of profound emotion one can hardly find expression for one's feelings ; but I feel thankful to think that this honour to our art has come at a time when Shakespeare is being honoured here. I only hope that I may have health and strength to continue my work, and to serve my loyal Public as loyally as I can. From the depths of my heart I thank all my kind friends to-night." He adored his sheaves of letters and telegrams, and I find them carefully preserved and cherished in two great volumes —taken care of as it was not his wont to take care. I am glad for the thousand kind senders' sake that he held them so dear.

After six years at Walpole House we suddenly left it— suddenly decided we could bear its far-awayness no more. I had grieved with many tears at leaving Sloane Street, but was

VIOLA TREE
From a charcoal drawing by J. S. Sargent.

perfectly complacent over the move from Chiswick. Not so Viola, who beheld with despairing eyes the ruthless wrenchings, the devastating, desecrating tramplings of the furniture-removers. To her it seemed sacrilege, for she had spent many a sweet and sacred hour in those beautiful rooms ; indeed, it was there that she plighted her troth to Alan, who won her for his wife after many vicissitudes. It was from our next house—All Souls Place—that, a year or so later, she was married. I think the day of her wedding was a great day in Herbert's life—great with pride, though great with pain, for he was losing what he adored.

All Souls Place was a corner house made entirely of windows, and drifting on and on into various studios, some of which belonged to us, and some to the painter, Sir David Murray. On Viola's wedding-day they were all open to us, and everybody we knew came flocking *et dona ferentes*. Indeed, it was just like Herbert's sensitive heart to bewail and be ashamed that people should think it necessary to send her such lovely and so many beautiful gifts. He said, " It seems so awful. We never give a party : but when we do, each guest has to give the wealth of Ind to come to it ! "

Respect for Herbert's name and admiration for Viola caused an immense demonstration when she was married, and the theatrical manager in Herbert could not help being elated by crowds so great that the traffic round about St. Martin's Church had for some hours to be diverted. I remember his darting to and fro all the morning from the theatre to the house ; I remember his sweet, glad face as he brought Viola up the aisle ; I remember how the tears rained down his cheeks when her friends sang their chorus hymeneal as she and Alan, man and wife, left our home.

The years are passing so quickly that one can catch but a flying gleam of them ; the mists around remembrance grow heavier even as our days do grow. Thus I am compelled to cast chronological order to the winds, and I am trying now only to recall the things that made us glad and proud and happy. One of these was Herbert's revival of *The School for Scandal*, with its glittering " star " cast. Dear, sweet Henry Neville, gallant and gay, you were one of the stars : you, grand actor, king of stage-lovers, whom as a child I had seen and hero-worshipped when you acted with Kate Terry : you who loved Herbert and whom Herbert loved.

What a miraculous cast ! Henry Neville, Edward Terry, Herman Vezin and Lionel Brough : those great names are now, alas ! erased from the world's programme : but Basil Gill, Robert Loraine, H. V. Esmond, Godfrey Tearle and Charles Quartermaine, you are all here to tell the tale of that happy and wonderful revival. Ellis Jeffreys played Lady Sneerwell as it has never been played before : she lifted it into a leading part. Then there was sweet Marie Löhr, fresh and fair as apple-blossom ; and Herbert as Sir Peter—Sir Peter of exquisite manners and exquisite humour, sensitive, intellectual, whimsical, lovable Sir Peter. Sheridan, I should like you to have seen Herbert's *School for Scandal !*

It is somewhat late in this dream of mine about Herbert to speak of one beloved by him who was vividly part of the theatre for many years—Percy Macquoid. He (and little less his wife, whom also Herbert loved) was responsible for many productions for us—from *Much Ado About Nothing* onwards ; and he it was who with " one hundred gallant gentlemen " gave Herbert in 1908 the golden Loving-Cup which was his treasure and his pride.

The dresses, furniture and scenery of *The School for Scandal* were designed and carried out for us by Percy Macquoid with loving joy in all their minutiæ ; indeed, everyone was wafted along by his enthusiasm—wafted in winged sedan-chairs. This brilliant revival crowded the theatre for more than a hundred nights. It was impossible for Herbert to keep it on, or it would have run right through the summer months and on into the autumn ; but this his plans forbade—to his great after-regret.

From the time that Herbert had his beautiful rooms in the Dome—a year or two after the actual opening of the theatre— it became more and more a custom for the children and me to forgather there on matinée days, to dine between the performances. Mrs. Browning, who had by now ceased to be the home cook and had become Herbert's housekeeper in the theatre, used to give us delicious food ; and Herbert's dresser used to whisk our plates and pour out our wine. In this Dome, too, all the plans were made, the plays were read ; and at one time, the outer room became an Infants' School! This was during the run of *Pinkie and the Fairies*—Herbert's first real Christmas play. I have said how great a love he had for children : and how great a feeling he had for festivals and feast days. He had always tried to have something at Christmas-time that children would like ; but now (I am going back to 1908) Mr. Graham Robertson brought him a real fairy play, and Mr. Frederic Norton made sweet fairy music to it. Ellen Terry was the queen of a perfect cast, which included Viola, Gwendolen Brogden, Philip Tonge, Iris Hawkins and Stella Campbell. It was a never-to-be-forgotten afternoon when Herbert, with his usual happy genius, made its first performance a sort of Christmas party given by Felicity and Iris. All the children we knew were bidden to bring their parents, and there never was such hilarious delight, so much music such as Swinburne loves when " laughs a child of seven." Elise Craven, you divine dancer from fairy-land, what an ovation you had ! Ellen Terry, how you were adored ! You little elves and sprites, birds, rabbits and the whole kingdom of a child's mind, how sweet and glad you made both old and young ! A mandate had gone forth that young children must no longer appear in stage productions, because it caused them to absent themselves from school, or something like that. But Herbert, with his accustomed " I can always get what I want " attitude, arranged a school for them in the Dome, with matron and teachers and all that the heart of a County Councillor could desire. Say, ye children of *Pinkie and the Fairies*, if you were not happy and well cared-for during the play's long run ?

It would be an ungrateful heart that did not remember Herbert's *Beethoven*, for it was a thing of surpassing beauty. The play was by Louis Parker, and it was hailed with delight by all lovers of the divine in music, of the great and true in art. I used to maintain that had it had but two acts instead of three (beautiful though the last act was, and music-haunted, perhaps, beyond all the rest)—had the play ended with that tragic moment of Beethoven's realizing his deafness—a moment which could have no beyond, for it touched the highest point of tragedy —the great public would have flocked to the play. As it was, it appealed to the few, the choicer spirits—and with them it ranked as one of the highest achievements of the stage. Herbert could not read one note of music and knew nothing about music *technically ;* but his *instinct* for it in relation to the needs of whatever play he was producing was marvellous. Many a fiery conductor has flung down his baton in a rage because Herbert has stopped him in the middle of a phrase, saying, " Stop *there* —exactly there." Wild appeals on the score of the score would fall on obstinate ears. " You must cut out all that tra-la-la-la- ing," he would say, imitating the sounds. The conductor would break his heart—the first violin his bow ; but Herbert had to be right. Well—everyone knew his intense feeling for music, but no one was prepared for his absolute worship of Beethoven. Yet he drank in every note ; and I believe his never-to-be-forgotten acting in the play was due to his great love of the heavenly music that pervaded it. The overture (Landon Ronald conducted for us on the first night) was the C minor Symphony. I had told him of Beethoven's own inter- pretation of those thrice-repeated tragic notes. " So Fate knocks at the door," he used to murmur as he listened, enchanted. The rest of the music was :

As *entr'actes :*—" Coriolan " and " Leonora."

As incidental music :—The Moonlight Sonata.
                The Fifth Symphony.
                The String Quartet (Opus 59).
                The song " Adelaida."
                Parts of the Ninth Symphony—

and, as Beethoven was dying, the " Ode to Joy " from the Choral Symphony. What a feast for music-lovers ! Sweet Evelyn d'Alroy of golden voice and serene and spirituelle personality, was the heroine. (She died, alas ! a year or two later.) Herbert loved the part of Beethoven, and it was his fixed intention, had he lived, to revive the play.

Two more plays, these not adaptations but original ones, came to us from the pen of Louis Parker, both of which—as different as the poles—had enormous success. Both in their turn brought grateful grist to a mill which was from time to time a little rusty. These were *Drake* and *Joseph and his Brethren*. *Drake* was a breezy, gladsome play, breathing Plymouth Hoe and a Peak in Darien ; and with one scene—the scene on board Drake's ship—which was a play, and a beautiful one it itself. It was grandly acted : Lyn Harding as Drake, Herbert Waring as Doughty, Amy Brandon Thomas as the maiden, Elizabeth Sydenham, and Phyllis Neilson-Terry as Queen Elizabeth—a *tour de force* from which she, in spite of her girlishness, emerged triumphantly. This gifted daughter of remarkable parents and ancestry was only seventeen when she first came to us, playing Viola at a special matinée to the Sebastian of her father, Fred Terry (who seemed, indeed, her twin-brother), in one of the most brilliant representations of this, his famous production of *Twelfth Night*, that Herbert ever gave. Phyllis was adorable in the part, without making us forget Lily Brayton ; adorable as Trilby, in a sensational revival of that play, without making us forget Dorothea Baird. But as Desdemona, which she played to Herbert's Othello, there can never be her equal. It was, indeed, a perfect exposition of that part : perfect in poise, in voice, in gentleness, in beauty ; and her Willow Song was divinely acted and sung.

There was a great deal of discussion about Herbert's Othello, and, indeed, about Laurence Irving's Iago. A writer in *The Daily Telegraph* (and I think it must have been our good and cherished friend W. L. Courtney) speaks of Herbert's performance thus :

" Such, as we understand him, is Shakespeare's Othello. Such is the man whom, in a performance of rare dignity and beauty, Sir Herbert Tree portrays. This Othello speaks having authority, and not as the scribes. He has the habit of command and great affairs. He is past the passions of youth, as, indeed, he says. He has not much of the days of gallantry. He speaks of Desdemona with great tenderness. He treats her with the gentlest affection. He is plainly all in love with her, but not after a young man's fashion of love. Through the long battle with Iago, the slow, irresistible onset of doubt was finely played. The whole is a performance of great nobility and a beautiful humanity and tenderness."

The production (Percy Macquoid and that great scene-painter, Joseph Harker, rioting among Carpaccio pictures) was of rare and exquisite beauty. Haunting music by Coleridge Taylor threaded in and out of the play, accentuating the dream-like loveliness of the scenery, accenting the passion and pathos and majesty of the words. I find an amusing letter from Herbert as to his " make-up " in *Othello* :

" I think Shakespeare meant Othello to be an Oriental, not a negro : a stately Arab of the best caste. This colour-question appears to be a controversial one, and while some Shakespearean scholars might want Othello to be black, others might want him to be the colour of a gentleman five-eighths white. Had I made him piebald, there would still doubtless have been some misgiving on the part of my friends the critics."

Allusion to Phyllis Neilson-Terry led me on to write of *Othello*, but *The Merchant of Venice* and *Henry VIII.* and *Macbeth* preceded it. Needless to speak of the entrancing production of what all the call-boys call *The Merchant*. (How Herbert and I used to laugh over the familiar stage-clipping of the titles of plays— *The Merchant, The Wives, The Ado, The Dream, Henry!* We were always expecting it to come down to one syllable : *Mac, Ham* and *Oth ;* but in this we were disappointed.) Talking of call-boys, what a loyal, lion-hearted race! How eager, how sympathetic, how helpful ! At least, it was ever so in Herbert's theatre.

Herbert made the setting of *The Merchant of Venice* a dream of loveliness, though naturally it cannot have surpassed Sir Henry Irving's memorable and poetic production. Herbert had one very wondrous effect of music, however, which was new and strange and compelling : the beautiful Jewish hymn that was lifted up, sonorously and religiously, against the light music of the revellers.

Ellen Terry's never-to-be-forgotten Portia (to Herbert her performance long ago with the Bancrofts : to me her performance with Henry Irving) had spoilt us both for all ensuing Portias ; nothing came up to our ideal. The nearest, strangely enough, was our daughter Viola, who acted the part once or twice only

in a Shakespeare Festival. After that she left the " legitimate "
stage to study for the operatic stage—to Herbert's disappointment and regret. He always said, " Viola would have made
a great actress." Well, there is yet time to prove the truth of
his half-humorous, half-earnest aphorism, " *I* am always right."
And Herbert's Shylock ? Picturesque, passionate, long-suffer-
ing ; by turns majestic and debased—he breathed the very
spirit of the Jew of the Middle Ages. Alternately he provoked
great pity and great scorn, and his large, wistful eyes seemed
to reveal the long, tragic history of a persecuted race. In the
earlier scenes and in the Trial scene—oh, marvellous presentment !—his acting was superb. (One need not say how he *looked*
—he *was* Shylock.) In the scene where he mourns Jessica's
treachery, his conception was one of genius : he strewed ashes
on his head, he lay writhing, moaning in the dust. Yet, on the
whole, I preferred Irving's Shylock, of the two great and memorable presentments. Martyr—Jewish martyr—though he made
him (which could not have been Shakespeare's intention), his
performance was undeviatingly picturesque, majestic and compelling. It was religious.

On the other hand (since I have ventured upon comparison),
Herbert's Wolsey in *Henry VIII.* was far finer than Irving's :
more dread, more grand, more poignant. No character in Shakespeare suited him better than this. It was greatly conceived,
greatly acted. The towering figure of Herbert Tree's Wolsey
must for ever remain a brilliant memory.

Percy Macquoid was Herbert's right hand in this production
—*Henry VIII.*—which, I think, in spite of its vast expenses,
was the greatest of all Herbert's Shakespearean successes. Mrs.
Macquoid, too, was enormously helpful, embroidering with her
own hands the tablecloths for the great Banquet scene, and,
if the truth were known, doubtless fashioning with those same
clever hands the gorgeous golden plate with which the long tables
groaned.

Arthur Bourchier can never have made a more palpable hit
than in his splendidly royal, royally roystering *Henry VIII.*,
and Violet Vanbrugh surely touched the highest point of her art
in her grand and beautiful Queen Katherine. Rich and glowing
production and acting of that richest, most glowing play—it

brought, in addition to its monetary advantage, a time of singular sympathy and contentment and graciousness—at home as well as in the theatre ; and I think we owed this in a great measure to the gentle yet strong personality of Violet Vanbrugh, whose lovableness and sensibility were strong enough to radiate happiness far and wide.

I confess that I did not think the part of Macbeth would suit Herbert (not that I had ever seen a Macbeth whom I thought ideal). But he could not be satisfied until he had essayed it, having a great love and reverence for the play. Accordingly he gave it, and gave one of his most wonderful productions. I did not tell him (or perhaps I did) how astounded I was at his Macbeth in the first three acts. (The last act demands a soldier, and that Herbert never succeeded in portraying.) But the scenes with the Witches, the Murder scene, the Banquo's ghost scene—these were rendered with a wild, tragic intensity, a very fury of the driven mind that made one's blood run cold. That is the essential effect that a great Macbeth must make : to make the blood run cold ! And the wistful, distraught face, the wistful, distraught voice in those immortal soliloquies : these were great acting, if ever acting was great.

Herbert and I once saw in Paris *Œdipus Rex* acted by Mounet-Sully ; it was one of the most memorable theatrical experiences of our lives. Of all actors, the Mounet-Sully of those days alone, to my mind, could give an ideal presentment of Macbeth, and I think Herbert thought this too. But would even Mounet-Sully have looked the wild and tragic, withal royal figure of a Northern King as Herbert did ?

And our holidays ? They were for ever changing ; and before trying to unravel the tangled skein of them, I ought to say that Herbert's idea of a holiday was to work harder than ever. For instance, during the run of Offenbach's *Orfée aux Enfers* (yes, Herbert was the first to revive Offenbach), in 1912, he took no rest : he merely plunged into a new adventure. After waging fierce war for years against the intrusion of the music halls into the kingdom of the theatre, suddenly, upon the altering of a comma in the law relating to both, Herbert made the *amende honorable* by consenting to appear at the Palace Theatre in a sketch ! (It should perhaps be called the *amende honorarium*, for he charged the recipients of his generosity one thousand pounds a week.) He chose Kinsey Peile's adaptation of Rudyard Kipling's lovely story, " The Man Who Was." The luridness, pathos and intensely dramatic nature of the little half-hour play— together with wonderful acting on the part of Herbert—made it a sensational success. (I have used that adjective " sensational " too often ; but I cannot find another word for the many successes Herbert had that set the Box Office humming and the world hurrah-ing.)

Having still time on his hands, he must needs take ship for Egypt (a ship, by the by, which made, to the utmost limit of the land, an overland route. Oh, would that flying had been the vogue in his day !—how his soul would have soared with the machine !). And he did not scour the desert or confiscate Cairo out of idleness. For his work's sake he wanted to know something of the yellows and blues, the jewelled dawns and spacious nights of the East.

Then, again, when *Drake* set him free, for he did not act in it, he first of all made a little tour in the provinces with *The Man Who Was*, and then rushed off to Germany *viâ* Paris, seeing plays, seeing theatres, seeing, as it seemed to us, a whole new world in the little space of fourteen days. Then Christmas comes—one of our wonderful Christmases, ever to be treasured in our memory, at Belvoir Castle. There our whole family was wont to be welcomed, feasted, made much of, royally entertained, year after year, for many happy years. Ah ! what love, what sweetness, what jollity, what perfection of hospitality we found there ! And scarcely had Herbert finished his Belvoir plum-pudding (like all nice men, he loved puddings and pies), than he started on a one-week's visit to New York and Boston—this not " for fun," though no doubt he had heaps of fun, but to see a play, and to negotiate for a possible season there. That magic-carpet of an exploit at an end, he must needs set out for Russia— taking with him his stage-manager, Stanley Bell, and sending telegrams from time to time, such as : " *Moscow.*—So lovely here ; why not all come ? " Or : " *St. Petersburg.*—Cannot you and Viola meet me Vienna ? " Such were his lightning ideas of lightning travel. He called this snatched voyaging of his " completing his neglected education." It was really part of his restless, resistless energy ; of a yearning, that knew no bounds, to know, to see, to encompass.

Herbert's return to work meant the production of a new play, which happened to be a complete failure ; and the inauguration of a month's Shakespeare Festival, in which, besides acting nearly all his usual parts, it pleased him to learn and play Mercutio to Phyllis Terry's Juliet. But he and I had seen an incomparable Mercutio in Charles Coghlan, and though he may have satisfied the public, I know he did not satisfy himself.

In the autumn of 1913 he produced Louis Parker's *Joseph and his Brethren*—ineffable, immortal story !—which, although a Biblical subject, was, to the astonishment of all the world except Herbert, who *willed* it so, licensed by the Lord Chamberlain. This play was—I must not say " sensational " again !—a delirious success ; beyond the wildest dreams of author and producer. And no wonder ! All the old Miracle plays and Mystery plays were set before us in this reverent melodrama, this sumptuous setting of a Psalm. It has been said that a play is always a success if it has appearing in it a dumb animal. This would account for the super-success of *Joseph and his Brethren*, for the Ark was ransacked to people its scenes—camels, oxen, sheep, asses and goats used to jostle one another in Charles Street, to the delight of the " queues " and to the gratuitous enjoyment of the passers-by. Wild beasts, too, were not wanting in their prowl ; but they, as someone said, were visible, though startlingly visible, only to the ear.

Herbert and I besieged Bushey (where she lived) and the Ritz Hotel (where she resided) in order to induce beautiful, brilliant Maxine Elliott, our loved friend, to undertake the part of Potiphar's wife. Who in the end ever said " No " to Herbert ? She came to us, and irradiated wickedness, tempered by so much loveliness as served to satisfy the severest censor. Herbert, needless to say, made a grand figure of Jacob—majestic, patriarchal, instinct with sacred and sublime dignity. Alas ! I used to say to him : " Why be ninety till you *are* ninety ? " He would answer, " It is better to be ninety when one is fifty than to be fifty when one is ninety." The play, its exquisite production, the difficulties of its being allowed, and the intrinsic beauty of the work itself had enormous *réclame*, and it filled His Majesty's for many months.

It was so like Herbert to dart from silver-bearded, majestic, patriarchal Jacob to flippant, solemn, ultra-modern, exuberantly vital Henry Higgins in Bernard Shaw's *Pygmalion*. But Herbert flung away his harp without a sigh, and eagerly put up the umbrella that stamped the new Wimpole Street hero. How well I remember the reading of *Pygmalion* in the Dome, and my passionate eagerness that Herbert should accept it ! He needed little persuasion ; the only doubt in his mind was whether he should play Dolittle, the Dustman, or the hero. It was I who insisted that, because no one on the stage could have acted the Dustman as he would have, yet that it was too *obvious ;* and that the original and unexpected thing was that he should be Pygmalion. Oh, and how right I was ! The play was produced and had phenomenal success—as it deserved, for it was a *wonderful* play, brimming with wit, brimming with drama. There were terrible scenes at rehearsals. Every day Herbert and Bernard Shaw and Mrs. Patrick Campbell used to turn one another out of the theatre and shake its dust off their feet forever. But the next morning saw them at eleven o'clock, serene in countenance and as polished in manners as in boots, there having been no sanguinary yesterday.

Pygmalion seemed as though it would run for ever ; but Herbert brought it to an end the third week in July, 1914, for at last he felt himself in need of actual rest. He made a faint attempt to arrange that someone should fill his place, but Mrs. Patrick Campbell had left the cast ; so the play was put upon the shelf to be revived, and Herbert set out, in a new car, to drive all the way to Marienbad. Luckily for him, and for us all, he never reached his destination. The yearly grace of these three weeks at Marienbad was always granted Herbert by his exigent family ; but after that he was bound by iron chains to join us wherever the children and I had pitched our tent.

I had a passion for taking houses—houses which we used to rent, and which were for ever being sold over our heads ; so that my mad nomadicity was my misfortune rather than my fault.

For two years we had a house, adored by the children, at Brancaster (that is where Alan and Viola met) ; for a year at Rottingdean ; for two years on the river at Sutton Courtney ; and at last (we have it still) a rambling house in Sussex, whose space and solitude were congenial to Herbert, as were the bosky dells and sheep-trimmed fields that surrounded it. Ah ! I can see him now, amazed and enchanted at millions of mushrooms, which he gathered with eager care and boylike ambition to win our game, " Whoever sees them first has the most." It amuses me to remember why, after a mere cottage and a barn at Sutton Courtney, I persuaded myself to take this enormous house at Robertsbridge. There had been a command gala performance at the theatre, and Herbert had had it decorated with thousands of noble swags made of laurel leaves and of golden and coloured fruits. The effect in majestic His Majesty's had been wonderfully beautiful, and I grieved to think such glory should be scrapped. So I conceived the idea of buying all those beautiful Italian wreaths and ropes, and set about finding a place to put them. Glottenham, with its long corridors and many spacious rooms, had evidently been built for them ; and it was settled. Alas ! I took the house before I bid for the wreaths—found they had been sold for thirty pounds to the man who made them (I think they cost a thousand pounds)—and I could only secure *three*. But those three are the making of one room to this day. It used to please Herbert to see them ; indeed, that one should admire and cherish and remind him of things that had been a careless, unremembered stroke of genius to him always gave him intense pleasure.

Here at Glottenham Herbert put together his book," Thoughts and Afterthoughts," a task which must have been onerous, but which caused him only unmitigated pleasure. Indeed, he took great pride and delight in authorship, and during the last fortnight of his life he was planning a new edition of a combination of both his books, " Thoughts and Afterthoughts " and " Nothing Matters." I need not say that we shall try to carry out his wishes.

To Glottenham, when June nights were so short that twilight merely faded into dawn, from time to time Herbert and I would make our way after the theatre, to join a " children's week-end."

"HAMLET."

Evelyn Beerbohm, Patrick Shaw Stewart, Billy Grenfell, Edward Horner, Dennis Anson—dear, blessed, sacred names—you were among the children.

One of " Maud's Follies," as they had come unkindly to be called, was a house I took because it was on the Seine (insane, said Herbert), because it was pure Louis Quatorze and absolutely beautiful, because it was " nothing a year " (like so many of our houses)—and because it was wise that the children should learn the art of French fishing. At the time I took the exquisite and elusive Maison du Canal I was acting in *Diplomacy ;* therefore it was only by travelling through Saturday night that I was able to devote Sunday to furnishing it. This I was perfectly content to do ; and by the summer-time Viola and Alan, Felicity and Iris were able to be there, Herbert joining them on his way home from Marienbad. They had a new and gladsome time, painting the little village of Pont de l'Arche red with their exploits and despoiling the Seine of its trout. It was impossible for me to go to stay until the following summer (1914), and we had not been there ten days before the War broke out. The return of four of us and of four scared English servants was difficult of accomplishment and full of adventure ; so much so that I was left behind alone on the quay at Dieppe (where panic-stricken holiday-enders had been sitting on their luggage for four days). I rejoiced at the delay because of the divine welcome Herbert gave me when, the next night, anxious and solicitous, he met me at Victoria.

His adventures when the War broke out were told me recently in a letter from Sam, our good and faithful chauffeur, some of which I quote :

" August, 1917.

" About the trip to Marienbad, or as far as we got. You can, I hope, piece together from me one or two things I remember. The dates you must verify, as I can't recollect them. We started the Monday at 8, crossed that night, arriving Sunday 8 a.m. back at Charing Cross (evidently went to fetch the car from France). We stopped Monday Folkestone, crossed over and motored to St. Quentin Tuesday, and spent the night there. I worked till 2 in the morning, so I remember that well. . . . I was

up early swearing at the waiter, and with every d—— he brought
another roll. Sir Herbert (he'd just come in) said I had better
leave off, or we should have all the bread there was. The French
were very excited, and in the Hotel all were wondering what Sir
Edward Grey would do. So Sir Herbert wired to London to Mr.
Langton to know if we should proceed—the answer to be sent
to Longwey. We left St. Quentin at 10 a.m., and there was
plenty of excitement in a small town (?) where we had lunch
between St. Quentin and Longwey. A run in the banks, numer-
ous peasant women taking things to market and gossiping outside
cafés. At the Customs (Longwey) the French had a chain and
an armed guard twenty strong. The Germans had only one man,
and there were no signs of any military movement till we got as
far as Colbing. We called at the Post Office—no telegram, so we
left word to forward to Luxembourg. But we never got it. In
the Luxembourg Hotel and garage everybody talked of war. Sir
Herbert said we were too civilized, and it would never come.
'A political game' he called it, or something like that. The
Germans said 'they were ready' and 'in nine days in Paris.'
They said *we* had the Suffragettes and the Irish question to keep
us out. Everybody was calm and confident and smiling—quite
the reverse from the French. In the French hotels they said they
were better prepared than in 1871. We left Luxembourg German
Customs for Frankfort—a good day's run. We saw lots of lancers
and noticed guards on the bridges. The waiter, where we had
lunch, tried to argue the point. He knew they would go to war,
and it would all end in two months ; he was in the ' Carlton,' so
he knew Sir Herbert. We arrived in Frankfort late on Thursday
evening ; the next day, Friday, we were starting, late—eleven
o'clock—for a short run. On Friday morning I had the car
washed, and I greased and fitted up. The town was seething with
excitement. Boys delivered newspapers every half-hour *free*,
I believe, announcing the latest. One that caused a lot, I remember, because the German proprietor of the garage told me the
British Fleet had sailed for an unknown destination. Everybody
came into the streets ; in fact, they must have had a presenti-
ment, for that seemed to sober them a bit. I went round at
ten—Sir Herbert was in bed ; round again at eleven ; Sir Herbert
still in bed, so I went to his room. I had had a talk with the

garage proprietor and I knew he was pumping me as to where we were going, because I told him a hotel in Luxembourg we never intended stopping at, and he informed me where we *did* stay. I told Sir Herbert the people were very excited, in fact worse than yesterday, and that the Russians had all gone home three days before. Lots of people—English—had left the hotel, going back home by the 8 train. He at last said he supposed he must get up, and I told him I was in favour of going home. He wondered why ! We had no telegram, but we suddenly thought of going to see the British Consul, and he took a cab there. I had got the car round when he returned—' half an hour.' He came up and said we were going home. Shots had been exchanged with France, and we could not get a train. He pointed to his breast and said, ' I can't tell you—something seemed to break inside me when I heard it was war—wicked !—wicked !—wicked ! ' I tried to make him have something to eat, but he could not, and he hardly finished his coffee. We got the luggage down and started, intending as the British Consul advised, to make for Holland or Belgium. We had a good run for an hour ; then the car fell away. We had some beer and a piece of bread and cheese to save time while the engine cooled. We put in a gallon of lubricating oil and decided that we must go slower or the car would let us down. I wished we had a good English car now ; but we dared not go faster then as the loss of oil varied. The road was most of way by the Rhine, but after the first three bridges (I am doubtful of the name, but a fairly large town) I was pulled up by soldiers with fixed bayonets. After a few sentences, Sir Herbert got out and started walking over the bridge. An officer climbed on the footboard and signalled me to go on—two soldiers in the back with fixed bayonets. So I said ' I am d——d if I drive this lot,' but Sir Herbert looked round and beckoned me to go over the bridge. The officer said ' Don't swear '—so I asked him if we were at war. He said ' No ' and he hoped we *never should be ;* but all cars were escorted over bridges so that they could not blow them up. The same was said to Sir H. when he came up. We were stopped now once every ten miles for our passports. I kept them handy as they sprang up and got their guns ready, and I've since thought they were loaded.

"We arrived in Cologne about 10—but before we got there I nearly ran over a child. It started across the road, and just missed it. The crowd ran for stones, but we did not stop. On the road children threw several stones, but only one or two hit the car. They also threw stones at it while we had tea, but they waved hands when we went. There were only a few dents in the panel. The crowd proceeding to the railway station made it impossible to get along faster than two miles an hour. I found afterwards it was to see the troops go by ; they were running through to France across a suspension bridge. We put up at a hotel a hundred yards off the railway station. Hotel Hoff or Koff. The place was so densely packed that it must have been half an hour—but it seemed ages to me, as I was certain I had a very little petrol and the engine had been running a long time. The mounted police did not worry about us, and I managed slowly to push through. They boo-ed a bit, but some sang songs ; in fact, they were a very light-hearted crowd. I went out (Sir H. was in the newspapers and was very anxious to get hold of an English paper) ; but was advised to go back to the hotel. A double-engine train ran every three minutes all night ; at least, I went to bed at one, and at five they were still running.

"I was up early next morning and went to the garage (five o'clock) and ordered petrol. I knew they were putting up the price, but the garage proprietor had lost all the English in the night. After trying to make him understand he condescended to inform me that I should get no petrol. I fetched the hotel proprietor. The Government had prohibited the sale from 10 p.m. the night before ! I reported to Sir Herbert and he at once decided that the train was the only thing. I went to the station, and the only train was eight—doubtful when another would start. We left the car in charge of the hotel proprietor, bought our tickets, and I saw all the luggage into the omnibus except mine, and that they would not bring, so I brought it myself. We walked to the station and we carried some of the luggage each, for the two men from the hotel to follow with the rest. Sir H. met a lady and gentleman (French) in the carriage. I can't remember their names, but ' a most wonderful lady ' wrote a marvellous article on the Suffragette question—against,

I believe. They came from Berlin, and both were very much upset. I believe she was some great artist in the theatre, or something, as I believe she said ' Herbert Tree ! ' when we went in. I waited several minutes till afraid the train would go. I said the luggage was not come yet, so we rushed outside the station, and the omnibus was starting back with our bags in it ! Sir Herbert was in a rage. Their excuse was (I believe it was the last train out) they thought we were going by a later train ; but from their manner it was a case of we were in a hurry and they intended keeping it. We had to detrain and carry our luggage, coats and rugs. A sovereign got us help towards the last hundred yards. How we toiled with that load of luggage ! We had to walk nearly half a mile to go through the farce of being chalked, ' Pass the Customs.'

" We parted with the lady and gentleman at Brussels ; I believe they were going to Paris. We had two or three lunches in the dining-car and several coffees ; the waiters seemed determined that we should not rest awhile. The corridors were packed with luggage and people—Americans, the greater part, and some noisy French students singing. Sir H. was greatly interested in a woman's case : English—three daughters married to German soldiers. She was coming to draw her money—a good round sum—and go back to Germany. She had lived long enough in Germany to believe them invincible. She admitted we had a Navy. Sir H. could not eat or drink any more, so he got the attendant to find seats so that he could get along to the front of the train. The attendant came back and started me off (outside the train) with two dressing-cases, coats and rugs. Off went the train, and I jumped in with the coats, expecting the porter would throw the dressing-cases in—but no. We sailed out and I saw them on the platform beside the porter. We eventually got them sent down. Arriving at Ostend, the boat had sailed. So we had to wait till 11 p.m. Saturday night. We had a fine crossing and arrived at daybreak in Dover Harbour.

" Those are all the incidents that I remember, and of course this is just dodged in, so excuse the way I have put it.

" Sir H. said that the time would come when the man who made war would be the first in the firing line ; London would be in flames, and all the best and strongest gone. He meant that by killing the robust and healthy, the nations of Europe would degenerate. We saw an old man mowing corn, and he painted a picture from that as we rushed in the train across Belgium. 'One man to have the means to send so many as food for powder ! '

" Yours respectfully,
    " SAM WORDINGHAM."

CHAPTER VII

ONLY the very young could ever know real happiness again after the outbreak of the War—a War that made through four long years a path to victory indeed ; but a path paven with broken hearts. The best, the dearest, the greatest ; the flower of England's manhood were falling like leaves in autumn ; and many a great-hearted gentleman, though never a soldier, grieved and was jostled until he joined the lóved, lost heroes who gave their lives in battle ; they climbed the steep ascent of Heaven ; he followed in their train.

Although theatrical London, for the first few days after the declaration of war, was fairly panic-stricken, Herbert kept his head, and immediately opened his theatre with the most patriotic play he had—*Drake*, acting in it himself. Thus was he able to give instant employment to a large number of people, and thus by giving all the profits to War Charities, with the generous co-operation of his author, Louis Parker, and his company, to render service to his country from the first. But we were all sick at heart. Too well we knew that there were grim and terrible days to come. After *Drake, Henry IV.* seemed likely to be in the spirit of the time, and Herbert revived it, but not with great success. I remember that on the first night of that, Lady Randolph Churchill, who was in my box, whispered to me of the fall of Brussels.

Thus passed the first half-year of the War, with its mornings ushered in for us by the glad, gay singing of a Flying Corps in training, whose route lay past our windows—mornings feverish with anxiety to see beyond the official news, the unofficial pro- phecies ; days that were made both sorrowful and glorious with the coming and going of ever-increasing khaki legions. One saw them swinging through the streets, a prayer on one's lips

161

and that shy, furtive waving of a half-concealed, tear-soaked handkerchief which said in plainest English : " You are our glory and our hope, but we don't want to upset you or ourselves by letting you know it."

Love and anxiety for those who fought for us make us all try to usher little shafts of light—endurance, self-sacrifice, added pitifulness and courtesy and devoutness—into our characters and life ; the very expression upon people's faces changed into something lovelier and more loving. The spirit of those who could only stand and wait was a fine and noble one. Whether in all cases it endured to the end, who shall say ? Confession may be, but I do not think that reaction is good for the soul.

In the spring there came, in spite of heavy news, a kind of revival of life and spirits ; a " give-the-boys-a-good-time-before-they-go-out " idea, and theatres began to be fuller now. Herbert gave a wonderful presentment of *David Copperfield* (adapted by Louis Parker), in which he doubled the parts of " Dan'l Peggotty " and " Micawber." This *tour de force* cost him not one instant's anxiety ; he slipped from one part to the other with amazing lightness and facility. It was a great success.

And in the winter of 1915 Herbert went to America—bitterly, how bitterly against my will ! But afterwards I learnt to think that he was able to do better work for his country there than here—indeed, it was allowed him by the great ones of the earth that he had done splendid things for the united cause in the United States, as the following letters show.

" April 3rd, 1917.
" MY DEAR TREE,
        " Very many thanks for your letter and for the enclosed extracts from your speeches. You have been doing very useful work, and you will rejoice, as we do here, that a decision has at last been taken, and that America has finally decided to come in and join us in this stupendous struggle for freedom.
                " Yours sincerely,
                        " D. LLOYD GEORGE.
" Sir Herbert Tree."

"March 30th, 1917.

"Dear Sir Herbert,

"I am much obliged to you for sending me reports of your speeches. Allow me heartily to congratulate you on the success of your efforts at this critical moment in the history of the English-speaking world.

"Yours sincerely,
"Arthur Balfour."

"Thou goest; to what distant place
Wilt thou thy sunlight carry.
I stay with chill and clouded face:
Ah! how long wilt thou tarry?
Where'er thou goest morn will be;
Thou leavest night and gloom to me."

This unknown, half-forgotten poem, which he used to love, goes on: "Bid souls of eager men awake; Be kind and bright and tender." And it exactly applies to him. When he left us, taking our youngest daughter, Iris, with him, taking with him his kindness and brightness and tenderness, taking the glint of his enthusiasm and eagerness and hopefulness, days became drab and dreary; in very truth he left night and gloom to me. (By the way, how he hated, all his life, things drab—thoughts, days, intentions, points of view: he wanted light and colour. The accompaniment of a little song of mine pleased him, because "It is so blue," he used to say.)

He came home for a few weeks in the autumn of 1916; came home in spite of our beseechings that he would take no such risk —for the submarine menace grew graver and graver. Contracts had been made in America that demanded his return, so it was a mere visit; one of his tread-mill holidays. He came in the very heart of the Zeppelin fury—a fury which found him absolutely calm and unafraid—he, who all his life had had childish, unconquerable terror of someone stealing up behind him in the dark! I remember that one night (the night that the Lyceum and the Gaiety Theatres and many another building had wrack and ruin dealt them) Iris and I left him at All Souls Place, as he wanted to stay at home and work, starting ourselves for the Haymarket

Theatre to see Henry Ainley in *Quinney's*. In the middle of the second act the dread sounds began which meant death, horror and destruction, here, there and everywhere. My first thought was : " Oh, why did we leave poor Herbert alone ? " Five minutes later he was in our box, having rushed through the known and unknown dangers of the streets ; perfectly heedless of himself —only eager to know that others were safe. Yes ; how strange an anomaly ! It was agony to Herbert to be startled—he would implore one *not* to startle him. In the presence of real danger or crisis there never was a braver man.

He was extraordinarily practical too, though the unthinking, unknowing called him " vague." Having learnt, or having appeared to learn, nothing, he could, at all events in his own profession, teach every man his trade. (Yes, he could even tell by touch an antique from a " fake " ; someone had idly told him the test, and when the time came he was ready with it.) He used, half bitterly and half excusingly, to cry out at rehearsal —when " properties " went wrong—when handles would not turn ; pistols would not go off ; thunder would not sound ; snow would not fall ; mountains would not be removed ; Hell would know no fury (as in *Faust*) : " There is nothing one cannot do oneself better than the man whose work it is to do it."

Herbert had no learning—had small Latin and no Greek—had read none of the books of science, philosophy, poetry, fiction, that other people live by, yet his instinct was so sure that he *knew* things. He was like an inspired Water-finder. With a desert of unexplored knowledge stretching about him, he always lighted on the little spring that gave the very draught he sought. If one quoted a good line to him, he would catch it up, repeat it, and never forget it. How proud I was if something that I told him turned itself to his use ! Yet he did not know what every child might know. On the day before his death he took from my hands Dr. Bridge's " Spirit of Man," which does not name the poets as it quotes. He read such an one as " Hail to thee, blithe spirit ! " or " Fair Attic shape," or " He prayeth best who loveth best ; " and musingly said : " That *is* lovely—I wonder who wrote it ! "

I used to say that he read but two novels during the whole of our married life : " Tess " and " Without Dogma " (though once on a motor journey to Margate he was absorbed in, and nearly finished, " The Card "). There may have been half a dozen more, but " Tess " and " Without Dogma " were Herbert's two novels. He must have mastered Dickens as a boy, for, though I never saw him read one, he seemed to be familiar with all Dickens' books. I do not believe he ever consistently read Thackeray, yet Colonel Newcome came as second nature to him, and all the names—Pendennis and Rawdon Crawley, Philip and Esmond, and the Four Georges—were as household words to him.

I find myself drifting into an analysis of Herbert's habit of mind. A foolish flow of thought, for love and reverence must ever needs blot out the faults and magnify the qualities of those we mourn, be they many or few. Indeed, of so great a man I could almost wish that his enemy, rather than his most loving friend, should appraise him. Kind and wise and generous ; gifted, far-seeing to the extent of being in advance of his time ; eager, affectionate, charitable ; strong, undaunted, original, of a great brain and of a child's heart—these must be allowed him, even by his detractors : " The enemies of Cæsar shall say this." Amid scholars, Herbert was never uneducated ; amid wits, he always shone. Among the simple, he was the most simple and understanding ; among " Our Betters " he was ever at his ease. His conscious dignity and pride forbade that marplot to good manners, shyness. Yet he had deference and reverence, and that inestimable humility which is governed by self-possession. He was neither iconoclast, socialist, nor revolutionary, though he affected so shabby a greatcoat that he was often accused of being all three. No ; he was to a great extent actually conventional—with a convention often put out of court by whimsicality and bubbling, irresistible humour. To those who loved him, his approbation was the most precious prize that could be dealt ; his rebuke broke one's heart. This was because he possessed, to an inordinate degree, Taste and Judgment. His taste was fine and delicate. Things coarse and ugly in conduct or idea were abhorrent to him ; they caused him a visible shudder of disgust. Long, long before the War, he declared that the domination of the execrable and the obscene in one of the leading capitals of the world was destined to undermine the civilization of mankind. He was proved right. And many years ago he said of Alsace-Lorraine : " Ah, yes, the children of Alsace learn their lessons in German ; but they say their prayers in French ! "

His judgment about the things of life (not about things theatrical, for he was often in fault in casting, in choosing plays and in rejecting plays—he has been known to refuse at least four of the greatest successes of his day) seemed always unerring to us. Severe, almost puritanical, yet always, if possible, on the side of joy, it became a household proverb with us : " Daddy shall decide." If, as too often happened, we acted without that decision, we were ill at ease, for there was always his own proverb —ridiculously and pertinaciously true : " I am always right."

Thus it came that to win his approval, to shine in his eyes, made splendour of any success ; to merit his scorn or disapproval, simply blackened life. To this day I remember the lash of his words when, carelessly as was too often my wont, I put on indiscriminate feathers and furbelows for a certain pàrt, and went to his dressing-room crying, not without expectant complacence : " Is this the period ? What do I look like ? " He answered, looking up from his own quiet, careful toilet : " A mad woman of *any* period."

Ah ! but the guerdon of his praise, how sweet ! If rare, how far the richer, making worthless the guerdon of others ! Not any applause or adulation that ever reached me have the pride and joy that he bestowed (during the last fortnight of his life) : " That interview of yours last June was the very best theatrical interview I ever read." I am ashamed to record such trivial things ; but they are bound about my heart.

My heart—oh ! that it could give words to the lovely, splendid life he gave me ; to the rich and joyous years I owed to him !

> " Love made me Poet
> And this I writ.
> My Hearte did do it
> And not my Witte."

Alas ! love has made me no poet ; but my Hearte cries out that in all my long life I never had a sorrow until I had the sorrow of Herbert's death. There were troubles, vexations, anxieties, jars and frets, shadows of the sorrows of others ;

these were as passing clouds that darkened for an hour a sunny, glorious life; but until I lost Herbert, I never knew a real sorrow. Only his leaving me made me acquainted with grief. Can love and gratitude give greater tribute?

Whitsuntide, 1918.

It was on Whit Sunday, a year ago, that you arrived in London from America, my Herbert. We knew of your landing in Spain, and of your being on your journey thence to Paris; but we were altogether uncertain as to the day and hour of your reaching London. That is why I did not wait at home for you—with that superstitious dread (all travel was still dangerous and uncertain) that if I lingered about for you, you would not come; for how eagerly we longed for, how fervently we had prayed for your safe return! Thus it came that though Viola was stationed at her own telephone, I at the telephone at Sutton Courtney, and Mr. Dana controlling the whole system of telegraphic and telephonic communication between Madrid and His Majesty's Theatre—yet, my dear, you arrived in London, and there was no one to meet you—you who had expected all our glad faces and glad words to glorify the gloom of Charing Cross Station! However, I think this momentary disappointment was the only one you had, for, in mingled triumph and anguish, I recall with what utter delight you took up the threads of your life in England—with what a passion of eagerness and fervour you instantly began to weave them into purpose and achievement.

It was evening—seven o'clock, I think—when, answering the telephone at Sutton Courtney, I heard your voice. " It's too good to be true! " I shouted; and you answered: " It's lovely to be home. Viola is here."

With characteristic eagerness he began at once to tell me of his adventures on his journey. His voice was gay and full of energy (a charming telephone voice—what an excellent thing in man!), and he began at once to thank me for such preparations as had been made for his home-coming.

And the next day—May the twenty-eighth—Herbert arrived at Sutton Courtney. Mr. and Mrs. Asquith were our hosts, and they gave him sweet welcome to the sweetest of all homes in the sweetest time of the year.

I remember his calm delight in English May-time. " Lovely "
were the buttercups, the birds, the river and the moonlight-
coloured hedges ; but I always think he cared more for the
achievements of man than the glories of nature. A yellow primrose was little more than a yellow primrose to him ; but he
literally ached with joy over a poem of Raymond Asquith's
which Elizabeth knew by heart. Over and over again he made
her repeat it, revelling in its wit, its cynicism ; dreaming
delightedly over its lines and phrases, and often starting up with
vigorous projects for its being published in America. All the
evening he kept us amused and enchanted ; I felt as though I
had never known him in a mood so boyish and light-hearted ;
but that mood seemed to last on for the rest of his few remaining
summer days on earth. After dinner he was the life and soul
of " parlour-tricks " ; at dinner, the life and soul of the talking.
He had so much to tell—and how blithely he told it !—of his
last months in America, of the President and Mr. Roosevelt
and Mr. Choate, whom he had lately seen ; of his strange journey
home by devious routes ; of his new rôle of King's Messenger
from Madrid to London ; of his victorious battle against Military,
Civil and Naval authority at Calais, which ended in his triumphant
journey to Dover, while all officialdom was dooming him to
Southampton *via* Havre.

During the next fortnight, at home, he seemed to be in daily
delight at the welcome given him. Every hour seemed to bring
him token of how much he was wanted, how much he had been
missed ; and—to my astonishment—for it was unlike him—
he accepted all the invitations showered upon him, and seemed
to have a new-born love for his home. Alas ! alas ! One morning,
as he started forth, he checked his light step upon the stairs,
paused, and said rather wistfully : " What a *charming* house
this is ! "

Summer weather, many " socialities "—some of which
included me, and some, such as The Pilgrims' Club and The
Other Club, which I used to drive him to (in a taxi, I mean, not
mentally)—made for him delighted days—but they were so
few !—in which he seemed continually amazed and overjoyed.
He accepted with childish glee and almost deprecating gratitude
the river of welcome that rushed to him.

One theatre we went to—*The Aristocrat*—and he saw George Alexander for the last time—George Alexander, who, though very ill that night, insisted upon acting because " Herbert is coming " ; and we lunched in their delightful house, with the Charles Wyndhams. We dined one night with the Henrys, sitting long in the June twilight of their garden, while Herbert, Sir Charles, Lady Henry and T. P. O'Connor (to whom Herbert was devoted) kept Carlton House Terrace ringing with their sallies ; a dinner at the Kennerley Rumfords', where again there was the garden and sweet and gay discourse, and where afterwards Clara sang to us. I remember these, but every day and every hour of his weeks of welcome and project were full of things that he enjoyed, that he was eager about. Everything was in train for gladness and such contentment as the War allowed ; and for what in reality contented him most of all (though he always declared himself by nature idle—he would insist that it cost him an effort to be up and doing)—hard work.

Then came his accident, and only seventeen days remained for him on earth. So slight a thing it seemed, and yet it was enough to crack that noble heart.

> " Not so deep as a well, nor so wide as a church-door,
> But 'tis enough, 'twill serve."

Except that it fretted him to be inactive, and that an occasional, quickly dissipated fear would cross his mind that it would be longer than a month or two before he walked and danced and ran, his last days were happy. The moment he was allowed to see people, to write, to dictate, to talk plans and business, he took advantage of every possibility, and was with difficulty persuaded that he could not keep public appointments by being carried hither and thither. He used to love people coming to see him, love the flowers and fruit that arrived, love letters and attentions, and all the petting everybody gave. Sir Alfred Fripp used to pay him a second, a non-professional, visit every evening after dinner, and this was always a time of great hilarity for us.

On the actual day of his death he woke unusually early— at five o'clock—and made himself quite happy, reading, perhaps for the tenth time, the play he was going to produce—*The Great Lover*. He said : " I shall not need to study the part at all ;

I know it already." He was full of a message which he had been asked to send to the Russian people, and equally full of plans for the day and for the morrow, and for many a day ; but here on earth no new day was to dawn for him.

I am bidden to be glad that his death was sudden ; that there was no lingering illness, no growing weakness, no dread of parting, no agony of farewells. Yes, for his sake, I would have wished that eager flame of life to be put out thus. But oh ! —the years of high endeavour, of happy fulfilment that seemed to stretch before him—the long road, smooth and wide at last, that he had set himself to traverse to his goal—how can one forbear to mourn, knowing his great love of life, to mourn that these were denied him ? Time and Faith can teach one not to question, but neither Time nor Faith can teach one not to grieve.

At the operation on his knee, two weeks before his death, when Herbert knew that he was being put to sleep, and just before he lost consciousness, he murmured : " I shall see you again ! "

I treasure this as your message, Beloved—the message you would have spoken to us had you known, in that July sunset, that your last, long sleep was hurrying upon you : " I shall see you again."

MY FATHER

By Viola Tree

July 7th, 1917.

SOMEONE, a man who had no particular reason to love him as we do, said to me : " Your father was quite the most irresistible man I ever met." That is exactly how I think of him—irresistible, absolutely dominating. From the time when I was little until now when I am more than grown up, the attitude of blind obedience and of abandoning all other occupation of the moment to do his will was absolute, even if in my heart I thought him wrong ; to me he was always a never-failing excitement, a surprise, an event.

That he was my father was and is wonderful, but somehow only secondary ; he bore no resemblance, so it seemed to me, to fathers as a race. We always heard his voice before we saw him, for he never came into the room, or, in Hampstead and Chiswick days, into the garden, without calling out loudly and penetratingly from wherever he was, " Viola ! " or " Children ! " This had the effect of a flourish of trumpets ; we all dropped our game or our lesson and ran to find him. I remember him best standing on the stairs or in the hall, always leaning on something ; sometimes he leaned on my head—always with his hat on, and wearing a big flamboyant coat, and carrying some very tall walking-stick (he had a succession of sticks) in his hand— he had really beautiful white disproportionately small hands.

Three things stand out clearly in my mind, proving how completely I was dominated by him, even to the point of casting out fear.

When I was very little, perhaps about four or five years old, I had the excitement of bathing with him in the sea for the

171

first time. I remember him saying to me, " Put your arms round my neck, dear, and I will swim out with you." Of course I obeyed, and we started off for the deep water. He then disengaged himself from my clutches and said, " Now float, dear," and I immediately and submissively floated.

A year or so later, when I had learnt to ride, the same thing happened again. It was the first day on which I was allowed out of the riding-school into Rotten Row, led by the riding-master on a leading-rein. Hardly had I overcome my first fears when over the horizon loomed my father on a large bay hireling, one hand on his hip—a favourite pose of his, even on horseback. His face lit up on seeing me, and he shouted, " Come on, dear, come and ride with me." I deserted my troupe, and my leading-rein, and trotted after him.

Then again, much later in life, as his prospective Ariel in *The Tempest*, I had to try the " wires " for the first time, and was timidly discussing with the professional on which foot to " take off." The wire was, I remember, uncomfortably hooked into my strait waistcoat, when he walked on to the stage. " I always know about these things, dear ; don't argue : fly ! " and he gave the order to the mechanic up above to let go. Without a murmur I flew, my feet dangling high above his head, and tingling like telegraph-wires at the sudden vibrations of his voice. " Very good, dear ; now sing ! " Up, up, towards the proscenium I soared, and managed, though with sinking heart, quaveringly to sing the first bars of " Where the bee sucks."

He hated hesitation or delay : " Are you coming along, dear ? " was his invariable formula. I would temporize feebly with " Where to, Daddy ? " " Oh, just out," he would say, but we found he always had a destination, and that destination the theatre.

About the time of the swimming incident we took a house on Hampstead Heath—rather a large house with a big garden and a lawn, overlooking many miles of green fields then unspotted by villas. I was still an only child, and therefore a spoilt child : all my mother's and father's holidays were planned for my pleasure, and their playtime was my playtime. Evenings, before they started for the theatre, and Sundays—always Sundays—were my great occasions. Sometimes they spoilt me to the extent of allowing me the grand treat of staying with them at Garlant's Hotel, which seemed to me a heaven of dissipation. It abutted on the old Haymarket Theatre, and he would go there for a night or two when his work kept him up too late for him to get back to Hampstead. He was ill there once with bronchitis, contracted on a terribly snowy night when he had to walk up the frozen hill, at which the one cab-horse rebelled. This was the only time I ever saw him ill; other people may remember that from time to time he had transitory illnesses, but I am sure this was the only time he was in bed for more than a few days: certainly no actor ever climbed to fame by filling the post of his understudy.

He was always desperately anxious that I should be truthful, and that I should never ask for money or presents. Once, in the kitchen-garden, I remember walking in abject misery behind him and my mother, who were discussing me in low tones, and she was crying because I had told a kind of lie about how many gooseberries I had eaten.

It was not really a lie, only apathy in counting the gooseberries, but he thought that just as bad, and they both decided not to forgive me that night. I went to bed in the terrible misery of children who can never argue because they have not the vocabulary, nor reason because they have not the experience; but in the end my father came up very late in the night with a plate of some nice thing or other from his supper.

The most beautiful of all young actresses came to see him to be engaged, perhaps for her first part. She had her pocket full of pennies, and as she strolled on the lawn I ran along by her side, and she offered them to me. After terrible misgivings I took them, but guiltily showed them to my father. His eyes became thunder-cloud blue, and he said almost fiercely : " You didn't ask for them, did you ? "

I cannot remember much more till we went to live in Sloane Street : there he used to dine every evening at home at five o'clock, and then to rest on the sofa in the back dining-room. My task was to put him to sleep by stroking his hair, and when I thought him " fast," to tiptoe out of the room, which I did with terrible contortions, for fear of waking him, taking twenty minutes to get to the door, often to be frustrated in the end by falling headlong over a rug or a cat—a great tragedy, as it would wake him, and I had to go back and get him to sleep again.

Though he was so dominating, almost domineering, about what he wanted us to do, and though we could not possibly have found it in our hearts to say " No," he always thanked us, even as children, for being with him : " So lovely, dear, your being with me."

When his own theatre was built, we necessarily saw less of him, and from the moment of laying the foundation-stone with a gold trowel, he regarded it as his toy, and he could never leave it. Like the engine-driver with his engine, who, I am told, is always, for love of it, screwing quite unnecessary screws to the sticking-point, he had to be at the theatre all day, merely to watch the works.

He was justly proud of it, as it gradually dropped its scaffolding and emerged, a tall, cream-coloured building, with a bronze dome, which we hoped would turn green with time. He and I used to look up at it, and then walk to the top of the Haymarket and look down at it, and one of us would say : " I think it's a little greener to-day, don't you ? "

The room he lived in—his " dome," as it was always called—was really the space under the dome where rats and fire-escapes would normally have been kept, but which he made into a wonderful place in which to live and work. It consisted of a high banqueting-hall, ending in rafters and what might have been a belfry, and a small inner room, which he always said was very characteristic of himself. This, however, was his own modest estimate, for it really was nothing more than an ordinary comfortable room, distinguished only by a frieze running round it, painted with scenes from *Twelfth Night, The Tempest,* and *The Taming of the Shrew.* Underneath the frieze were bookshelves containing great big useful illustrated books, with a mass of hopeless presentation copies bearing such titles as " Shakespeare through an Old Stager's Spectacles," " Sardanapalus : A Tragedy in 8 Acts." The interesting books and papers were piled up with his methodical untidiness on chairs, sofas and desks : the room had a nice glow of hard work ; there was nothing stale or burnt out about it. Many happy meals of Mother and the children, between matinées and evening performances, were eaten here; Mother used to call these meals " Sir Herbert Tree at Dome." He had a nice childish feeling that he could shut his two great doors, and feel he was out of the world. He used to tell the story—one of his loved stories—of Sir Squire Bancroft, who, when first shown the theatre, exclaimed with gloomy wit, " All those windows will have to be cleaned," which, indeed, they had, and sometimes the theatre, from being so immense, did prove a slight burden to him after the compactness of the Haymarket. Not only had he to keep an enormous staff at work there, but he could not put on many plays which he would have liked to produce, especially modern plays. Still, he loved the place, and never could keep away from it long. Even on my wedding-day, when we were driving to St. Martin's Church, I, very typical and rather sedate (for me), with veil and train poised ready for my spring on to the red carpet, he turned to me suddenly in Regent Street and said, " Will you drive me down to the theatre first, dear ? " And so at the stage-door I, the bride, sat watching his beloved figure—flamboyant coat-tails, hat, stick and all—vanish through the swing-doors, only to return a few minutes later having found out that all was well. I was so glad afterwards, as it would not have seemed natural for me to be driving with him and not to stop there. It was not in the least want of consideration for me or disregard of the deep happiness of the day ; indeed, he always said that it was one of the proudest days of his life.

He had real sympathy both in joy and sorrow, and yet so much of the child in him, that he loved all silly games and imitations, making rhymes, drawing, counting wheels, and making up stories about passers-by. All this made him the most wonderful friend and companion, for he was not only entertaining, but being entertained ; like Falstaff, he was not only witty himself, but the cause of wit in others, and I think there is no higher praise than this.

Not quite an outdoor man, no ; he boasted, on the contrary, that he could do without exercise entirely, yet he loved riding and swimming, if they happened to be within reach, and what he called " going through the air, dear," the actual pleasure of movement, walking very quickly (as my legs got longer and longer they never quite learnt to keep up with him without an occasional run), or going in a motor with bare head, to feel the wind in his face—not trains, which he couldn't bear because they stopped at stations. Continually I have known him at some quite ordinary place, like Crewe, lean out of his carriage and say to some innocent passing official, " Can't we be getting along now ? "

He was absolutely natural and unaffected, though people who knew him only a little were inclined to think the opposite. He would go past them wrapped in a cloud of ideas, his face turned neither to the right nor to the left, but his light eyes expressing what was going on in his brain. He therefore appeared to look through people and things ; but this mannerism was not, as some people say, a mask to hide his real feelings, but, to use his own expression, in order to " switch himself off." Sometimes at the beginning of one of his big enterprises, when things threatened to go wrong, his staff, hoping against hope, would whisper, " It's all right ; the chief won't notice." But the chief always did notice ; he could " switch himself on " the moment he liked, and very little escaped him.

He hated artificiality and make-believe, or anything trivial, or what he called flippant, so much so that some of our modernest effects in art seemed to him false and unintelligible. He would open his eyes very wide, and wave his head from side to side, as if to say, " Why ? Why ? " However, some of the really great modern things, notably Gordon Craig's *Hamlet*, which he saw in Moscow, he admired infinitely. He described this as a wonder of gold kings and courtiers from which background the tiny black figure of Hamlet detached itself—described it as he alone could, very slowly, sometimes using gestures to fill the gap of words, which made us hold our breath for fear of losing the sense.

Two parallel lines, they say, never meet, and it seems cruel that these two great figures, Craig and himself, born to work together, should have been parted by a sea of misunderstandings, though they occasionally tried to throw rocket signals to each other across the void. Together they would have been gigantic. . . .

Technical terms he never knew ; they always bothered him, and sometimes he had a difficulty in making himself understood at rehearsal. He would point, for instance, at a refractory light and say, " That one, that one there ; it gives no light ; " instead of " Don't check your battens," or whatever it might be ; or, again, " More mystery, more mystery," which the stage-manager, in his capacity of interpreter, would translate in a raucous whisper to the limelight-man above as " Biff your Number Threes." But in his own way he did all and every kind of work himself, never relying on mere " departmental work " so far as the stage was concerned. Even with the music, of which he had no technical knowledge, he had marvellous instinct, often to the point of suggesting to the composer exactly what he wanted. His colleagues were constantly amazed by the quickness and inspiration of his suggestions. " It's so awful to be right every time," he frequently said, after having won a tussle against exceeding odds of experts.

Beauty—to realize beauty was his great object, but he could not find beauty, as some of us can, in ugliness, crudity, or queerness, and the subtleties of symbolism seemed to him mere mediocrity and cheating the public. " These things will soon be Bakst numbers, dear," was his comment to me on what was, I must say, one of the least beautiful of the marvellous Bakst ballets.

No one was less vain than he about his personal appearance, or cared less what he wore. When his tie had lost its pristine splendour, he used to take me with him to the little shop next to his barber's, and say, " I want a tie ; " then he put on the first one offered him, and left the old one on the counter. All his shopping he did like this.

Of course we all loved his looks, and would not have changed anything of them : when he was not tired, his eyes were very blue, and he had perfect teeth, which showed very much when he laughed, a real out-and-out laugh, to arouse which one went through anything ; even to make him smile was worth a lot, and his staff tried every conceivable trick to amuse him. For all his carelessness he would from time to time feel dissatisfied with his appearance, and I remember his once trying to describe to me a young actor whom I had not yet seen : " He has the sort of looks I ought to have had."

When he was going to be drawn by Mr. Sargent I went with

him to the studio; knowing that he was very diffident about his looks and that Mr. Sargent was terribly shy and modest about his work, I was afraid that, left to themselves, they would never set to and get to work.

The moment he had stepped on to the daïs, I said to him : " Look towards the window, Daddy." He did so. Mr. Sargent became covered with confusion. " Don't strain, don't strain ; you will never be able to keep that pose." My father seemed surprised, and answered : " No, no, it's quite natural." This defiant turn of head and illuminated look was normal to him, before whose mind's-eye processions of popes, jugglers, and sinister servants holding peacocks in the leash passed continuously to the accompaniment of music, sad, strange, or grotesque. His most beautiful production, *Herod*, was probably built up like this, while he was driving through the streets, or carrying on a polite conversation.

I cannot help speaking of him as an actor, though others will have better things to say. Still, I have had my part in that side of his life, and I like to recall what so many of his comrades felt—what a wonderful person he was " to meet " (to use theatrical parlance) on the stage. Once again, he was always an adventure, an excitement, one never knew quite what he would do ; but it was always the right thing to give inspiration to one's next line. I believe it has been said that the greatest technicians of the stage don't become their parts, but mechanically drill their faces and their emotions. This may be, but it was not so with him : he actually became the part he was playing —that is why he was never the same from night to night, and why sometimes he appeared to be " walking through his part." With him it was everything or nothing : he was either living the part over again, or else completely out of it. His genius for make-up was always remarkable, but it was always helped— much more than people thought—by this quality of " getting inside " the character he was playing. As Gringoire he actually felt thin and hungry ; as Svengali he felt magnetic, dirty and musical ; as Beethoven he felt small and square, with big, strong, rather stumpy hands.

I think I shall always remember the last act of *Richard II.* as my best time with him, because in it we did not seem to be

HERBERT TREE
From a charcoal drawing by J. S. Sargent.

on the stage—we were showing what we really felt about things :
that there was an audience looking on didn't seem to matter. I
played the Queen—very badly, except for the one scene, in
which I became myself. I had to wait for his coming (Act V.,
Scene I. A Street) with Aumerle :

> THE QUEEN : This way the King will come ; this is the way
>   To Julius Cæsar's ill-erected tower——

After this I looked instinctively to see my father come out,
very simply and rather tired, dressed in black, and each time it
seemed as if he were surprised to see me standing there, and as
if we were really to say good-bye to each other for the first
and last time.   Then I fell on his neck, and said my speech sobbing, because at that moment I was not Richard's Queen but
my father's daughter—all alone on the great isolation of the
stage, for Aumerle and the super halberdiers had vanished like
shadows to the dark corners. He never could begin his speech
at once—he was so worried by my tears, as I looked at him
through blinded eyes. By and by I put my head down on his
shoulder so that he might begin—then only his voice came loud
and ringing like a clarion :

> " Join not with grief, fair woman, do not so,
>   To make my end too sudden : learn, good soul,
>   To think our former state a happy dream. . . .
>   In winter's tedious nights sit by the fire
>   With good old folks, and let them tell thee tales
>   Of woeful ages long ago betid ;
>   And ere thou bid good-night, to quit their griefs,
>   Tell them the lamentable tale of me,
>   And send the hearers weeping to their beds. . . ."

All it meant to me was, " Don't cry, Viola ; tell them I wanted
to do what was fine," and then and there I used to see myself
by some fireside in Norfolk or Kent, telling no lamentable tale,
indeed, but the proud story of his life's work and of his wonderful vitality. . . .

It can only do good to us to speak of him often, and perhaps —who knows ?—it may do good to him and make his life beyond more vivid and less misty. For myself, I think continually of the spirits of the grandparents in " The Blue Bird " —insisting, " Come back, back to us every day ; don't forget us ; come back, children." . . .

MEMORIES

By Iris Tree

THEATRES have lost their meaning for me now—I have known one theatre so well, and have loved it so long, it has run through the chain of all my memories, but now the link is broken. When I was a child the theatre was a refuge from lessons, mutton and rain, a place whose mystery was never dimmed by familiarity, a place of sliding curtains and endless doors, a corridor of echoing adventures.

So many times I have run up the noisy stairs that resounded with armoured footsteps, ladies humming tunes and rustling dresses, despairing voice of the call-boy—" All down for the first act, please "—I have chased down the passages, round the empty dress circle, into my father's room, where people were always waiting, and where there were so many pictures to look at.

And then the dressing-room itself, where my father sat before his mirrors, whitening an eyebrow, building a nose, haggering his face with delicate lines and laughing with us the while, dictating letters, calling for people.

It was the busiest, most whimsical, most fairylike room ; into it entered the man of cares, ambitions, of worldly hopes, and worldly weariness, emerging as some creation of a poet's fancy, an incarnation of fables, jests and tragedies. No longer man, but a spirit to move among men's hearts, to hush them to tears and revive them to laughter.

In and out people darted, harassed, mechanical, having momentarily lost all personal identity to become the stops and wires of my father's will.

He was a great despot in the theatre, no tyrant could have been more exacting, though no ruler more beloved.

It was only when he had left the theatre that he seemed to put on his more human mood.

Those long drives with him through the park, through melancholy suburbs, through sunset-lighted roads, and back again in the lamplight.

My father, though he professed to love the country, in reality had no sympathy for rustic living, he would tell me as we drove along how wicked country people were, pointing with a sinister finger at some criminal or merely idiotic face, and assuring me that Cockneys were the only good people.

When he stayed in country houses, after the first hours of dozing upon lawns, and climbing stiles, he would go back to the house humming a tune and furtively looking for the Bradshaw.

In America, when we saw the Grand Cañon together, he stood on the cliff with a smile of puzzled wonder at the barren beauty of those abysmal twilights and torch-like peaks, for he could only see them as the solemn background of human existence, the vast theatre of man's emotions, labours and progress. But there was no life in the scarred hollows beneath us, so he turned away with relief to the little Indian camps huddled among the snow.

It was to London that he belonged, or rather his brain and body belonged to London, though in his spirit I think he belonged to no land ; he seemed like an exile from some country whose name he had forgotten, but whose beauty came back to him and left his eyes bewildered at gazing upon things to which he had no kin. Most men bear traces of their environment, are typical of some place or age or coterie, but he seemed always the singular being, a wanderer from far roads whose dust had not dimmed his face, a seeker for some star whose rays had dazzled his eyes.

It was this aloofness that gave him a curious distinction among all gatherings of people, in all streets of all cities, so that strangers would turn to watch him questioningly, wondering whence he came.

He had a great admiration for the gipsies and their music, and told me that he had once resisted an impulse to visit them, lest he should become too fascinated by their life and unable to return to his own.

He so seldom spoke of his inner life, of his personal sorrows and joys, but on rare occasions, walking or driving, he would tell me of the things he had done, of his love of the pine, woods, of Hungarian music, of his youth, of sad days and gay.

And he seemed in these shy reminiscences to be a different person, someone I had never known.

It was the personal side that he showed least to people. I think that he was too sensitive to speak of the things that touched him most, and this made it difficult to probe deeply into thoughts with him.

I remember him less as a father, though he was the most wonderful father, less as a man, though he was the most lovable of men, but more as a mood, a voice, a gesture toward fancy, and light, and imaginative adventure.

His voice, which had that far, clear quality of voices on summer waters, his laughing eyes under brows that frowned from the habit of thought, and his hands that were more expressive than his words, and seemed as though they would draw on the air the thoughts that flashed upon his mind—these things I remember so vividly that I lose the detail of our days together.

But I have many memories of him ; lighted moments of his happiest moods, when all our smiles were kindled from his ; quiet evening hours when he was very tired and would talk wistfully of things and finally fall asleep ; triumphant nights of success and pleasure, when he would charm the dullest company from their monosyllabic small-talk to glitter with the highlights reflected from him, when he seemed to be dancing to some inward tune, and recalling old days whose ghosts had become fairy in his memory.

When we were children he used to take us away from our lessons to play with him, telling the governess that he had hated lessons, that he never read books, and that most education was useless. He told us fairy-tales, and never scolded us unless we had been rude or unkind. He liked simplicity, and used sometimes to cry at something that seemed very beautiful to him.

He was a rebel at heart and hated all forms of oppression, slavery and injustice, though another side of him revelled in ceremonies, legends, and the magnificent pageantry of tyrants.

His ideals were Tolstoyan, his temperament despotic, so that he was always spiritually opposed to things that his body accepted. I used to tell him for fun that he was a tyrant, and he would laugh guiltily and deny it.

We played all sorts of games together, talking in invented languages, quarrelling in Cockney, and one day we pretended to be ordinary people, but in the end he sighed and said : " It is no use, dear, I cannot help behing exceptional."

He loved food—æsthetically—and while lunching at some provincial hotel where, as he said, yesterday's cold chop is served on the family Bible, he used to invent Caligulan dishes, and deck the table so magnificently with his imagination that we would completely forget the chop.

It was distasteful for him to eat alone, and he told me that solitary eating was a grave symptom of the criminal mind.

He liked doing useful things like opening tins and bottles, murmuring : " I always know about these things," adding, when he had failed : " Ah, very good, patent non-openers."

He was so proud of our bungalow in California because he had found it himself and engaged the servants. All day he wandered through its rooms and generously gave the largest to me for my bedroom, but I saw him admiring it wistfully, and gradually it became his bedroom instead.

We used often to ride together on the rugged California hills. He insisted upon using the wooden property saddle constructed for Macbeth and would gallop all the way. He made great friends with the cowboys to whom he repeated his most obscure epigrams.

How hard and how long he worked at Los Angeles ! Sometimes for eighteen hours a day, in the heat of the sun, in the glare of the studio lights, until I used to marvel at his extraordinary vitality, his power to wade through fatigue, and when he had reached a resting-place, to laugh, make merry, write, create, discover new horizons.

In his own theatre it was the same, his energy seemed the pillar upon which everything rested.

Everyone loved him, or seemed so dependent on his personality that they lost theirs during his absence.

The grey stage at rehearsal with its dim figures moving
about in restless groups, seemed suddenly electrified by his
presence. Lights flashed from the roof, telephones rang, disasters
occurred, laughter, despair, sudden inspiration—everything—
began. I think that only those who saw him at work, building
his productions with such loving eagerness, raging, commanding,
almost mesmerizing people to perform his will, could realize
his genius in the theatre.

For I am sure that he had genius, although, perhaps, unaided
by great technique or intellectual knowledge, it was, if anything,
too instinctive and untempered by scholarly reserve.

There was something in his art akin to fascination, one could
criticize his acting, but no one could deny the power and wizardry
that he exercised over the imaginations of his audience.

I never liked him so much in the ordinary manly parts of
soldier, peasant and conventional lover. It seemed false when
he said : " Lend me a fiver " or " Old chap," and became the
plain blunt man. It was in those parts of sinister fancy, of
whimsical humour, of nightmare and dream, that he let his
spirit loose, leaving the audience haunted and bewitched.

He had a strange faculty for stirring the imagination by
little touches, as in Fagin's asthmatic cough before the opened
window, which made one almost feel the fog rolling in from the
river, the taste of dust and the smell of mouldering walls. The
clenched, awkward gestures of Beethoven, the thin, slightly
affected voice of Richard II., which gave a strange, pitiful
beauty to his weakness, the snarling woes of Shylock, whose
passions seemed tearing at themselves rather than at his enemies.

He could not be cynical or merely clever in his acting, and
when he was playing Macbeth for the cinema the directors were
amused and slightly irritated by his insisting upon knowing
his part perfectly, putting into his voice all the impassioned
quality it had on the stage. " I could not act unless I *felt* the
words," he said, and they knew it was true.

So deeply did he love his art, so entirely did he give himself
to the public, that I felt at times that he had no life outside the
theatre ; that daily anxieties and pleasures were fictitious things

for him, and the only realities lay in his work, and in the hearts of his audience. . . .

My father . . . More than anything I felt and feel about him is a shining quality of light, the power of shedding and receiving its rays.

And now that light so suddenly blown out has left its glow upon our memories, kindling the darkness that his going left within our hearts.

FROM A BROTHER'S STANDPOINT

By Max Beerbohm

On a wintry and damp afternoon, in the year 1908, I was stand-ing on the doorstep of my mother's house in Upper Berkeley Street, seeing off a man who had been lunching with us. A taxi stopped at the curb, and my brother Herbert stepped out of it in the dreamy yet ample and energetic way that he had of stepping out of taxis. " Oh, how are you, Mr. Tree ? " my friend greeted him. " I ? " said Herbert, shaking the proffered hand and gazing around him. " I ? Oh, I'm radiant ! "

My friend, when I went to see him a few days later, said to me that this epithet, if any ordinary man applied it to himself, would doubtless seem rather absurd, but that Herbert's use of it was perfectly right and proper : he looked radiant, it was obvious that he felt radiant, and he told the simple truth in saying that he *was* radiant. My friend, having spoken thus, looked in the glass and, I remember, sighed.

Herbert was for many reasons an enviable man, but I think that what most of us most envied him was that incessant zest of his. Nothing ever seemed to derange for one moment that large, wholesome appetite for life and art. Difficulties that would have crushed any man of no more than ordinary power to cope with them were for Herbert a mere pleasant incentive— or rather, as he was the last man to need any incentive, a mere pleasant challenge to be lightly accepted and quickly dealt with on the way to something else. The gigantic risks of His Majesty's Theatre never, so far as I could see, caused him to turn a hair. He was glad if things were going well ; if they weren't, he had a plan for making them do so within a few weeks. He could look Ruin in the face and say, " Oh, I'm radiant " ; whereat

Ruin always slunk away, drawing her hood over her face—foiled again.

First impressions are sharpest, and in describing anybody it is always from them that one would wish to start. But when first I saw Herbert I was too young to be impressed by him in any way. I was but a few hours old ; and when those few hours had become a few years, Herbert was already one of the accepted figures on my horizon. He was nineteen years older than I, and, as I have no memory of anything that was going on before my fourth year, he must have been quite twenty-two at the time of which I have faint glimpses. My parents, and my sisters and I, lived in Clanricarde Gardens, a cul-de-sac off the Bayswater Road—a double row of houses that seemed to me far taller than the modern sky-scrapers seem. Herbert seemed very tall, too, and his hair was of a very bright red, at which I used to look up, up, with interest. It would seem that his hair had touched the imagination of other children before me. In the early 'seventies young laymen were apt to be less wholly lay than they are now ; and Herbert, at the age of eighteen, had felt it his duty to preach in the Sunday-school of a neighbouring church, and had ceased to do so only when the children, presuming on his lack of sternness, began to call him " Ha'porth o' Carrots." It was not until many years later that the tuitional instinct revived in him and led him to found the Academy of Dramatic Art.

Besides teaching on Sundays, Herbert was also learning on week-days. My father was in the City. He was for many years a corn merchant, and subsequently started a journal, *The Evening Corn Trade List* (which was carried on after his death in 1892 and only recently ceased to exist). His three eldest sons, Ernest, Herbert and Julius, all graduated as clerks in his office. I doubt whether any one of them learnt much there, or was solemnly expected to learn much there. My father, though devoted to his own work, had the most liberal of minds, and was, I imagine, very well content that his sons should do as they willed. It was not their will to stay for ever at their desks. Ernest had a desire for sheep-farming in the wilds. He went out to Cape Colony, married, and made his home there. Julius went to explore Patagonia, explored it quite thoroughly, and wrote a delightful book about it. Herbert wanted to go on the stage. That, in those days, was a wild, an awful inclination, and somewhat horrified even my father ; insomuch that Herbert confined himself to a whirl of amateur theatricals. In this whirl he had so much success that by the time he made his first appearance in public all fatherly misgivings had vanished, giving place to fatherly pride.

The Globe Theatre was, I believe, the scene of that first appearance. And, as the year of it was certainly 1878, I can claim to remember Herbert as he was before the seal of his profession was set on him. But, as what I remember is so scanty—just that memory of a bright redness high up—my boast had better be that I remember him in days long before he had set his seal upon his profession. In 1879, or thereabouts, I had acquired a habit of drawing pictures ; and what I liked about Herbert, whenever he came to see us, was that *he* could draw pictures, too. I think I liked him all the better for that our styles did not clash. I drew *and* painted—especially painted. Herbert used pencil only. The subjects I chose were soldiers, policemen, cottages, and knights in armour. These subjects he would sometimes assay, but only to please *me :* they did not really interest him, and his handling of them was (I still think) inferior to mine. What he excelled me in was Mr. Gladstone and Lord Beaconsfield. He could draw either of them equally well in profile or in full-face, and as the features of both of them were very familiar to me in *Punch*, whose cartoons I was fond of colouring week by week, I was in a position to appreciate his skill. I was a Conservative, and Herbert (to my wonder and grief) a Liberal. Yet his Lord Beaconsfield amused me not less than his Mr. Gladstone. My mother, too, was very fond of watching him draw, and for her he used to draw all sorts of people— people whom he had recently met. " This is Whistler, the painter," he would say, or " This is E. W. Godwin," or " Here's Oscar Wilde, the poet." Henry Irving, however, was his favourite theme. And I remember him saying, one day, with some importance : " The Routledges have asked me to dine on Sunday night, and Irving is to be there." Whereat I communed with myself : " Dinner ? On *Sunday* night ? " Mr. Edmund Routledge had the house opposite to my father's, and on the following Sunday, at my bed-time, I looked out at those lit windows, looked long at them. I was fascinated, in spite of myself, and, much as I pitied Herbert for being so unlikely now to go to Heaven, I was also envying him not a little, too.

I wanted to grow up quickly and belong (on week-days) to the great world in which Herbert was moving. And of that world I was soon to have a closer, more inspiring glimpse than had been vouchsafed by the Routledges' lit windows. I think the date of this glimpse was in March, 1882. I was now nine years old, and went to a day-school that was graced with a whole-holiday every Saturday. Herbert nobly invited me to spend a Saturday morning with him. He had rooms in Maddox Street, sharing them with his friend A. K. Moore. I remember a room that seemed to me rather shabby (I had expected marble columns), and I remember the smell of the smoke puffed continually from A. K. Moore's pipe. I did not like this smoke, and did not form a high opinion of A. K. Moore. I did not know that he had greatly distinguished himself at Oxford, and that he was destined to write very brilliant leading articles for *The Morning Post*. And even had I known these things I should still have regarded him as the man who smoked that pipe and stared at me and laughed again and again at the notion that Herbert had so small a brother. Herbert himself went on writing at a table by the window ; but this preoccupation I excused, for he told me he was writing something for—*Punch !* And he told me that in a few minutes he was going to take his manuscript—and me !— round to Bouverie Street and show us both to Mr. Burnand. At about this time Herbert wrote several skits for *Punch*. One of them, I know, was on the " interviews " given to reporters by Oscar Wilde during his American tour, and another was on the press-notices of Mrs. Langtry's impersonation of Lady Macbeth. Excellent fun they were—and are, in the bound volume. It may have been one of these two skits that Herbert was writing on that marvellous morning in my life. I remember A. K. Moore looking through the manuscript and laughing, but doubting (which seemed to me just like him) whether Mr. Burnand would put it in.

There were no marble columns even in the office of *Punch* itself ; but there was, and I saw him with my own eyes, Mr. Burnand ; and he seemed to me the more greatly a prince of men because he was not smoking, and because he sat in a chair that swung round towards us in a most fascinating manner, and because he did not laugh at me. I liked also Mrs. Bernard Beere, the famous actress, to whom, after another drive in a hansom, I was presented as she lay, in the middle of a large room somewhere, on a sofa of crimson velvet, with a great deal of lace around her head, and an enormous bunch of hothouse grapes on a small table beside her, and a company of important-looking men standing and sitting around her. I liked her for giving me so many of her grapes ; but my enjoyment of these was somewhat marred by the more-than-A.-K.-Moorish mirth of one gentleman at the smallness of " Beerbohm Tree's brother." This gentleman was of immense height and girth ; and I was just old enough to think of saying, and just too well-brought-up to say, that *I* might as well laugh at the bigness of " Beerbohm Tree's friend." I did but look fixedly at the striped shirt-collar that he wore ; and later, when, in another hansom, Herbert told me that the gentleman was Mr. Edmund Yates, I merely said that I did not like his striped collar.

The greatest event of that great day was yet to come : we were to lunch at Herbert's club. Was it the " Arundel," perhaps ? The " Savage " ? I know not. I cared not. It was Herbert's club, and I lunched in it, and was presented to the great Mr. Godwin in it. At first I thought he must be " a conspirator," for he wore a large black cloak and a large soft black hat. But he had the most charming manners, and treated me as an equal, and I quite agreed with the opinion, so often expressed by Herbert in those days, that Godwin was a Master. I left the club in company with these two, and Herbert, after hailing a hansom for me and paying the driver, gave me a ten-shilling piece. To have gold seemed to me at that time hardly less wonderful than it would seem in this age of paper. That gold piece soon became some mere silver ; that silver, vanishing copper ; but the memory of those hours with Herbert was a treasure to be jealously hoarded.

Herbert was (then and always) a hero to me. But, let me add, Julius was a god. And he was not so because he had explored Patagonia (remote and savage things had no magic for me), nor because he had written a much-praised book about

Patagonia (I was not literary), but because he was so cool and calm and elegant. Herbert seemed always to be in a hurry, Julius never. Herbert would overpay and dismiss his hansom whenever he came to see us, and at his departure would whistle frantically and piercingly for another. Julius always kept *his* hansom waiting, hour after hour. And *his* hansom was always one of that new and lordly kind, padded throughout with black leather, and fitted with two little looking-glasses, and drawn by a spirited horse, and driven by a not tipsy driver. Herbert talked excitedly, and used to pass his hands through his hair, and leave it all standing up on end. Julius never raised his deep voice, and never put any expression into it, and his straw-coloured hair lay around his head as smoothly as satin. Herbert's necktie was often on one side, and his top-hat always lustreless, and he never had a flower in his buttonhole. Julius had always a gardenia or Parma violets, and his hat was dazzling, and his linen was washed in Paris. Also, he had a moustache. Not to have that when one was grown up seemed to me to argue a deficiency in sense of fitness. I knew that Herbert, being an actor, had to be clean-shaven. But I felt that I myself, if hereafter I had to choose between being an actor and having a moustache, should not hesitate. Not in virtue of his acting, but rather in virtue of himself, was Herbert a hero to me. More than once, schoolfellows of mine had said to me : " Your brother's an actor, isn't he ? " They had not said this in a tone implying actual condemnation. But——

In some early month of '84 my classification of the two brothers underwent a sudden change. Herbert became a god, Julius sank to the level of a hero. For Herbert was engaged to be married ; and being married had always seemed to me an even finer thing, a thing even more essential to the full glory of the adult state, than having a moustache. My father and mother, my sisters and I, were all of us equally enthusiastic about Miss Maud Holt. She and Herbert used to come and lunch in Clanricarde Gardens every Sunday, and these Sundays were great days. Miss Holt was so charming and amusing. Also, she used to play and sing to us ; and I can see Herbert now, hanging over the piano, rapt, in devotion. A goddess, decidedly.

JULIUS BEERBOHM.
From a painting by Zorn.

But the greatest Sunday of all was yet to come. In September Miss Holt came to stay with us in Kent, in the house where we were spending the summer holidays. Herbert was in London, acting. He was due to arrive only on the bridal Sunday. Of the preparations for that day, I recall especially the two triumphal arches of flowers and branches, one at the gate of the garden, the other at the gate of the little church hard by. These were conceived and erected by the gardener and his brother ; and I remember the surprise I felt when the gardener's brother said to me : " They're not what you might call awful grand, but they're what you might call rustic." To me they appeared awful grand. Under the garden-gate's arch, on the Sunday morning, I posted myself a full hour before Herbert was expected to arrive. I was to be his " best man," and so delicious was the foretaste of that duty that it could not be too long for me. When at last he appeared, I was glad to see that his hat was of almost Julian splendour ; but he looked so pale and excited that I gasped out instinctively : " Have you lost the ring ? " I felt, god though he was, that it would be rather like him to have lost the ring. However, all was well. The wedding was conducted as smoothly as the most exacting " best man " could wish. And at the wedding-breakfast there were sillabubs, my favourite dish. I remember Herbert saying that they sounded Biblical—" And Sillabub, the son of Sillabub, reigned in his stead," a remark which shocked but amused me.

The reason for my being best man was that Julius was away in Spain. A few weeks later, we heard that Julius, too, had married. It seemed to me, when presently I saw her, that his bride was as delightful and wonderful as Herbert's. Julius rose from his brief abeyance among heroes. Julius was once more a god.

In the years that followed, as I grew in understanding, and was somewhat able to understand what a play was about, I acquired a greater respect than I had had for the art of acting. And particularly did I admire and applaud Herbert's exploits in that art. Such a preference was natural ? I think it was not due wholly to my affection. I was just old enough to appreciate something of that elastic subtlety, that unflagging imagination, which Herbert brought to the task of his every embodiment.

I could see the enormous difference between him and the ordinary " sound " actor, and why it was that his fame was so great now, and always becoming greater. No boy now ever asked me if I had a brother who was an actor. It was known that I was a brother of Beerbohm Tree, and the knowledge was fraught with awe—awe that perceptibly deepened when, in the year of the first Jubilee, Herbert became a Manager.

Ripened judgment has not inclined me to think *The Red Lamp* the greatest play ever written. But I thought it so on its first night—the first night of Herbert's management. And I saw it seventeen times, without changing my opinion. Herbert always let me sit in his dressing-room during the entr'actes, and there I met many of the most interesting men of the period —none of whom, however, interested me so much as Herbert. *Partners* and *The Pompadour* pleased me almost as much as *The Red Lamp*, and so did the plays that came after ; and it seems to me, as I look back, that even during term-time, when my body was at Charterhouse, my soul was in the Haymarket Theatre.

I think the magic of the Haymarket lost something of its power for me when I left school. Oxford was so wondrous in itself. My soul was undoubtedly there during term-time. But in the vacations I was constantly at the theatre, and I stayed often, with an unfailing sense of romance, at the house that Herbert now had in Hampstead. A very lovely old house it was, with low-ceiled rooms and plenty of chintz ; and with plenty of garden ; and with Bully Boy, the celebrated bulldog of *The Dancing Girl*, ugliest and most beauteous of beasts ; and with Viola, not the least charming of children. And supper was so very late up there, after the theatre down yonder ; and break-fast so very late, too, and dinner so very early. Early though dinner was, there was never a day when I didn't feel sure that Herbert would be late for the theatre. It had always been an odd thing about him that his restless energy seemed to be coupled with a perfect vagueness as to time and place and distance. He did, it is true, carry a watch, and often looked at it ; but one never could believe he had drawn any deduction from it. And yet he was never late for anything that mattered. His punctuality was a great mystery. It would seem that he had some kind of queer instinct that saved him the trouble of taking thought. And it would seem that he had this in regard to other things than time. I never saw him read a newspaper ; yet he appeared always to know just what was going on all the world round. He had read fewer books than any man I have ever known; yet I have known few men of letters who had a keener discernment of good writing, or a keener delight in it. He had no standards of comparison to guide him. He had merely an innate sense of literary form.

He was, also, an acute judge of human character. Almost everybody prides himself on being that. Herbert had the rather rare distinction of being it. I think that the correctness of his judgment of the people he met may have been due partly to the unperceiving manner he had—that "radiant" but abstracted and roving regard of his. It was apt to put people off their guard. Nor was this the only way in which Herbert's famous "vagueness" was useful to him. Especially after he became a manager, and was accordingly beset by all manner of people with axes to grind, it was immensely useful to him in saving him from committing himself. It was an escape from the necessity of using the dangerous word *yes* or the unpleasant word *no*. And when his vagueness became a by-word and a legend, he humorously cultivated it for its own sake— cultivated it partly, too, perhaps, because it seemed to fit in so well with the unworldliness on which he prided himself.

Unworldly he was, in so far as he had, like all artists, an imaginary world of his own. And he was unworldly also in the sense that he cared little or not at all for money. He was, however, amongst other things, a very capable man of the world.

Of his shrewdness wrapped in vagueness I can give an example that befell me one day while I was staying with him in Hampstead. He asked meditatively what I intended to *be*. I reminded him that I was going to the Bar. "Ah . . . The Bar. . . . You at the Bar. . . . I should have thought you'd better be a—a sort of writer, and then, perhaps," he added, "drift into Diplomacy." This was merely his way of saying what the average man would have said thus : "You haven't a single one of the qualities that make for success at the Bar. But I fancy you might do well in journalism." Or more likely the average man would but have advised me to cultivate the acquaintance of solicitors, and would *not* (as I hadn't ever attempted to write anything) have guessed that I had a bent for writing. The delightful touch about " drifting " into the Diplomatic Service was added merely to please himself and me.

He liked the company of very young men. For them his manner was apt to shed much of its indirectness. With them, being himself so young at heart, he was always, I think, more at his ease than he was with men not very young. He liked their ingenuousness and their pomposity. He revelled in drawing them out. Whenever I took this or that fellow undergraduate to a play at the Haymarket, Herbert always invited us both to sup at the Garrick. We used to wonder at his power of sitting up into the small hours, and the not so small, without a trace of fatigue. We didn't know how much we amused him.

Until I was twenty-two I had never seen Herbert for more than a few hours or days at a time. During the first three months of 1895 I saw him continuously. For he took me with him on his first tour to America. My sister-in-law has said, in speaking of the voyage out, that Mr. Lionel Brough and I went below after the first day and were not seen again. This is an unintentional injustice to the memory of Lionel Brough. I only wish he had not been so perfectly, so exuberantly good a sailor as he was. He and I shared a cabin. The sea was very stormy indeed. For three days and nights I remained in my berth. I preferred the nights to the days, for then Brough was sound asleep in the berth beneath me, and even the sight of Brough's saucy little yachting-cap, swaying to and fro on its peg whenever I opened my eyes to the dim lamp-light, was preferable to the knowledge that Brough himself might at any moment come breezily in at the door with that same cap surmounting his fresh pink face and his crisp silver hair. He was the kindest of men, and was always coming down from the smoking-room, laden with the scent of that meeting-place, to cheer me up for a few minutes. He was the bluffest of Yorkshiremen, and the best of professional *raconteurs*, and he was always asking me : " Have yer heard the one about the parson's bullfinch ? " or " Have yer heard the one about the coal-heaver's ticket to Blackpool ? " or " Have yer heard the one about the old lady who didn't like shrimps ? " Also, he wore in his scarf a large and unusual pin which I think he thought might act as a talisman for me against sea-sickness. He had recently appeared in some " command " performance at Windsor, and " This," he would tell me, " is the pin Her Gracious Majesty gave me ; " but somehow it always made me feel worse.

On the last three days I was well enough to be on deck, nevertheless, and to share something of Herbert's delight in the look of the Atlantic, and something of his immense excitement as to what America would be like, and something of the incidental pleasure he took in the intentness with which crew and passengers gazed on the actor-pilgrim. I remember that on the day before landing he went to have his hair cut by the ship's barber, and how amused and pleased he was that the man said : " This is a bit of a responsibility for *me*, sir ! " To the last day of his life, he never was habituated to fame. The stares of passers-by, eulogistic letters from strangers, invitations to preside over meetings and things, snapshots in the illustrated press—it was a sign of his abiding youngness that such things, though they befell him so abundantly, never lost for him the savour of freshness. They seemed always to take him by surprise and make him the more " radiant." And it was characteristic of his complexity that he was greatly amused at his own naïveté. He once handed me a letter from a stranger who had seen him act on the previous night. " That's very nice," I said after reading it. " Very," said he. " I can stand any amount of flattery so long as it's fulsome enough."

To the magic of New York, on our arrival, he was instantly responsive. He was not the sort of tourist who takes a home-made tuning-fork about with him and condemns the discords. He regarded himself not as a responsible judge, but as a quite irresponsible flitter-through. He liked the over-heated rooms and the over-iced streets, liked not only the slow, low voices of the New York men, but also the piercing voices of the New York ladies, and also the fabulous expensiveness of cabs, and the manners of street-car conductors, and being expected to make a speech after the play's last act but one. Nor was Chicago

too grim for him, nor Boston too prim. Almost every member
of his company had brought over a tuning-fork. There was a
great deal of grumbling and growling, especially during railway
journeys. Herbert was a shining example of adaptability,
and I had never admired him more. What an appalling amount
of work and play he had to go through ! Yet from early morning to late night, or rather to early morning again, he was never
out of temper. In some of his work it was my mission to help
him. I had been given the post of private secretary (with salary).
But my mission was rather a failure. The letters that I wrote
in his stead were so carefully thought out and worded that many
of the letters sent to him could get no answers at all. After
two or three weeks (Herbert insisting, however, on my retention
of full salary) one of the regular managerial staff, a less scrupulous
writer, took over the main part of my duties.

    People often said of Herbert that he lived nineteen to the
dozen. Twenty-nine is the number I would use in speaking of
his life in America. And that number was too high for even
him to touch with impunity. At the end of the three months,
after the series of farewell performances, farewell speeches, farewell banquets and what-not, Herbert did, soon after the boat
weighed anchor, say he thought he would go to bed rather early
to-night ; and for two or three days, as my sister-in-law has
related, he *stayed* in bed—he ! After which he arose, and was
the life and soul of the liner. The concert to be given on the
last evening of the voyage was organized by him as eagerly
as though his whole future career depended on its success. But
from this task, as from all his tasks, he derived plenty of light
amusement by the way. I shall never forget the conversation
between him and a very earnest, a very " ahr-nesst," actor who
had volunteered to recite Mark Antony's funeral speech. On
the afternoon of the day before the concert this actor invited
Herbert, and Herbert invited me, to a rehearsal of the speech,
down in the dining-saloon where the concert was to be held.
He posted himself at the end of the saloon, in front of the organ-
screen, folded his arms, and for a while regarded Herbert and
me, very sombre and beetle-browed. " Friends," he suddenly
began in a voice of thunder. It would have been fatal for me to
catch Herbert's eye. " Romans," he resumed. " Country-

men "—" One instant, Mr. * ! " cried Herbert's voice.—
" Well,- Mr. Tree ? "—" An idea has just struck me. Didn't
Antony address the crowd from *above* ? "—" From the rostrum,
Mr. Tree."—" Rostrum, yes—rostrum. My idea is this : How
would it be if "—Herbert pointed to the organist's gallery—" you
spoke your speech from that little place up there ? " Mr. *
looked up, considered, nodded his head gravely, and was about
to disappear up the winding staircase. " One instant, Mr. * !
Another idea ! What did Antony *wear* ? "—" A toga, Mr. Tree."
—" Toga, yes—toga." Herbert had already snatched a tablecloth off one of the tables ; and I know not which face was the
more solemn—the face of that actor while Herbert draped him,
or Herbert's face. For some reason or another, Mr. * decided
that on " the night," as he called it, he would not wear costume.
But he did actually, when the time came, deliver his speech
from the organ-loft, with terrific effect. There was, however,
a rather awkward moment when he reappeared at the foot of
the winding staircase. Major-General Sir Somebody Something, who was acting as chairman and sitting in the middle of
the front row, sprang up and went to shake him warmly by the
hand. The Major-General was warded off with a fierce gesture.
The end was not yet. Antony had but, as in the play, come
down among us to read Cæsar's will. " If you have tee-arrs,
prepare to shed them now," and so forth.

Such expressions as " the night," just quoted by me, never
were used by Herbert. He disliked slang. And especially did
he dislike theatrical slang. To him the theatre was always
a thing romantic and marvellous. " Knowingness " about it
jarred his sensibility. But he did, as it were, study theatrical
slang, feeling a horrid fascination in the subject. " Do you
know," he once asked me, " what they call the curtain ? They
call it ' the rag.' " And he began to improvise various phrases
around this expression ; one of which was : " My boy, the rag
came down on mud," meaning " The play failed on the first
night."

Herbert, when he was in the vein, was a fine improviser.
His wit was a thing carefully thought out, and if he were going
to say something witty he would keep you waiting a moment
or so. But his humour was all spontaneous, and came, unlike

that of many humorists, not in spurts, but in a stream. I have said that he was self-conscious, though "radiant," in general company ; and so he was. But his self-consciousness quickly melted away when he was alone with friends at a dinner-table or supper-table. He was, for all his shyness, an essentially sociable man, not merely in the sense that he liked to be often with many people, but in the further and rarer sense that he liked to be with anybody rather than be alone. If he were alone in a hansom or a taxi, and saw on the pavement *any* man he knew, he would stop the vehicle and offer that man a lift. Whenever he came to our house, he would always, as I saw him off, say that he was going to such-and-such a place and ask me to go there with him. I do not, in telling this, mean that I was no fitter company than *any* man. But I am afraid that as the years went by, and the gap between our ages was accordingly contracted, each of us found himself even more shy in presence of the other than he was wont to be with people at large. An old friend of Herbert's once said to him and me, in the course of a dinner in the " Dome " of His Majesty's : " You two, when you're together, always seem to be in an attitude of armed neutrality." I suggested to Herbert that " terrified love " would be a truer description.

It was a great thing to me, the love that I knew in my heart he had for me in his. I do believe he took as much pride in my little career as I took in his big one.   " Big " is a word that attaches itself in my mind to so much concerning Herbert. His body was big, and his nature big, and he did so love big things ! Mountains, cathedrals, frescoes, Shakespeare, summer skies, Wagnerian opera—his spacious temperament welcomed everything of that sort. Things on a small scale, however exquisite, did not satisfy him. I doubt whether even His Majesty's Theatre was quite big enough according to his standard.

A curious and little-known fact about that theatre is that by reason of me it had a narrow escape from never existing at all. When Herbert was in Philadelphia, Paul Potter's dramatic version of Du Maurier's *Trilby* was being acted at one of the theatres there. The book had had a tremendous " boom " in America. The play was a great success. I went one evening, as emissary of Herbert, to see it and report on it. My report

"SVENGALI."

across the supper-table was a very brief one, to the effect that the play in itself was utter nonsense and could only be a dismal failure in London. Thus I, in my wisdom ; whereby impressed, Herbert put *Trilby* from his mind. Six weeks later, in New York, two nights before we embarked for England, he gave his final performance at Abbey's Theatre, and on the next night accordingly was free to visit one of the other theatres. He thought he might as well go and see *Trilby* . . . and it was on the proceeds of his production of *Trilby* in England that His Majesty's presently began to rise.

For twenty years after its completion it was a source of immense happiness to him ; it enabled him to realize his dreams ; it fulfilled him. He achieved there things that he could not have attempted elsewhere ; and these were the things nearest his heart and most agreeable to his ambition. I shall always be thankful for His Majesty's. For my own pleasure in play-going, let me admit, I prefer small theatres. And for my own delight in the genius of Herbert as actor I liked His Majesty's less than the Haymarket. Robust though he was in mind and in body, it was not in sweeping effects that his acting was pre-eminent. The full strength of his art was in its amazing delicacy. His humour and imagination, and his beautiful power for pathos, found their best expression in ways that were subtlest. Subtleties have a hard time on a large stage, in front of a large auditorium. Herbert had to adapt his method to his surroundings. He did this with great skill and success ; but I often wished he had not to do it at all. Apart from his acting—and his acting was but one of the many parts of him—I am entirely glad for him that he had His Majesty's.

I think that in the last years of his life he grew to care less for acting. His versatility had ranged over so vast a number of diverse interpretations. What new thing was there for him to do ?—for him, to whom the notion of marking time was so utterly repugnant ? Especially after the outbreak of the War did I notice in him an impatience of his work. The last time we met was at my mother's house, just after his return from America. He was looking, as usual, splendidly well, and was full of animation. But in all his talk there was not a word about acting.

I shall always miss him.   He was a great feature in my life, and I am always wishing him back again.   But I am grateful, for his sake, that he died in the fullness of health and vigour. I am glad that but two moments before his death he was talking and laughing, paring a peach for his dessert.   When I saw him, early next morning, he lay surrounded already with the flowers he had been fondest of.   His face was both familiar and strange. Death, that preserves only what is essential, had taken away whatever it is that is peculiar to the face of an actor.   Extreme strength of character and purpose was all that remained and outstood now.   But at the corners of the lips there was the hint of an almost whimsical, an entirely happy smile.   And I felt that Herbert, though he was no longer breathing, was somehow still " radiant."

A SKETCH

By Edmund Gosse, C.B.

In attempting to obey my friend Max's command that I should send him a sketch from memory of his brother Herbert as I remember him, I am struck in the first place by a difficulty which I never met with before, namely the insecurity of such impressions in the case of an actor. That is to say, while the recollection of what a man of some other class looked like may be simple and direct, that of what an actor was is bound to be complex, and confused with his manifold impersonations on the stage. Of most actors whom I have slightly known I should instantly refuse to make any portrait whatever, because I lose their reality in their assumed parts. Is there any real person at all, any bundle of genuine characteristics left, one asks one's self, under the Protean disguises? If I try to give some faint portrait of Herbert Tree, it is because I think that, in spite of all the costumes and all the attitudes, an unusually hard core of personality did survive, and even actively protrude, in him.

I never had the privilege of knowing him intimately, but we were acquaintances for more than thirty-five years. I recall no occasion on which he was not courteous, considerate and friendly, but our relations were never intimate, and long periods divided our successive meetings. I never had an opportunity of coming to close quarters with his character, and my little sketch must be purely superficial. It seems to me that the complicated aspect of the actor, of which I have spoken, affected him externally, for I find it hard to bring into accord two visions of him, the one of a certain dandified elegance, the other sturdy, four-square and a little Batavian. In youth,—for he was still

young when I met him first,—he had not arrived at that im-
pressiveness which he achieved at last. He was then, in fact,
—with his red hair, his pale complexion and faint eyes,—the
reverse of impressive off the stage, and I think he may have
adopted what I call his " elegance " of manner in order to remove
this deficiency. At all events, as years went by, his increased
solidity of form and authoritative ease of address made him more
and more a " figure " in social intercourse ; and he developed
a style in conversation which was quite his own, and of which
he was not in possession when I knew him first.

Unless my memory is all at fault, it was the mother of
Sisera who invented the artifice of asking a question that she
might answer it herself. Herbert Tree was a master of this
trick. He was the Rosa Dartle of conversation. Vaguely,
dreamily, in that odd sonorous whisper that seemed to come
from the hollows of his skull, his face turned upwards and his
lips bent down, he would propound a question, sometimes pre-
posterous, sometimes naïvely puerile, and would employ the
silence of surprise which followed it by answering it himself with
great solemnity and yet with a twist upwards at the end which
provoked a continuation of the argument. He liked to air a
shadowy sort of paradox, and watch the result. If the quip
was respectfully accepted, he was pleased ; if it was scornfully
rejected he was not less pleased. His object never was to
instruct, but to stimulate interest. (I speak, of course, of his
private conversation, for I am told that, professionally, he was
an excellent instructor.)

His sense of humour, and his expression of it, were remarkable, but he gave one the impression of not being very sure of
the effect of what he might be led to say. He was witty, partly
I think by studious cultivation, but he was whimsical by nature,
and his wit was an offshoot of his whim. He tossed his arrows
up into the air, and sometimes they hit the bull's-eye miraculously ; sometimes they did not. I have heard him say things
that were deliciously apropos, and with a rapidity of mind that
was exhilarating ; but I have also heard him murmur things
that were almost fatuous ; and he seemed to lack personal
criticism in this respect. This was doubtless the reason why
there was always debate behind his back whether Herbert Tree

was " clever " or merely silly, the truth being that he could be both, or at least that he could divagate into a sort of dreamy, aimless irony which gave the impression of silliness. I am not sure that there was not often a method in those quaint sallies, for he was a past master in the practice which is called " pulling the leg " of a victim.

Herbert Tree possessed in high cultivation the art of narrative. He recounted ludicrous incidents with a gravity, and with a picturesqueness, which were diverting to an extreme degree. The very last time I had the pleasure of meeting him in private, he had lately returned from an excursion to California, where he sought out a hermit-colony of film-performers, who conducted their mysteries in some forest, far from the eye of man. Herbert Tree, who was of course expected, reached a clearing of this woodland, when he perceived at a distance, drawn up in a half-moon against a background of trees, a large company of actors and actresses. He walked towards them, like Agag, delicately, and feeling very shy, for they made no movement, but, as he came nearer, a little boy of some eight years of age, bearing the word WELCOME embroidered in large letters across his abdomen, advanced out of the crowd, and broke the death-like silence by ejaculating in a loud shrill voice, " Glad to make your acquaintance, Sir Tree ! " This episode was narrated by the great actor, with imperturbable gravity, while we rocked in helpless laughter.

A TRIBUTE

By Louis N. Parker

THIS is a modest nosegay laid on the grave of the great manager, great actor, and, above all, great friend. If my own affairs seem to crop up unduly, that is because they have been linked closely with him during many years, and because I can only speak of him according to my own individual knowledge and experience.

My first acquaintance with Sir Herbert dates back to the evening of the 17th April, 1876 ; when, with other " earnest students of the drama "—let me rather say, with other enthusiastic young pittites—I waited at the pit-door of the old Prince of Wales's Theatre in Tottenham Street, to see the first performance of *The Merchant of Venice* under the Bancroft management. Edward Rose, who had already written and published a blank-verse play on Columbus, and was later to dramatize " Under the Red Robe " and to write many other successful plays, was of our party, and had brought with him a tall, thin, fair-haired youth, whom he introduced as " young Beerbohm," and who claimed our respectful admiration as an amateur actor who was shortly to appear in a real London Theatre (the Duke of York's in Holborn) as Achille Talma Dufard in *The First Night* (" Le Mari de la Débutante ").

That passing acquaintance went no further at the time. Our little group was dispersed. I retired to my musical life in the provinces ; Tree went through the usual mill of the young actor. But although I did not hear of him again for many years, his striking personality, casual though our meeting had been, had impressed itself upon me very vividly. The circumstances under which we had spent the evening together contributed to keep memory clear. It had been the occasion of Ellen Terry's return to the stage after a long absence, and I think none of us had ever seen her before. To see Ellen Terry for the first time, in the full glory of her youth and beauty, was an experience never to be forgotten, and the companions who shared in that delight became for ever a part of the experience. Thus Tree and the others lived on in my memory as if I had met them for the first time in the radiance of a spring morning.

In 1881 to my astonishment I recognized Tree in the shape of Lambert Streyke in *The Colonel*. Now he was a well-known actor, while I was still a humble pittite, and I did not venture to recall myself to his recollection. Nevertheless, the fact that I had sat next to him five years before gave me a personal interest in him, and from that time forward, as he clomb from rung to rung up the slippery ladder of popularity and fame, I watched him from my obscure corner with that curious enthusiasm which many laymen who have never crossed, and have no hope of crossing, the threshold of a stage-door, feel for some actor or actress of their choice. In my case it was silent hero-worship carried to the extreme limit of self-denial ; for I never even wrote to ask for his photograph.

I did not see him again till 1884, when he was playing Paolo Macari in *Called Back*. One is forced to cultivate the Muses on a very little oatmeal in the pastoral provinces, and one's ideas of what is going on in the theatre can only be gathered from the accounts of the critics. I think the critics of those days went into more detail, took more trouble, and had, perhaps, a broader outlook than the critics of to-day. Perhaps also they had more sympathy with the drama, and, more particularly, with the art of the actor. Mr. William Archer was writing profound and interesting studies which it is an illuminating pleasure to read even now ; Mr. Clement Scott was making and unmaking reputations ; Mr. Joseph Knight was pouring his scholarship and his vast experience into his notices ; and Mr. Moy Thomas and Mr. Addison Bright were keenly on the look-out for new talent, and did not hesitate to say when they had found it. None of these writers wrote to display his own wit at the expense of the subject of his criticisms, and there seemed to be nothing of the malice, finding expression in cheap epigram, which, I fear, can be traced in some of the dramatic journalism of to-day. At any rate, in spite of my remoteness from the theatrical hub, I knew that Tree had arrived ; that he had become one of the hopes of the theatre, especially in parts of a weirdly romantic sort.

In 1887 Tree went into management at the Comedy Theatre. This fact speaks volumes for the strides he had made, for his courage, and for his faith in his own star. Only eleven years had passed since he stood outside the pit-door of the Prince of Wales's, and here he was, one of London's leading actors, the manager of a West-End theatre, and a personality in the artistic world.

I had lately begun—led thereto by accident—to try to write alleged plays ; so I took my courage in both hands and sent him the first play I ever wrote. The amazing thing happened. Instead of a more or less polite rejection, Tree sent me seats to witness *The Red Lamp*, and asked me to come and see him in an interval between the acts. I am not dwelling on that evening as an episode in my autobiography, but I think it of interest as illustrating a less well-known phase of his character. Already at that comparatively early date he had an established reputation as a wit, and he was the companion of wits ; he had the " grand manner " (bestowed upon him, I do believe, in his cradle), which never left him ; his performance, his surroundings, entirely novel to my unsophisticated eyes ; the fact that he was a manager ; then, my unconquerable shyness, the knowledge that I was a yokel from unknown wilds—my self-consciousness, in short—added to my infirmity, which was already pronounced —all these things struck me dumb, paralysed me, and made me, I must imagine, the most ungainly and unpromising candidate for dramatic honours who ever stepped across a manager's threshold. Nothing, I suppose, can be more discouraging than to have an epigram received with an uncomprehending " What ? " Yet, instead of dismissing me with courteous in-difference, and consigning me to prompt and permanent oblivion, Tree encouraged me with undeserved praise and held out hopes for the future which sent me home glowing with happiness and

HERBERT TREE
ABOUT 1887.

determined to do or die. Thus, at our first interview, I unconsciously struck the vein of simple humanity in him, and of spontaneous good nature, which I was later to learn was the bed-rock foundation of his character, but which he frequently disguised under a humorous mask of artificiality and *préciosité*. Moreover, from that evening onwards, undiscouraged by my unprepossessing début, by my half-successes or complete failures, he never let me slip out of his ken or withdrew his friendship or his support, or ceased to egg me on to renewed effort. My dramatic beginnings were not such as to hold out any hope that I should ever be of the slightest use to him ; yet in 1894 he engaged me to adapt Ludwig Fulda's " Der Talisman " (*Once Upon a Time*). That was a fiasco. No matter. He had no sooner opened Her (now His) Majesty's Theatre than he commissioned me to adapt Richepin's " Le Chemineau " (*Ragged Robin*), which turned out quite as unsatisfactory as *Once Upon a Time*, in spite of a most engaging performance on his part and a very remarkable one on the part of Lady Tree.

Tree was not discouraged, but I was ; and for a long time I left His Majesty's Theatre untroubled by my manuscripts. I felt the canvas was too large for my inexperienced brush. The next experiment was an adaptation of Réné Fauchois' *Beethoven*. The subject appealed very strongly both to Tree and to myself, but the adaptation of the French play was a very difficult problem : it is a beautiful poem, in which Beethoven figures as a rather verbose and very declamatory old gentleman. While retaining as much as possible of the beauty of the original, I tried to get a little nearer the historical Beethoven. I have seen the play instanced as a failure. That is very considerably overstating the case. It was not even financially a failure ; but at His Majesty's a play had to make a great deal of money even to pay its way, and *Beethoven* did not attract the ordinary theatre-going public sufficiently to fulfil that purpose. That public did not know, and did not want to know, anything about Beethoven. " What's Beeth-uvven ? " said the man in the street, and did not pause for an answer. This was a pity, for Tree never gave a finer, simpler, more carefully considered, or more sincere performance, than in the title-part. In mere externals he achieved a great *tour-de-force*. Many doubted his physical fitness for the part ; for Beethoven was a short, stocky, square-set little man, with dark eyes. I shall never forget our gasp of surprise when Tree made his first entrance at the dress-rehearsal : a short, stocky, square-set little man, with dark eyes. His head was Beethoven's head. I have two portraits before me as I write : one of Beethoven and one of Tree in the part, and it is difficult to tell which is which. In many cases the effect of even a wonderful make-up evaporates after the first three minutes, and the actor's own individuality forces itself through the disguise. In this instance it was not so. Tree had got into the skin of the part ; he was in earnest ; and he maintained and even increased the illusion to the very end of the play. He seemed-to have absorbed the mind of Beethoven. His performance illustrated in a remarkable manner his facility for assimilating arts with which he may be assumed to have had no working familiarity. He was, for the time being, the master-musician, the inspired composer, and the expert craftsman could find no flaw in the technique of his performance. During the course of the play Beethoven was shown in the act of composing, of thinking out a composition ; he was shown in the very afflatus of musical inspiration. The actor was required to express this almost without the help of words, while the orchestra interpreted the working of his mind. We went to Beethoven's own sketch-books for our material : the sketch-books in which he jotted down germs of musical thought during his solitary walks ; erased them ; turned them this way and that ; until he had found the one right way. Tree's facial expression, every movement of his body and of his extraordinarily eloquent hands, fell spontaneously into perfect agreement with the complicated music. His audience was enabled to see into the composer's mind, was initiated into the arcana of musical inspiration. We felt we had surprised Beethoven himself in the act of composing. Again, in the scene in which Beethoven ultimately realizes his deafness, the actor was, as I can testify from experience, absolutely, tragically, true to nature. Comparatively few people witnessed this performance ; for the love and comprehension of fine acting had given place to admiration for lingerie and the worship of the clown who grins through a horse-collar ; but those who did, remember it as one of the greatest and most perfect of Tree's achievements.

Tree was an indefatigable worker. If he only lived sixty-three years according to the calendar, he lived one hundred and twenty-six measured by the work of an average man. There is an impression that a successful actor-manager's life is one of elegant indolence, tempered by epigram ; and I think Tree loved to encourage that impression. To a careless observer he never seemed to be doing anything ; never seemed to want to do anything ; seemed always more interested in something quite beside the matter in hand—in anything, rather than that. I think he liked to have it thought that his theatre ran itself ; that the plays were rehearsed in odd moments ; that he learnt his own parts while shaving ; that all his time was spent in lotus-eating. He would wander away from a rehearsal to listen apparently with the deepest possible interest to one intolerable bore after another. When he had had as much of the bore as even he could stand—and he suffered bores gladly—he would pin him to the lapel of the busiest man he could find on the spot, and meander away chuckling. When he was travelling, even with the purpose of acquiring local colour, he never seemed to look at anything. He said he never opened a book. He pretended he had no sense of time. All this was merely an attitude it gratified his sense of humour to assume *pour épater le bourgeois.* He must at one time or another have devoured books ; for there was no subject he was not familiar with. I never knew him miss an appointment of any importance. He showed, when the moment came, that he had absorbed the essentials of any place or country he had visited. We went to Egypt together to get hints for scenery, and he made me miserable because he seemed to see nothing. I discovered later that he had seen everything, and retained everything, much more clearly than I, who had worn myself out in sight-seeing. One day, in 1910, he drifted into my work-room in his usual accidental, nonchalant, unexpected way, and casually, as though it were nothing at all, asked me to help him " produce " (that is a hateful word, but I can think of no other) *Henry VIII.* People talk lightly about working day and night. We did work day and night, and on the day and night of the dress-rehearsal I was done for ; had to be carried out of the theatre; went to bed and stayed there ; but Tree played the endless part of Wolsey as if he had had nothing else to do and nothing else to think of.

Long before this I had lost my stupid self-consciousness where he was concerned and had grown to know him pretty intimately. This intimacy was increased by my intercourse with him in connection with *Drake, Joseph, David Copperfield* and *Mavourneen*. I saw him under all sorts of circumstances and among all sorts of people, and I had long ago discovered that under the Tree of legend, the Tree who was constantly letting off verbal fireworks, paradoxes and epigrams, there was a kind, affectionate, simple, child-like man with a heart of gold ; the most lovable man I have ever met ; the most aggravating man, too. But though his "aggravatingness" sometimes put one in a fury, the fury was instantly disarmed by his perfectly sincere surprise that one could be angry. At the climax of the most horrific quarrel, when we had littered the stage with each other's fur, he would slip his arm through mine and say, "Now, L-N, come and have supper," as if nothing had happened. What could one do with a man like that, except love him ? His affectionate nature compelled affection and would take no denial. When once he had thought it worth while to conquer your shyness or reserve, you were his friend and he was yours, for all time. The whole staff of his theatre proved that. There was not a man employed in it, whether before or behind the curtain, who would not gladly have let himself be cut in little pieces to serve " The Chief." A rehearsal might begin at 5 p.m. on one day and end in total exhaustion at 7.30 a.m. the next morning. What of it ? Did anybody go on strike ? Not a soul. They began again at 11 a.m. the same day. The word fatigue did not exist in his vocabulary nor in anyone's who was working with him. His enthusiasm for the play in hand remained at fever-heat until the curtain had fallen on the first performance. Then he wanted to get to work on the next. I believe his ideal of theatrical life would have been six weeks of strenuous rehearsal and one performance. He was always, without cessation or interruption, reaching out for the new thing ; the thing that had not been done before ; the thing no one else had ever thought of ; the thing that seemed impossible.

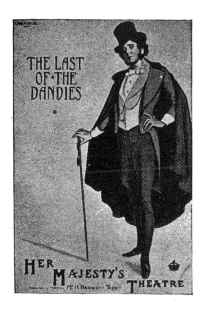

"D'ORSAY."

A poster by Charles Buchel.

By permission of]   [*The London Stereo. Co.*

"FALSTAFF."

Photo by]   [*Floyd, N.Y.C.*

"MACBETH."

Photo by]   [*F. Burford.*

"SHYLOCK."

His theatre was his world, and to it he devoted his life. He loved the building itself and he was proud of it, as well he might be. To have kept such a house open and flourishing so many years; to have made it the leading playhouse of the English-speaking world was, *pace* the faddists who consider no man successful who is not bankrupt, a great achievement. His theatre was his kingdom; he treated it royally; he treated his colleagues royally; and he treated his public royally. With all the business acumen he and his staff brought to bear on the conduct of the great house, there was always an indefinable air of princely hospitality about His Majesty's. The public felt that they were getting something beyond their money's worth, in the way of comfort, of consideration, of elegance.

He took a special pride in honouring his foreign colleagues. The Théâtre Français can testify to that, and so can all foreign authors and players who visited London during his management, even if they were previously unknown to him. As his pride in his profession was intense, so he loved to show his foreign guests that they were properly appreciated and duly honoured.

I am not here concerned with Tree's wit, with his felicity of repartee, with his quips and quiddities. Those who only knew him as a brilliant jester did not know him at all. It is but a poor creature who survives in nothing but his *bons-mots*, and Tree should not be classed with Theodore Hook. I have read with amazement certain obituary notices by self-styled intimate friends (many of whom, in the familiar intercourse of thirty years, I never saw in his company) in which this facet of his character was magnified to the distortion of the whole portrait, while the serious work of his life was only passingly alluded to, and then with invidious comparisons and insidious qualifications.

Tree was a happy man; his nature was sunny; his disposition was to look on the bright side of things, and, if the side turned towards him happened to be gloomy, to set to work and brighten it without loss of time. That characteristic helped him to face occasional managerial failures with equanimity. If anything bored him it was what he himself called " an obstinate success," for the reason that it delayed some cherished scheme

He shirked no duty however unpleasant, and evaded no responsibility however irksome ; on the contrary, he turned the duty into a pleasure and the responsibility into a further occasion of happiness for others and therefore for himself. He bore no grudges and had not an iota of malice. Even the intentionally offensive caricature of a buffoon could not provoke him ; if the buffoon seemed essential to the cast of his next play he engaged him. I think he enjoyed every moment of his life, and would not have had one moment other than it was. He squeezed the last ounce of work and enjoyment out of his day, and his day seldom ended before its morrow was well on its way. While I am certain he had no thought of dying, I am equally sure he died as he would have wished : in harness, with his energies undiminished, and in the act of planning the future. On the day of his death he was busy engaging performers for the play he was soon to produce, and he was looking forward to that with as much interest as if he had been about to make his first appearance as an actor. He had preserved the joyous spirits, the ambitions, yes, and the illusions of youth. He believed in everybody until they deceived him—and then he pensioned them. He was, in short, a large-minded, tender-hearted, impulsive, generous gentleman, and as such he will ever be remembered by those who knew him and loved him.

War has passed a reeking sponge over the drama, and for a time the gap caused by Tree's death will not be appreciated. But soon others besides his intimates will notice the hiatus. The English Theatre has lost something more than a great actor or a brilliant manager ; it has lost a leader ; it has lost its dispenser of open-handed hospitality ; it has lost, as you might say, the head of its household, who splendidly did the honours on great occasions ; who, on all occasions, was hot in defence of his art and proud of his profession. His Majesty's Theatre was a great institution with a great gentleman at the head of it. But it is not only the theatre that is bereaved ; England has lost one of her representative men : a man whose name was famous all the world over, even where his personality was unknown.

All the foregoing I had set down a few days after his death. Upon re-reading it nearly four years later, I see nothing I wish to omit : I only see that I have conveyed little of the sense of personal loss which I—and how many others !—feel. That increases daily. A joy has gone out of life. I constantly catch myself saying, " I must tell Tree that," or " Tree would like that idea," and then I remember that the place he occupied in my world is a great blank.

FROM THE STALLS

By Desmond MacCarthy

Sometimes between spectator and actor there grows up a kind of one-sided personal relation. I call it a personal relation because it is not merely on the part of the spectator an appreciation of the actor's art ; it includes sympathy with the actor himself, as he is conceived to be behind the parts he acts, and it may carry with it almost a delusion of intimacy. Although I never in my life spoke to Sir Herbert Tree, I felt as if I knew him well. It made me sorry when he came to grief in a part ; it added to my interest when he notably succeeded ; it even made me sometimes follow him a little way along the street, that I might enjoy the form and flourish he put into the simple business of progression ; it made a casual face-to-face encounter with him significant, so that I would afterwards recall his restless, dream-glazed eyes which looked at objects in a steady imperceptive way as though he was staring at his own thoughts, and that bar above them, which, it is said, tends to lift its possessor an inch or two above the solid ground. He attracted me as a character at once flamboyant and extremely sensitive ; I thought of him as a man immensely friendly, and sympathetic, yet immensely self-absorbed. These conjectures, whatever their value, at least attest that interest in me, and interest, though it is no guarantee that a critic will reach right conclusions, helps him at least to fix his attention on his subject. Herbert Tree was an enthusiast ; the comments which follow are by no means entirely composed of laurels, but on the grave of an enthusiast we need lay no artificial wreaths.

For a long time before his death Herbert Tree, if his profession can be said to have a head, was the head of his profession ;

he had succeeded to the position once occupied by Irving. It was not what it had been during the hey-day of Irving's career, for His Majesty's was never a focus of all that was considered choicest, most inspiring and most enterprising in dramatic art, as the Lyceum had once been. It was never so important, partly because it had no Ellen Terry, but chiefly because that tradition had begun to lose prestige with the imaginative public. His Majesty's, under Herbert Tree's management, frankly forewent the claim to be the last word in dramatic art. It stood instead for the grandly, lavishly popular in that line. For years it represented the central British conception of the drama when it is taken seriously, just as the Savoy Hotel represents the British conception of magnificence taken seriously; that it also reflected Herbert Tree's ideal is both true and untrue.

In judging his career, the first thing to remember is that he was an imaginative, romantic man, and (though this found no expression in his productions in their entirety) a subtle man. His subtlety of feeling peeped out in the by-play of his own acting. He might have been a greater actor, if he had had enough self-confidence to believe that what he could do best was more worth doing than bringing off effects which, in his youth, he had been taught were the triumphs of an actor's art, or even perhaps if his methods of production had not entailed such innumerable preoccupations which had nothing to do with acting. But he lived in an uncritical age, and he was ambitious. He set before him, as an aim, that pre-eminence in the theatrical world he did in fact attain, and in attaining it many aptitudes, all clamouring for exercise, found satisfaction ; the artist in him acquiescing —as far as we could see from stalls—without painful struggles. It was easy for him to keep to the high road leading to a big success, for two reasons.

In the first place he was pre-eminently a social man, not a solitary one. He had that temperament which saves a man from becoming a crank, but at the same time makes it hard for him to trust those slight evanescent promptings which must be listened for and obeyed, if he is to find himself completely as an artist. Although he had obviously plenty of confidence in his talents and courage in undertaking the most diverse parts, I doubt if he had in him that hard kernel of arrogance which has made it easier for less gifted, less original men to get the best, and only the best, out of themselves. Emotionally, he was a prime example of what is called the artistic temperament, but intellectually I suspect him of having been sceptical, with more than a touch of dilettantism, which, while it injured his art, must have made him a most charming companion. In the second place it was easy for him to follow the high road to popular success, because the Lyceum tradition did give enormous scope to his emotional, artistic temperament. The performances at His Majesty's were not merely bids for full houses, they were the gifts of an enthusiast. They were on a scale far too minutely lavish to be commercial, and the effect was often magnificent and impressive, giving pleasure and exhilaration to thousands. It was the whole tradition that was wrong, not the way he carried it out ; in that he displayed a wonderful amount of invention. The editions of Shakespeare issued at His Majesty's were more sumptuously bound and richly illustrated than any the Lyceum had produced. The mistake was to suppose that, say, *Antony and Cleopatra* could be improved by introducing a thrumming, aromatic kind of music, or that the mystery and attraction of Cleopatra herself could be reinforced by a symbolic transformation scene, in which a Sphinx loomed out of the blackness to die into it again. Very fine that Sphinx was, I remember ; but I also remember that it called down louder applause than any other scene in the play, which proves there was something very wrong.

The result of all this accumulation of commentary and illustration, however ingenious or lavish, round a play was often to slow down its action intolerably ; and while attempting to interpret Shakespeare to the eye, the production too often failed to interpret him to the mind. Thus it was that, in company with several other critics, I found myself, when Shakespeare was on at His Majesty's, shouting : " Sir Herbert Tree's carriage stops the way ! " Yet I was also aware that there was no better test of the degree in which anyone possessed the finer fibres of appreciation than his attitude towards Herbert Tree's own acting. Indeed, I sometimes used the topic of his acting as a method of discovering if anyone with whom I happened to converse about acting had, or had not, genuine sensibility. In many of his interpretations there were features to which anyone, who was master of the elements of criticism, could object—extravagancies it required only rudimentary acuteness to ridicule ; but did my interlocutor also respond to the light, quick indications of character, to the flashes of insight, illumining those impersonations, to the generous impetus, the self-forgetful audacity with which the actor had thrown himself into his part ? Or did he merely direct a destructive sniff at the whole performance ? That was the test. Partly because the methods of production at His Majesty's were rightly being questioned, partly on account of the too obviously histrionic side of Herbert Tree's technique, it became in some circles almost a mark of discrimination to depreciate him indiscriminately ; his severest critics being, perhaps, those kind of people who, holding some of the more common among sound opinions upon the art of acting (either honestly acquired or picked up secondhand), feel an instinctive need to protect the weakly growth of their own sensibility by hedging it round with sweeping condemnations. But cautious criticism without the faintest tincture of generosity —who would care a fig for it ? Certainly not Herbert Tree.

He was essentially a romantic actor, perhaps the last exuberant descendant of Romanticism flowering on the English stage. Anyone looking at the pictures of bygone green-room celebrities, of the Kembles, of the Keans, of Macready, will perceive at once in their grandiose postures the naivety of their appeal, the simplicity of their trust in an instant response on the part of their audiences to whatever is histrionically noble, prodigious, extreme. Stop for a moment in front of, say, the picture of Kemble as Hamlet, holding in his hands the skull of Yorick, or read the description of Fechter in the part : " Lymphatic, delicate, handsome and with his long flaxen curls, quivering sensitive nostrils, fine eye, and sympathetic voice, he perfectly represents the graceful prince." . . . " It is," says George Lewes, speaking of Fechter's performance, " the nearest approach I have seen to the realization of Goethe's idea,expounded in the celebrated critique in *Wilhelm Meister*, that there is a burden laid on Hamlet too heavy for his soul to bear. The refinement, the feminine delicacy, the vacillation of Hamlet are admirably represented ; and it is only in the more tragic scenes that we feel any short-coming." Here is the fore-runner of Tree's Hamlet with the wandering, pathetic eye (the very words might almost fit his Hamlet), just as that much criticized incident in his performance, his kissing the hair of the unconscious Ophelia, was the derivative of Kemble's farewell in the " get thee to a nunnery " scene, when Kemble used to fling himself at her feet and cover her hands with kisses before rushing from the stage. The triumphs of dead actors live for us only in pictures, in half-obliterated tradition, and in the pages of the few dramatic critics who happen to be still readable on account of their style. We believe in the dignity of Kemble's declamation, in the power of Macready's pathos, in the thrilling fury of the elder Kean and the marvel of his voice, because critics like Hazlitt and Lewes have described them ; and no doubt we do right to believe. But it does not follow that there was not also much in their acting to which we would not have taken exception, though it was pleasing and satisfactory to their contemporaries. We know that these famous ones also clipped and altered the text of Shakespeare ; we observe that they were praised for the ingenuity of " their business " (precisely the kind Tree was always inventing), and we suspect that their expression of emotion was pitched in a very high key indeed. Garrick was amazingly natural in comedy, but there are indications that even Garrick's tragic acting was to our taste overcharged. " Would you not, sir," asked Boswell, " start as Mr. Garrick does, if you saw a ghost ? " " I hope not," Dr. Johnson replied. " If I did, I should frighten the ghost." What I wish to suggest is that the astringent atmosphere of the 'nineties and early twentieth century, which was not favourable to the romantic, expansive side of Herbert Tree's art, would have probably nibble-nipped also the reputations of some of his famous predecessors. To Tree's Hamlet we much preferred the fastidious, scholarly, airy-gallant Hamlet of Forbes-Robertson, which lightened the heavy shadows of the play and braced up the drooping figure of the traditional " gloomy Dane," whose utter abandonment to self-pity and display of pride in feeling an exile in this world, were features more immediately sympathetic to bygone audiences than to us. If Lewes complained that there was too much of the cambric

"RICHARD II."

handkerchief in Macready's much-admired Hamlet, no doubt we should have done so too.

I used to wish that someone would write a play for Tree with Alfred de Musset as the hero. He would have been at home in the part of a poet who is as proud of his sorrows as a soldier of his scars ; and much at home in a world where genius was marvelled at, not analysed, and men and women, the tight-waisted beaux and wide-skirted ladies of old fashion plates, first exchanged glances at such respectful distances, approached each other with such elaborate delicacy and adored with such despairing admiration. What an audience too those men and women would have made for him ! Perhaps this wish was suggested by his admirable rendering of intellectual feminine-ness and exalted self-pity in Richard II. ; but my purpose in mentioning it is to hint that in judging his talent and in placing him among his predecessors and contemporaries, it is important to think of him as an actor trailing with him into the twentieth century clouds of romanticism, from which, for our eyes, the glow and colour had in a measure departed. But if he was pre-eminently a romantic, the next thing to note about him is that he was a character actor ; and it was in the exercise of this side of his talent that his subtlety showed itself.

A character actor is one who does not excel chiefly in playing certain recurring situations, but in building up before our eyes a definite human being. Tree possessed the power of conceiving character in a very high degree. Of all his contemporaries he had the largest share of this author's gift. But an actor must, of course, also possess the faculty of representing the characters he understands. His gift of conceiving character may, as it does in dramatists and authors, outrun his power of representing it to the eye and ear, which power is limited in the case of every actor by his temperament and physique. In the case of Herbert Tree his power of understanding character was far wider than his power of representing it ; and his extraordinary skill in making-up, in which he was unmatched, often tempted him to play characters which were outside his temperamental and physical range. He had not the animal vigour which is necessary to great excellence in violent tragedy or in robust comedy. He could make himself look like Falstaff ; he understood and revelled in the character of Falstaff, but his performance lacked fundamental force. Hence the contradiction in his acting : his performance as a whole often fell short of high excellence, yet these same impersonations were lit by insight and masterly strokes of interpretation, which made the spectator feel that he was watching the performance of the most imaginative of living actors. He had understood the character marvellously well. The same phenomenon would occur in parts in which the author himself had put next to nothing. It is well known that Tree practically created the part of *The Private Secretary*, which amused many thousands of people for several years, actually supplying many of the lines which were quoted whenever the character was mentioned. Take, again, a very bad play he produced at His Majesty's, *Colonel Newcome*. From the first act, when the old soldier quavers out an old-fashioned song, while the young men are laughing at him in their sleeves, to the last, when he dies in an almshouse surrounded by a few loving friends, the play was one long attempt to work in us the handle of the pump of tears. Sir Herbert Tree himself worked at that handle hard. But a scene comes back to me which illustrates how fine and subtle in the midst of cheap sentiment his acting might suddenly become. This scene was one in which the Colonel's old nurse, hearing he had been ruined, came to return to him some little presents of value which he had given her in his prosperity. The pathos of that situation was obvious. What was remarkable in this scene between the two old people was the way in which Sir Herbert Tree's gestures somehow expressed the comfort it was to them both just to be near each other ; the kind of unconsciousness with which he caressed her, as though the vagueness of old age had recreated in him the instinctiveness of childish affection. Only an imaginative actor could have given the scene that beauty. Sometimes when the sentiment of his parts was subtle he succeeded with an ease and completeness which, owing to the absence of emphasis, seemed often to escape the notice of critics ; sometimes when it was crude he was apt to intensify its crudeness by abandoning himself to it utterly, and this did not escape them.

His production of *The Enemy of the People* was an example at once of his weakness as a producer and of his rare gift for comprehending character. To liven Ibsen up he introduced some foolery. He chose a very little man to play the part of " the representative of the compact majority," so that there should be a funny contrast between his own stature and this minute actor's. (There was some foolery, too, over the burgomaster's hat.) But his own acting in the part of that homely and courageous prophet, Dr. Stockmann, was masterly and subtle. He was perfect in the impassioned, indignant harangues, in representing Stockmann's incredulous distress of mind, his readiness to drop any number of points if only people will listen, a readiness which looks so like want of dignity but springs from sincerity. How admirably he acted the ruefulness with which Stockmann surveys his torn clothes and gravely concludes that " a man should never put on his best trousers when he goes out to battle for freedom and truth ! " That Tree comprehended his character completely was shown in the way he brought out to perfection that rare and touching humour which expresses itself in ways and words so like those of a person who has no humour, that people without a sense of character do not see the difference. When he was thundering from the platform about stuffy, selfish, ignoble homes, he had a characteristically subtle inspiration. Katerina, Stockmann's nervous, devoted wife, is sitting beside him. She has tried all along to prevent her husband embarking on his unpopular campaign, and her efforts have always drawn the same remark from him : " Really, Katerina, you are a most extraordinary woman." In the middle of this harangue about stuffy homes he put his hand for a second on her shoulder. It is hard to describe a gesture that is exactly right, but this one at that moment said as plainly as words : " Of course, my dear, that is not a hit at you." That momentary gesture expressed perfectly the relation between husband and wife. I recall it because it illustrates his gift of comprehending character.

A character actor has, of course, like an author, a limited repertory of characters whom he can make live for us. There is always a central type which an author does better than any other, and from which he cannot wander far without losing his inspiration. This is still more obvious in the case of the actor who must use his body and physical temperament in creating character. Reviewing the many parts Tree played and noticing those in which he excelled and the points at which he excelled in others, it is not difficult to fix upon that type : it was a character who had something of the artist in him and in whom the artistic temperament readily took a histrionic form. He loved to impersonate, and excelled in impersonating, characters who, in varying degrees, were the play-actors of their own emotions. Dandies, in the spiritual or literal sense, he understood and sympathized with ; mannered elegance, intellectual coquetry, humorous tenderness, self-defensive irony, cunning grace, self-conscious pathos, delicate familiarity, he could express perfectly. His Hamlet was satisfactory in the passages which these phrases recall ; his Macbeth impressive only where Macbeth resembles most a literary man ; it was the " qualis artifex pereo " strain in the character of Nero which attracted him to the part ; his Othello, Antony (in *Antony and Cleopatra*), Shylock are forgotten, and best forgotten. But his genius for representing one who takes advantage of a gush of spontaneous emotion to heighten it for his own ends, made his Antony in *Julius Cæsar* a performance of the highest excellence. For the same reason he triumphed, though his elocution was seldom perfect, in the delivery of the stage harangue ; that over-stippling of his effects which sometimes spoilt them at other junctures, on these occasions added the grace of spontaneity to what he uttered. He understood the orator, the actor, the artist whose emotions are his own material, and the half-sincere advocate. It was his sympathy with the man who dramatizes his own woes, and his comprehension of the shifting connection between the heightened pose and genuine feeling beneath, which made his Richard II. so admirable. He understood well, too, the curious corruption of sincerity which may result, and pitied the weakness of such men compared with unimaginative men of action ; that pathos he conveyed to us excellently well. The conscious courteousness of Richard II., his flashy imperiousness, the delicacy of his untrustworthy nature, his exquisite gentleness, his spiteful arrogance so inconsistent with it, his theatrical humility and his rapid transitions of mood, never found a better interpreter. Richard is essentially the man who, when disaster comes, seeks refuge in being the spectator of his own tragedy, whose heart is only gracious and alive while he is looking on at his own destiny, but in action becomes cowardly and mean. The reason why this piece of acting has not been better remembered is that his audiences were too busy gaping at the amazing pageantry of the performance to remember or talk about anything else.

He was always better in representing weakness than strength, passivity than resolution, failure, whether of the faithful or ignoble kind, than victory. He was admirable in the expression of that irony which is the revenge of the beaten or the refuge of the helpless. He was not a good interpreter of lovers' parts and he avoided them, but he could express an intimate tenderness extremely well. One characteristic of his acting—and it distinguished him from most of his eminent contemporaries—was that he always acted from his imagination. He flung himself neck and crop into his parts. Sometimes the results were disastrous, but even on these occasions there was always discernible that effort to become entirely the part which is the foundation of good acting. How strong the romantic was in him was shown not only in his choice of parts, but in his technique. He believed in inspiration. He was to the last an improvisor, trusting to the emotion of the moment. Opinions about him differed so widely, partly because different people had seen him on different nights. He was sentimentally reluctant to register and reproduce mechanically an effect he had once achieved on the spur of the moment ; instead he waited for the impulse to recur again. In this he differed from a great actor like Coquelin, who, having once adjusted an intonation or a gesture to a hair's-breadth, stereotyped it, so that if one saw him in the same part years later, the impression was exactly the same. The artistic impulse in him being far more emotional than intellectual, he was attracted by exaggerated situations, and this preference often prevented him from making full use of his finer faculties. He was not his best when he put on yellow tights and greaves and hung a skin about him and pretended to be Ulysses ; and, astonishingly effective as his Svengali and Fagin were, such parts did not show what was most moving in his acting—his fantastic humour and the extreme delicacy of his insight into the pathos of certain characters and situations, which made him the most imaginative of contemporary actors.

HERBERT TREE—MY FRIEND

By C. Haddon Chambers

It was in 1887 that I first met Herbert Tree. I was then writing magazine stories for a livelihood, and had made only one or two timid adventures into the dramatic field. I knew Tree but very slightly, and when I met and was stopped by him one day in Panton Street I was not unimpressed, for he was already in management at the Comedy Theatre, and the world of London was not unaware of his potentialities. After the conventional greetings, he said : " Have you ever thought of writing a play for me ? " Frankly I hadn't, not even in my wildest day-dreams. To this day I don't know if he was serious, but to doubt it at the moment I felt would be poor policy. " No, but I will," I said, and we parted. I went home to my rooms over a milk-shop in Bayswater, aflame with ambition for the first time in my life. In four months I had completed my task as represented by " *Captain Swift*, a New and Original Play in Four Acts."

In the meanwhile Tree had left the Comedy Theatre, and his long and brilliant management of the Haymarket had begun. I duly carried my manuscript to him, and am unable to remember if he expressed his surprise, or, as I had hoped, his overwhelming joy. He promised a reading, however, and I discreetly retired to my suburb from a sanctum which had, apparently, already become the shelter of grave interests. Three months later I was given my hearing to Tree alone at the Haymarket Theatre. Probably my methods of reading have improved since those days, for by the time I reached the end of Act II. our managerial hero was aweary, and retired from the unequal contest in favour of the Leicester Square Turkish baths. I had not ridden after recalcitrant cattle in the Australian wilds fruitlessly, however, and presently I appeared loin-clothed and manuscript in hand in the " hot room," where I gently but firmly imposed the remaining two acts of my play upon the great manager's tired hearing.

Naturally, Tree accepted the play, and the youthful author's joy was unbounded ; but there were rocks ahead. They were represented by Comyns Carr, the literary adviser, and Hastings, the stage manager. One day, when I sat with Tree in his room at the Haymarket, there entered to us Hastings, manuscript in hand. " Well, what do you think of it ? " asked Tree. " Damned rot ! " said Hastings, throwing the manuscript heavily upon what he imagined was a table, but was really my heart. He hadn't thought that the slender young fellow by the window might be the author, and I never knew, when Tree introduced us, whether he blushed behind his impenetrable beard. And then there was Joe Carr, afterwards one of my dearest and most sympathetic of friends. He was a hard nut to crack, for he had no admiration of or belief in the play whatever. Not only so, but he was able to advance his reasons with great eloquence, weight and wit, and with copious quotations from the alleged authorities ; and he permitted no misguided reticence to restrain him from doing so in the presence of both manager and author. I can see him now in that room overlooking Stafford Street, walking up and down, arguing my play away with an unfailing flow of words, and cutting my newly-opened career from under my feet. Carr, with his lion head, his flowing beard, his fine diction and choice of words, and his obvious sincerity, was nothing less than formidable. " He's back at the Bar," I thought, and I quaked for Tree. Suddenly I felt Tree's blue eyes on me. They unmistakably expressed sympathy that I should be present to hear all this bad news about my play. Carr's back was turned at the moment. I deliberately winked at Tree. (I have always thought since that that wink was the match that kindled our long friendship.) He burst out laughing. " What are you laughing at ? " asked Joe, turning quickly. " I am laughing," said Herbert adroitly, " because I have an idea. If Chambers doesn't object, we'll give his play at a trial matinée." I didn't object.

I needn't write of the matinée here, or of the subsequent career

Photo by]   [*Alfred Ellis.*

HERBERT TREE
ABOUT 1889.

of *Captain Swift*. Everybody knows the story, and of how the attractive and tragic ex-bushranger became one of Tree's great modern creations. I wrote my second play, *The Idler*, for him within the year, but, although he pondered it for some months, Tree didn't see himself in the character provided, and I took the play to George Alexander, who made it his first production at the St. James's and gave a superb performance of the protagonist. But Tree's judgment was sound, all the same, for " Mark Cross " was an unsuitable character for his own particular gifts.

Tree and I were again associated in a production a very few years later. The play was *John-o'-Dreams*, and it was a great success, the only drawback being that its run had to be interrupted on account of agreements previously made for Tree's first visit to America. The production gave rise to a correspondence in *The Times* which created a considerable stir at the time. An anonymous correspondent denounced the play as having an immoral tendency. Tree was most indignant, and on account of the style of the letter, and for other reasons, he was convinced the writer was Clement Scott, with whom at the time he was on indifferent terms. Well do I remember my dinner with the Haymarket manager at Kettner's that evening before the performance. Fortunately the restaurant was empty at that hour, for Tree's fighting blood was up, and he was able to walk about between courses and compose his answering letter aloud. " I shall say," he said, snatching a pencil from behind the ear of the bewildered waiter, " I shall say, ' And here I seem to detect the ink-stained forefinger of an old journalist hand ' " (how he loved a phrase !), and down it went on the back of the menu card. But Scott (if it was Scott) was also a fighter and phrase-maker, and the day after Tree's letter appeared we had a shrewd retort from the anonymous one which began something like this : " Spoon-fed with the theatrical pap of suburban epigrammists, Mr. Tree——" and so on.

" Who are the ' suburban epigrammists ' ? " asked Outram Tristram, the author of *The Red Lamp*, and our familiar friend.

" Well," said Tree, " you and Haddon both live in Bayswater."

I was not wholly unassociated with one other verbal mêlée

in which Tree and Scott were actors a little later on. One
evening Comyns Carr took me to sup with him at his club. It
chanced that during the day I had noticed an advertisement in
a daily paper extolling the attractions of Bexhill-on-Sea. The
advertisement concluded something like this : " And as the
celebrated dramatist and critic, Clement Scott, writes :

> " ' Bexhill-on-Sea is a haven for me,
> Whene'er my nerves are depressed ;
> For there's a retreat where you golf and you eat,
> And you sleep and you dream and you rest.' "

The thing had struck me as priceless, and as affording
delightful material for light entertainment, and when we sat
down to supper I handed the advertisement to Carr and drew
his attention to its glories. Joe, who had the mischievous heart
of a boy, fell upon it with glee, and was presently reading it
aloud to several men at the supper-table. These included
old Joe Knight, who was one of Scott's close friends. Carr's
humour, of course, took the form of considering the effusion as
a serious contribution to modern poetry ; but Knight, who
didn't see the joke, and who was also induced to read the verse
aloud, permitted himself to be drawn into an argument as to
whether the lines " scanned." Some of the members of the
company were frankly amused, while others were with Joe Knight
in failing to see any fun in the thing. Then Tree entered the
room, and quickly catching up the spirit of the joke, joyously
carried it shoulder-high for a couple of hours. About one o'clock
Scott himself appeared at the supper-table, and then there was
the devil to pay. Jokes, jibes, phrases, witticisms and retorts,
courteous and otherwise, whizzed over the supper-table. Scott,
also a fighter, hit back with characteristic energy, and his par-
tisans were not unvocal. And yet, although noisy, the affair
was seemly, with an absence of any real malice or rancour. As
for me, I continued to maintain an attitude of aloofness, for I
was not only the youngest member of the party, but a guest ;
but I hugged to myself the knowledge that I had been instru-
mental in starting the fray, which, had it occurred in the bush,
whence I had recently come, would have resulted in many a
bloody nose. As it was, the party broke up about four a.m.
in the highest spirits and the most orderly confusion, and Carr,

Tree and I dropped each other at our respective homes from a most reactionary four-wheeler. As our American friends would say, " Some night ! "

John-o'-Dreams was the last play I wrote for Tree, although I sometimes threatened him, and he was genuinely anxious for more work from my pen. He undoubtedly should have had it had he remained at the Haymarket. But he built himself the magnificent theatre opposite, where " big " plays were needed, and about that time I had drifted into writing comedies whose production called for a small stage. I wrote *The Tyranny of Tears* for Wyndham, but I don't think Tree ever had an opportunity of seeing it. He saw *Sir Anthony*, however, and was very enthusiastic about Weedon Grossmith's and his own nephew, Evelyn Beerbohm's performances. And he saw du Maurier's production of *Passers-by*, and wrote a most generous appreciation for it in the Press.

Meanwhile the silver cord of our friendship remained unloosed. It found no active expression in the way of our seeking each other's society, or in correspondence. In its thirty years of life I don't believe we exchanged more than half a dozen letters. But there was a subtle, tacit understanding between us which enabled us to pick up the threads of interest at a moment's notice. We rarely arranged to meet—we just met, and were glad. Sometimes we were together when he was making holiday. That I found excellent, for he was always alive and always joyous. The fields, lanes and sands over which I am just now walking daily, I have ridden over with Herbert many and many a time. Although no player of games, he loved the open air, and loved exercise, more particularly on horseback. He distrusted himself, and justly, as a sailor ; but in the old days, given amiable weather, he would put to sea with me in my boat and remain undismayed while I handled the sheets and tiller.

One morning, about seven years ago, Tree called me up on the telephone. " I hear you are going to New York again," he said. I admitted it. " Would you mind if I crossed on your ship ? " he asked. Naturally I didn't. I was delighted. On the following Saturday we met at St. Pancras Station. Lady Tree and Henry Dana were there to see him off, and " Please take care of Herbert," whispered Lady Tree to me apart, and " Don't

let the dear old chief get into bad hands," similarly whispered
Dana. " Nobody ever wants anybody to take care of me ! "
I said to Tree when we had steamed out of the station. " No
one would take on the job, you rascal ! " he replied.

During the first two days at sea the weather left everything
to be desired, and Tree kept his state-room—a large one on the
top deck—most of the time, reclining upon his sofa and expressing
weariness of life. He was not actually ill, but his distrust of
himself was of the gravest. After luncheon on the third day
out I chanced upon a very old and valued friend playing cards
in the smoking-room. I got an idea. I went to Tree's cabin
and sat by his " couch forlorn." " Herbert," I said, " you are
not actually ill."

" No," he said wearily, " but——" and he made a face.

" You need rousing," I said.

" No doubt," he replied.

" And I have found the man to rouse you."

" Who's your friend ? " he drawled.

" One Blank," I announced.

" What does he do ? " asked Tree.

" Everything and everybody," I answered. " Tom Blank
is one of the world's great men. You are a great man," I added
hastily, " great enough to permit me to say that Tom is an even
greater one. He's a citizen of the world, and has been everywhere and crossed every sea. He's travelled more boats than
you've even read the names of. His life has been an endless
romance. He's been a slaver, a buccaneer, a pirate. He's a
born and unbeaten fighter, and has a generous soul. He's been
the hero of vendettas in the South, and the ever-dangerous poet
of camp fires in the North. He has undoubtedly killed persons,
and persons have undoubtedly endeavoured, but vainly, to kill
him. For the rest, he is one of the most formidable of living
men, is a ripe Shakespearean scholar, and talks almost as well
as he plays cards. In a word," I concluded, " he is your
man."

Despite some feeble protestations from the invalid, I went
in search of Blank, and presently brought him to the cabin,
explaining *en route* that my friend was feeling seedy and needed
cheering up. The introduction was an event. Blank was

six feet two and built to perfection—a terrific man, but withal
a genial. " Let me introduce my friend, Mr. Blank," I said.
With splendid friendliness Blank offered a monstrous hand,
a portion of which Tree grasped. " How do you do, Sir Tree ? "
said Blank. " I'm sorry you're feeling a bit *de trop.*" That
nearly finished Herbert. It's a terrible thing to want to laugh
when you mustn't. His eyes blazed with humour, and he was
fain to bite his writhing lips. To help him out, I quoted genially :
" Sooner or later mountains meet." Then we all laughed, and
the situation was saved.

Needless to say, Tree and Blank became tremendous pals
from that moment, and spent most of the rest of the voyage
in each other's society. There is no doubt that Blank's extraordinary personality and amazingly adventurous career fascinated the actor, who for long after begged me to write a play
with Blank as the central figure for Tree to impersonate.
And then, of course, a supper had to be given by Tree in his
state-room in honour of his new friend. (Was ever a more
hospitable fellow, or a better host !) There were present, in
addition to the twin stars, the purser, the ship's doctor, Walter
Jordan (the American manager) and myself, and a glorious time
we had. Songs were sung, Shakespeare was recited by the yard,
personal adventures were told and accepted without question,
feats of strength and agility were performed, bottles and glasses
were kept amove, and cigars and cigarettes aglow until you
could have carved your name in the atmosphere. It was, indeed,
a merry party, and no one was happier than our ex-invalid host.
The sitting was an abnormally late one, and the last item I am
able to remember was that of Tom Blank demonstrating to
Tree how a man may be tied into a knot and rendered helpless
before the administration of a *coup de grâce.*

The mention a little earlier in these notes of Tree's fondness
for a phrase reminds me that during the voyage to New York
he quoted to me with some pride of authorship an aphorism he
had recently coined and made a careful note of. It was " A
sense of humour is the love-child of intelligence." I was duly
impressed, and I regarded the revelation to me as a literary
confidence ; but I was soon to remark that it was a confidence
which my most human old friend was willing and even anxious

to share with anyone who came along, and I heard him repeat it at least a dozen times before we left the ship. Shortly after our arrival, it chanced that we were both invited to a small luncheon-party given at what is generally known as the " Millionaires' Club." I chanced to be a little late in arriving, and found the company already at table. When I had made my apologies the expansive millionaire on my right said : " Pity you were late, Mr. Chambers, for your friend Sir Herbert was very amusing over the cocktails." I remarked that Sir Herbert was always amusing and asked for details.   " Well," said my neighbour, " among other things he said that a sense of humour is the love-child of intelligence."

" Splendid ! " I cried ; and, noting that Tree, who was sitting opposite to us, and to whom I was indebted for several items of raillery on board ship, was listening eagerly, I added : " But what does it mean ? "   " Well," drawled my millionaire, " you may search me ; but it sounded good, all the same."   No one laughed more joyously than Tree himself.

Yes, Herbert Tree's sense of humour and of the fun of life were certainly inexhaustible. So also were his courage and endurance under difficulties. It was only a very few years after the incidents I have mentioned that he and I were again in New York and seeing each other constantly, and I shall never forget the splendid courage and masterly skill with which he met and overcame a grave reverse on his arrival. His arrangements for and production of *Henry VIII.* at the New Amsterdam Theatre a few weeks later represented a managerial accomplishment of the highest order. The success of the revival was at its height when I sailed for England. Tree gave me a farewell supper—and a farewell supper it proved to be, for I never saw him again. It was characteristic of him that the beginning and end of our long friendship should have been expressed in terms of hospitality—the hospitality of his theatre and the hospitality of his heart.

Of Herbert Tree it may be truly said that he achieved his ambition. He gained the topmost rung of the ladder of his craft. He won his way by his own tireless efforts to the throne of his own particular world. He lived where he wished only to live, in the heart of life, giving all he had to give, and receiving with equal gratitude or hardihood the gifts or the knocks that came his way. He was a success, and he mostly went as one rejoicing ; and had his passing been less sudden, his last supreme glance back upon the varied, difficult and brilliant way might have constrained him to quote from one of his earliest successes : " I've had a good time here. Good-bye ! "

TO THE MEMORY OF A FRIEND

By Gilbert Parker

To write about Herbert Beerbohm Tree is hard and it is easy. It is hard because he was a man of the most varied accomplishments and unexpectedness, of the most fertile brain and vivid temperament, of delightful contradictions, of genuine enthusiasms and high ambitions, and it is difficult to get a well-balanced point of view of him ; and yet it is easy to write of him, for he had rare charm of manner, with versatility and rather ragged eloquence, nimbleness of mind and fine perceptions. To his last day he was a boy in spirit. He would not have been old if he had lived to be ninety. He had the secret of perpetual youth of the Spirit. He had his ups and downs of temperament, but hope and faith were his constant comrades, and with a flash all gloom would vanish, and he would snap out some witty phrase which would lift him up again. He had the gift of levitation.

The last time I saw him was in the month of February, 1917, in the house of a friend in Washington, the United States. He had come over to see me from Philadelphia, and to hear me read to him the play, *The Money Master*, which James Bernard Fagan did from my book of that name. If he had lived I think he would have produced it, and he would have played the weird part with that whimsicality and distinction of which he was a master. He returned to England and in a short time he was dead. It was a sudden and a painless death, but he left behind him a host of admirers and innumerable friends, who were deeply pained at his going and who still miss, and will for very long miss, his buoyant, piquant, powerful and distinguished presence. Faults, of course, he had, as who has not ! But his chief fault to my

236

Photo by]   ["*Daily Mirror.*"
          " MICAWBER."

Photo by]   [*The Dover Street Studios.*
          " THE MAN WHO WAS."

Photo by]   [*F. Burford.*
          " ZAKKURI."

          " ISIDORE IZARD."
       A drawing by Charles Buchel.

mind was the boredom that success brought him. He hated playing one part for a long run, in spite of the monetary benefit, because his active temperament was always planning something new. The artist in him was impatient with the arrest of progress—wanted to move on to other experiments and bolder flights.

I suppose no man ever lived who worked harder or who had a greater gift for work. I saw very much of him in the days when he removed from the Haymarket Theatre to Her Majesty's Theatre, and the ceaseless toil and responsibility never damped his spirits. He kept alive and vigorous and hopeful, although he was taking on a theatre which was larger than any actor in London had ever had, and of which the fate was most uncertain. He never lacked faith and hope ; he always believed in the theatre, and I am proud and sorry that my play, *The Seats of the Mighty,* opened it. I am proud because it was a great theatre and a great honour to have presented therein its first play, and sorry because I did not believe it could have a big success. From the Isle of Jersey I wrote to Tree, and begged him not to produce the play, and pointed out that the proper sort of play to open a great theatre like that was one by Shakespeare. His reply was a wire which said : " See *Daily Telegraph* to-morrow." He had paid me advance royalties, and I had not the power to prevent him from producing it ; but the mistake of the play was in making a bad Frenchman like Doltaire the central figure, and leaving Moray, the English hero, in the background too much. Tree's delight in the part made him make this decision, and it was bad for him and his theatre, I think. It had been first produced in Washington, the United States, and then I saw that nothing could make the play a big success. When it was again produced in New York, I was convinced of it ; but Tree still had faith and hope. That was one of his characteristics, when he had made up his mind to a thing it was hard to move him. It was one of the secrets of his success, one of the reasons why he left behind him a great reputation and a considerable fortune.

He did what Irving did—he risked much financially to make Shakespeare a success, and if his comparative wealth was not made out of Shakespeare's plays, he won for himself a bigger

reputation. England and the Empire have reason to be grateful
to him, for he kept the flag of Shakespeare flying when few
others dared attempt it in London. He is the only actor of our
time, except Irving and Sir Frank Benson, who has continuously
and persistently presented Shakespeare's plays, and Benson
worked chiefly in the provinces. The scenic splendour of
Tree's productions has never been excelled by any actor of our
day, his fidelity to histrionic truth was remarkable, his sense of
the theatre was natural and intimate.

No one on the stage could inform a whimsical and weird part
with such an air of verisimilitude as Tree. His striking and
effective Shylock, his Malvolio, his Svengali, his Gringoire, his
Micawber, were examples of this rare art, with many others.
Yet with all his versatility and immense adaptability and appreciation, he had not the heroic gift as had Edwin Booth or Salvini,
but he had gifts which they did not possess, and as an actor he
was greatly beloved by the theatre-going public. With Irving's
death he became, naturally, the head of his profession, and
Wyndham, Hare and Bancroft, actors of a somewhat older
school, accepted him in that light. His tireless energy, with
his instinctive perception, his talent for arranging things in a
dramatic way, his tremendous circle of acquaintances, renowned
and humble, his tact and finesse, made him a natural leader,
and he was strongly supported.

The people of England do not know, I think, that on his last
visit to America he spoke constantly from the stage at every
performance on the war and against the Huns, though there
were many Germans in his audiences. He had the courage of
his convictions. I read many of these speeches, and they were
Imperial in the right spirit, when the United States was slowly
but surely making up her mind what to do. So the last year of
his life was spent as an actor out of his own country, and yet as
a kind of missioner for the Entente. For this special service
his fellow-countrymen owe him a great debt.

One is glad to know that his theatre still prospers, and that
there is worthily maintained within its walls the beautiful spec-
tacular side of Tree's work, but the place will never, in one
sense, be the same again. When people enter it, they will think
of Tree and of his twenty-two years of splendid work there, and

just as the Lyceum became associated always with Irving's name, so will His Majesty's be linked with that of Tree. He has left behind him a wife, one of the wittiest and most brilliant women alive, and very able and clever children. What their sorrow is we can guess. Sir Herbert Beerbohm Tree's work was well done. One cannot say he died too young, but the gods loved him, and he did die young—in spirit, in heart, in imagination. I recall with joy the hours spent in his company, always vivid, human and stimulating, and I mourn his loss. We only fully realize what a notable figure he was among us now that he is gone. "After life's fitful fever he sleeps well." But his name and fame live still.

FROM THE POINT OF VIEW OF A PLAYWRIGHT

By Bernard Shaw

A TRIBUTE to Tree from the playwright's point of view is a duty of such delicacy that it is quite impossible to be delicate about it at all : one must confess bluntly at the outset that Tree was the despair of authors. His attitude towards a play was one of whole-hearted anxiety to solve the problem of how ·to make it please and interest the audience.

Now this is the author's business, not the actor's. The function of the actor is to make the audience imagine for the moment that real things are happening to real people. It is for the author to make the result interesting. If he fails, the actor cannot save the play unless it is so flimsy a thing that the actor can force upon it some figure of his own fancy and play ˏthe author off the stage. This has been done successfully in several well-known, though very uncommon cases. Robert Macaire and Lord Dundreary were imposed by their actors on plays which did not really contain them. Grimaldi's clown was his own invention. These figures died with their creators, though their ghosts still linger on the stage. Irving's Shylock was a creation which he thrust successfully upon Shakespear's play ; indeed, all Irving's impersonations were changelings. His Hamlet and his Lear were to many people more interesting than Shakespear's Hamlet and Lear ; but the two pairs were hardly even related. To the author, Irving was not an actor : he was either a rival or a collaborator who did all the real work. Therefore, he was anathema to master authors, and a godsend to journeymen authors, with the result that he had to confine himself to the works of dead authors who could not interfere

240

with him, and, very occasionally, live authors who were under his thumb because they were unable to command production of their works in other quarters.

Into this tradition of creative acting came Tree as Irving's rival and successor ; and he also, with his restless imagination, felt that he needed nothing from an author but a literary scaffold on which to exhibit his own creations. He, too, turned to Shakespear as to a forest out of which such scaffolding could be hewn without remonstrance from the landlord, and to foreign authors who could not interfere with him, their interests being in the hands of adapters who could not stand up against his supremacy in his own theatre. As far as I could discover, the notion that a play could succeed without any further help from the actor than a simple impersonation of his part never occurred to Tree. The author, whether Shakespear or Shaw, was a lame dog to be helped over the stile by the ingenuity and inventiveness of the actor-producer. How to add and subtract, to interpolate and prune, until an effective result was arrived at, was the problem of production as he saw it. Of living authors of eminence the two he came into personal contact with were Brieux and Henry Arthur Jones ; and I have reason to believe that their experience of him in no way contradicts my own. With contemporary masters of the stage like Pinero and Carton, in whose works the stage business is an integral part of the play, and the producer, when he is not the author in person, is an executant and not an inventor, Tree had never worked ; and when he at last came upon the species in me, and found that, instead of having to discover how to make an effective histrionic entertainment on the basis of such scraps of my dialogue as might prove useful, he had only to fit himself into a jig-saw puzzle cut out by me, and just to act his part as well as he could, he could neither grasp the situation nor resist the impersonal compulsion of arrangements which he had not made, and was driven to accept only by the fact that they were the only ones which would work. But to the very end they bewildered him ; and he had to go to the box office to assure himself that the omission of his customary care had not produced disastrous results.

Just before the production of my play we lunched together at the Royal Automobile Club. I said to him : " Have you

noticed during the rehearsals that though you and I are no longer
young, and have achieved all the success possible in our respective
professions, we have been treating one another throughout as
beginners ? " To this, on reflection, he had to assent, because
we actually were, relatively to one another, beginners. I had
never had to deal with him professionally before, nor he with
me ; and he was quite unaccustomed to double harness, whilst I
was so accustomed to every extremity of multiple harness, both
in politics and in the theatre, that I had been trained to foresee
everything and consider everybody. Now if I were to say that
Tree foresaw nothing and considered nobody, I should suggest
that he was a much less amiable man than he was. Let me
therefore say that he never foresaw anything or considered
anybody in cold blood. Of the foresight which foresees and
faces entirely uninteresting facts, and the consideration which
considers entirely uninteresting persons, he had as little as a
man can have without being run over in the street. When his
feelings were engaged, he was human and even shrewd and
tenacious. But you really could not lodge an indifferent fact
in his mind. This disability of his was carried to such. a degree
that he could not remember the passages in a play which did not
belong to or bear directly upon his own conception of his own
part : even the longest run did not mitigate his surprise when
they recurred. Thus he never fell into that commonest fault of
the actor : the betrayal to the audience that he knows what his
interlocutor is going to say, and is waiting wearily for his cue
instead of conversing with him. Tree always seemed to have
heard the lines of the other performers for the first time, and
even to be a little taken aback by them.

Let me give an extreme instance of this. In Pygmalion the
heroine, in a rage, throws the hero's slippers in his face. When
we rehearsed this for the first time, I had taken care to have
a very soft pair of velvet slippers provided ; for I knew that
Mrs. Patrick Campbell was very dexterous, very strong, and a
dead shot. And, sure enough, when we reached this passage,
Tree got the slippers well and truly delivered with unerring aim
bang in his face. The effect was appalling. He had totally forgotten that there was any such incident in the play ; and it
seemed to him that Mrs. Campbell, suddenly giving way to an

Photo by]

HENRY HIGGINS IN " PYGMALION."

[F. Burford.

impulse of diabolical wrath and hatred, had committed an unpro-
voked and brutal assault on him. The physical impact was
nothing ; but the wound to his feelings was terrible. He collapsed
on the nearest chair, and left me staring in amazement, whilst
the entire personnel of the theatre crowded solicitously round
him, explaining that the incident was part of the play, and
even exhibiting the prompt-book to prove their words. But his
moral was so shattered that it took quite a long time, and a
good deal of skilful rallying and coaxing from Mrs. Campbell,
before he was in a condition to resume the rehearsal. The
worst of it was that as it was quite evident that he would be just
as surprised and wounded next time, Mrs. Campbell took care
that the slippers should never hit him again, and the incident
was consequently one of the least convincing in the performance.

This, and many similar scenes that are told of Tree, will not
be believed by experienced men of business. They will say curtly
that it is no use trying to stuff them with stories like that :
that running a theatre like His Majesty's must have been a big
business, and that no man could possibly have done it for so
long without being too capable and wide-awake to forget everything that did not amuse or interest him. But they will be quite
wrong. Theatrical business is not like other business. A man
may enter on the management of a theatre without business
habits or knowledge, and at the end of forty years of it know
less about business than when he began. The explanation is
that a London West-End theatre is always either making such an
enormous profit that the utmost waste caused by unbusinesslike
management is not worth considering, or else losing so much that
the strictest economy cannot arrest the process by a halfpenny
in the pound. In an industrial concern the addition of a penny
to the piecework rate or the hourly time rate of wages, the
slowing of a steam engine by a few revolutions, the retention of
a machine two years out-of-date, or the loss of fifteen minutes
work in the day by unpunctuality, may make all the difference
between profit and bankruptcy. The employer is held to rigid
conditions by a stringent factory code enforced by a Government inspector on the one hand and by a jealous trade union
on the other. He is the creature of circumstance and the slave
of law, with so little liberty for sentiment and caprice that he

very soon loses not only the habit of indulging them but even the sense of possessing them. Not so the manager of a theatre. Tree was accustomed to make two hundred per cent. profit every day when he was in luck. With such a margin to play with, it was no more worth his while to economize or remember uninteresting things than it was to walk when there was a taxi at his beck. When his theatre was built for him, the equipment of its stage, apart from the electric lighting instalment, was exactly what it would have been a hundred years before, except that there were no grooves for side wings. If every employee on the premises had come an hour late every day and had received double wages, the difference in profit would have been hardly worth noticing. A theatre is a maddening plac* to a thrifty man of business, and an economic paradise to an artist, because there is practically no limit to the waste of time and money that may go on, provided the doors are open every night and the curtain up half an hour later. But for this necessity, and a few County Council bye-laws, an actor-manager would be as unbridled as Nero, without even the Neronian check of a Prætorian Guard to kill him if he went beyond all bearing.

There is no denying that such conditions put a strain on human character that it can seldom sustain without injury. If Tree's caprices, and his likes and dislikes, had not been on the whole amiable, the irresponsibility and power of his position would have made a fiend of him. As it was, they produced the oddest results. He was always attended in the theatre by a retinue of persons with no defined business there, who were yet on the salary list. There was one capable gentleman who could get things done; and I decided to treat him as the stage manager ; but until I saw his name in the bill under that heading I never felt sure that he was not some casual acquaintance whom Tree had met in the club or in the street and invited to come in and make himself at home. Tree did not know what a stage manager was, just as he did not know what an author was. He had not even made up his mind any too definitely what an actor was. One moment he would surprise and delight his courtiers (for that is the nearest word I can find for his staff and entourage) by some stroke of kindness and friendliness. The next he would commit some appalling breach of etiquette by utterly ignoring their functions and privileges, when they had any. It was amiable and modest in him not to know his own place, since it was the highest in the theatre; but it was exasperating in him not to know anyone else's. I very soon gave up all expectation of being treated otherwise than as a friend who had dropped in; so, finding myself as free to interfere in the proceedings as anyone else who dropped in would apparently have been, I interfered not only in my proper department but in every other as well; and nobody gainsaid me. One day I interfered to such an extent that Tree was moved to a mildly sarcastic remonstrance. "I seem to have heard or read somewhere," he said, "that plays have actually been produced, and performances given, in this theatre, under its present management, before you came. According to you, that couldn't have happened. How do you account for it?" "I can't account for it," I replied, with the blunt good faith of a desperate man. "I suppose you put a notice in the papers that a performance will take place at half-past eight, and take the money at the doors. Then you *have* to do the play somehow. There is no other way of accounting for it." On two such occasions it seemed so brutal to worry him, and so hopeless to advance matters beyond the preliminary arrangement of the stage business (which I had already done) that I told him quite cordially to put the play through in his own way, and shook the dust of the theatre from my feet. On both occasions I had to yield to urgent appeals from other members of the cast to return and extricate them from a hopeless mess; and on both occasions Tree took leave of me as if it had been very kind of me to look in as I was passing to see his rehearsals, and received me on my return as if it were still more friendly of me to come back and see how he was getting on. I tried once or twice to believe that he was only pulling my leg; but that was incredible: his sincerity and insensibility were only too obvious. Finally, I had to fight my way through to a sort of production in the face of an unresisting, amusing, friendly, but heart-breakingly obstructive principal.

We finally agreed that I should have been an actor and he an author; and he always sent me his books afterwards. As a matter of fact, he had a very marked literary talent, and, even as an amateur, achieved a finish of style and sureness of execution that was not always evident in his acting, especially when, as in the case of Pygmalion, he had to impersonate a sort of man he had never met and of whom he had no conception. He tried hard to induce me to let him play the dustman instead of the Miltonic professor of phonetics ; and when he resigned himself to his unnatural task, he set to work to make this disagreeable and incredible person sympathetic in the character of a lover, for which I had left so little room that he was quite baffled until he lit on the happy thought of throwing flowers to Eliza in the very brief interval between the end of the play and the fall of the curtain. If he had not been so amusing, so ingenious, and so entirely well-intentioned he would have driven me crazy. As it was, he made me feel like his grandfather. I should add that he never bore the slightest malice for my air of making the best of a bad job. A few days before his death, when he was incredibly young and sanguine, and made me feel hopelessly old and grumpy, he was discussing a revival of Pygmalion as if it promised to be a renewal of the most delightful experience of our lives. The only reproach he ever addressed to me was for not coming to Pygmalion every night, which he thought the natural duty of an author. I promised to come on the hundredth night, adding rather unkindly that this was equivalent to not coming at all. The hundredth night, however, was reached and survived ; and I redeemed my promise, only to find that he had contributed to my second act a stroke of comic business so outrageously irrelevant that I solemnly cursed the whole enterprise, and bade the delinquents farewell for ever.

The fact that Tree could do and be done by thus without bloodshed, although he had all the sensitiveness of his profession, and all the unrestrained impulsiveness of a man who had succeeded in placing himself above discipline from the beginning of his adult life, shews that he was never quite unpardonable ; and though this, to the world that knows nothing of the theatre, may seem more of an apology than a tribute, those who know the theatre best will understand its value. It has to be considered, too, that the statement that he did nothing unpardonable does not imply that he did nothing irreparable. Almost all the wrongs and errors of the West-End London theatre are like the wrongs and errors of the battlefield : they cannot be undone. If an actor's or an author's chance is spoilt, it is spoilt for years and perhaps for ever : neither play nor part gets a second chance. I doubt whether there is an actor-manager living who has not done both these wrongs more than once. Tree was no exception; but as the result, like that of the elephant sitting on the hen's eggs, was never intended, it was impossible to bear malice for long. I have seen him try to help a very able Shakespearean actor, and, incidentally, to help Shakespear, through what he thought a tedious scene, by pretending to catch flies, with ruinous consequences to both player and Bard. He put a new complexion on Brieux's *La Foi*, with effects on the feelings of that illustrious author which I shall not attempt to describe. He meant equally well on both occasions.

And here I come to a source of friction between authors and actor-managers which is worth explaining with some care, as it bears on the general need in England for a school of physical training for the arts of public life as distinguished from the sports. An author who understands acting, and writes for the actor as a composer writes for an instrument, giving it the material suitable to its range, tone, character, agility and mechanism, necessarily assumes a certain technical accomplishment common to all actors ; and this requires the existence of a school of acting, or at least a tradition. Now we had no such provision in the days of Tree's novitiate. He had not inherited the tradition handed down at rehearsal by Phelps to Forbes Robertson ; nor was there any academic institution with authority enough to impress a novice of his calibre. To save others from this disadvantage he later on founded the Academy of Dramatic Art in Gower Street, which now supplies the want as far as an unendowed institution can. But he had to do without teaching himself. Like Irving, he had to make a style and technique out of his own personality : that is, out of his peculiar weaknesses as well as his peculiar powers. And here he sowed dragons' teeth between himself and the authors. For no uncommissioned author can write for an idiosyncratic style and technique : he knows only the classical one. He must, like Shakespear, assume an executant who can perform and sustain certain physical feats of deportment, and build up vocal climaxes with his voice through a long crescendo of rhetoric. Further, he assumes the possession of an English voice and an English feeling for splendour of language and rhythm of verse. Such professional skill and national gift are not accidents of personality : they are more or less within every Englishman's capacity. By themselves they will no more make an actor than grammar and spelling will make an author, or fingering and blowing a bandsman ; but one expects every actor to possess them, just as one expects every author to parse and spell correctly and every bandsman to finger and blow properly.

Tree, like so many of our actors who have picked up their profession on the stage without systematic training, found that he could not produce these stock effects. When they were demanded by the author, he had to find a way round them, and, if possible, an interesting way. Thus he had not only to struggle against his handicap, but to triumph over it by turning it into an advantage. And his handicap was not a light one. Instead of that neutral figure which an actor can turn into anything he pleases, he was tall, and built like nobody else on earth. His Dutch extraction gave him an un-English voice, which, again, was like nobody else's voice and could not be disguised. His feeling for verbal music was entirely non-Miltonic : he had a music of his own ; but it was not the music characteristic of English rhetoric ; and blank verse, as such, had no charm for him ; nor, I suspect, did he credit it with charm for anyone else.

The results were most marked in his Shakespearean work, and would certainly have produced curious scenes at rehearsal had the author been present. No doubt it is an exaggeration to say that the only unforgettable passages in his Shakespearean acting are those of which Tree and not Shakespear was the author. His Wolsey, which was a " straight " performance of high merit and dignity, could be cited to the contrary. But take, for examples, his Richard II. and his Malvolio. One of the most moving points in his Richard was made with the assistance of a dog who does not appear among Shakespear's *dramatis personæ*. When the dog—Richard's pet dog—turned to Bolingbroke and licked his hand, Richard's heart broke ; and he left the stage with a sob. Next to this came his treatment of the entry of Bolingbroke and the deposed Richard into London.

Shakespear makes the Duke of York describe it. Nothing could be easier, with a well-trained actor at hand. And nothing could be more difficult and inconvenient than to bring horses on the stage and represent it in action. But this is just what Tree did. One still remembers that great white horse, and the look of hunted terror with which Richard turned his head as the crowd hooted him. It passed in a moment ; and it flatly contradicted Shakespear's description of the saint-like patience of Richard ; but the effect was intense : no one but Chaliapine has since done so much by a single look and an appearance for an instant on horseback. Again, one remembers how Richard walked out of Westminster Hall after his abdication.

Turn now to the scenes in which Shakespear has given the actor a profusion of rhetoric to declaim. Take the famous " For God's sake let us sit upon the ground, and tell sad stories of the death of kings." My sole recollection of that scene is that when I was sitting in the stalls listening to it, a paper was passed to me. I opened it and read : " If you will rise and move a resolution, I will second it.—Murray Carson." The late Murray Carson was, above all things, an elocutionist ; and the scene was going for nothing. Tree was giving Shakespear, at immense trouble and expense, and with extraordinary executive cunning, a great deal that Shakespear had not asked for, and denying him something much simpler that he did ask for, and set great store by.

As Malvolio, Tree was inspired to provide himself with four smaller Malvolios, who aped the great chamberlain in dress, in manners, in deportment. He had a magnificent flight of stairs on the stage ; and when he was descending it majestically, he slipped and fell with a crash sitting. Mere clowning, you will say ; but no : the fall was not the point. Tree, without betraying the smallest discomfiture, raised his eyeglass and surveyed the landscape as if he had sat down on purpose. This, like the four satellite Malvolios, was not only funny but subtle. But when he came to speak those lines with which any old Shakespearean hand can draw a laugh by a simple trick of the voice, Tree made nothing of them, not knowing a game which he had never studied.

Even if our actors came to the stage with complete executive mastery of all the traditions and all the conventions, there would still be a conflict between the actor's tendency to adapt the play to his own personality, and the author's desire to adapt the actor's personality to the play. But this would not make any serious trouble between them ; for a good part can be played a dozen different ways by a dozen different actors and be none the worse : no author worth his salt attaches a definite and invariable physiognomy to each variety of human character. Every actor must be allowed to apply his own methods to his own playing. But if, as under our system, an actor, instead of laying the foundation of a general technique of speech and action, is driven, by the absence of any school in which he can acquire such a technique, to develop his own personality, and acquire a technique of exploiting that personality which is not applicable to any other purpose, then there will be friction at rehearsals if the author produces his own play, as all authors should. For the actor will inevitably try to force a changeling on the author. He will say, in effect: " I will not play this part that you have written ; but I will substitute one of my own which is ever so much better." And it will be useless for the author to assert himself, and say : " You *shall* play the part as I have written it." If he knows his business, he will see that the " will not " of the actor really means " cannot," because the author has written for a classical technique which the actor does not possess and cannot learn in three weeks, or even three years. It is better to let the actor do what he can : indeed, there is no alternative.

What Tree could do was always entertaining in some way or other. But, for better for worse, it was hardly ever what the author meant him to do. His parts were his avatars ; and the play had to stand the descent of the deity into it as best it could. Sometimes, as in my case, the author understood the situation and made the best of it. Sometimes, no doubt, the author either did not understand the situation or would not make the best of it. But Tree could not act otherwise than as he did ; and his productions represented an output of invention on his part that may have supplied many deficiencies in the plays.

One of his ambitions was to create a Tree Don Quixote. He used to discuss this with me eagerly as a project we might carry out together. " What I see," he said, " is a room full of men in evening dress smoking. Somebody mentions the Don. They begin talking about him. They wonder what he would make of our modern civilization. The back wall vanishes ; and there is Piccadilly, with all the buses and cabs coming towards you in a stream of traffic ; and with them, in the middle, the long tall figure in armour on the lean horse, amazing, foreign, incongruous, and yet impressive, right in the centre of the picture." "That is really a very good idea," I would say. " I must certainly carry it out. But how could we manage the buses and things ? " " Yes," he would go on, not listening to me after my first words of approval : " there you see him going down the mountain-side in Spain just after dawn, through the mist, you know, on the horse, and——" " And Calvert as Sancho Panza on the ass," I would say. That always surprised him. " Yes," he would say slowly. " Yes. Sancho, of course. Oh, yes." Though he had quite forgotten Sancho, yet, switching instantly over to his Falstaff line, he would begin to consider whether he could not double the two parts, as he doubled Micawber and Peggotty. For your true actor is still what he was in the days of Bottom : he wants to play every part in the comedy.

But the heart of the matter (which I have been coming to slowly all this time) is that the cure for the disease of actor-managership (every author must take that pathological view of it) is actor-author-managership : the cure of Molière, who acted his plays as well as wrote them, and managed his theatre into the bargain. And yet he lasted fifty-one years. Richard Wagner was author-composer-conductor-manager at Bayreuth : a much more arduous combination. Tree should have written his own plays. He could have done so. He had actually begun to do it as Shakespear and Molière began, by tinkering other men's plays. The conflict that raged between him and me at the rehearsals in his theatre would then have taken place in his own bosom. He would have taken a parental pride in other parts beside his own. He would have come to care for a play as a play, and to understand that it has powers over the audience even when it is read by people sitting round a table or performed by wooden marionettes. It would have developed that talent of his that wasted itself in *jeux d'esprit* and epigrams. And it would have given him what he was always craving from authors, and in the nature of the case could never get from them : a perfect projection of the great Tree

personality.   What did he care for Higgins or Hamlet ?   His real
objective was his amazing self.   That also was Shakespear's
objective in Hamlet ; but Shakespear was not Tree, and therefore Hamlet could never be to Tree what Hamlet was to Shakespear.   For with all his cleverness in the disguises of the actor's
dressing-room, Tree was no mere character actor.   The character
actor never dares to appear frankly in his own person : he is the
victim of a mortal shyness that agonizes and paralyses him when
his mask is stripped off and his cothurnus snatched from beneath
his feet.   Tree, on the contrary, broke through all his stage
disguises : they were his robes of state ; and he was never happier
than when he stepped in front of the curtain and spoke in his own
immensity to the audience, if not as deep calling unto deep (for
the audience could not play up to him as splendidly as that), at
least as a monarch to his courtiers.

    I trust in this volume he may find his bard, as Elliston found
Charles Lamb.   It is my misfortune that I cannot do him justice,
because, as author and actor, we two were rivals who regarded
one another as usurpers.   Happily, no bones were broken in the
encounter ; and if there is any malice in my description of it, I
hope I have explained sufficiently to enable the reader to make the
necessary allowance and correction.

    December, 1919.

Photo by]   [C. Vandyk, Ltd.

HERBERT TREE 1914.

AN OPEN LETTER TO AN AMERICAN FRIEND*

By W. L. Courtney

You ask me to give you some idea of Herbert Tree—what principles he stood for in art, what was his contribution to the English stage, what was the basis of his personal popularity. And I find it hard to give you satisfactory answers, for two reasons, one of which has to do with you and the other with myself. Let me take the latter first. I have been a friend of Tree for more than a quarter of a century—a rather intimate friend, with whom he would discuss matters concerning which he would remain silent with others. He talked freely with me because he thought (and I hope he thought rightly) that I would understand him and sympathize with him. Therefore, now that he is dead, you may be sure that I shall instinctively take his part, and though I may suggest certain lines of criticism, I shall naturally be inclined to laudation rather than censure. I was fond of Tree, and because he had a real affectionateness of disposition—which sometimes he carefully disguised—companionship with him was always easy and pleasant, and to me delightful.

And now let me turn to your side of the question. I take it that judging Tree entirely from the outside, you have sometimes wondered why, on this side of the Atlantic, we thought so much of him. You were aware that his first visit to America some years ago was more or less of a failure, and that his idiosyncrasies struck people in that continent more forcibly than his positive qualities. On the occasion of his last visit you were minded to make exceptions and discover differences ; you tolerated his Cardinal Wolsey, though the slow delivery of

* First printed in *The Fortnightly Review*, August, 1917.

his speeches irritated you ; you admired the sumptuous manner
in which the play was set on the stage, though sometimes you
thought that the frame was too ornate for the picture.   When it
came to Thackeray, you frankly rebelled.   You considered his
Colonel Newcome *not* the ideal of an English gentleman, but the
laborious effort of an actor to look like it ; it seemed to you
that the pathos was wrong, the humour sometimes misplaced,
the sentimentality too much in evidence.   You never saw Tree
in Dickens, did you ?   I ask because in *David Copperfield* Tree
gave two performances, both of them admirable.   He was both
Dan'l Peggotty and Micawber, and of the two I think the Peggotty
was the better.   He was also a very vivid and picturesque
Fagin.   And the moral of my remark is that the pathos of Dickens,
the humour of Dickens, the sentimentality of Dickens suited Tree's
art better than the similar qualities (which exist in a very different
form) in Thackeray.   If Tree had been a reader of books—he
emphatically was not—he might have understood Thackeray
better.   You cannot get at the author of " Vanity Fair " from
the outside, or by any ingenious or brilliant *a priori* methods ;
you have got to live with him in prolonged intimacy ; his books
must be at your bedside ; his curious, elusive spirit, half-preacher,
half-cynic, must be your constant companion.   With Dickens
it is different.   You can have a very good bowing acquaintance
with Dickens and do him little or no injustice.   His characters
have the melodramatic tinge and strike one easily and forcibly.
They are not pure creations of the Comic Spirit like some of the
characters of Thackeray and Meredith.   Farce, sheer, undiluted
Farce, enters into them so largely that for stage purposes they
suit admirably an actor with a frank liking for caricature.

And that reminds me that you have not seen—I do not think
I am wrong—Tree's Falstaff or his Malvolio.   You have missed
a good deal, though, perhaps, you would have had the uneasy
feeling that these, too, bordered on caricature.   But did not
Shakespeare intend them for caricature ?   I am thinking for the
moment of Falstaff in the *Merry Wives of Windsor*, not of the
hero of Eastcheap.   In the historical plays Falstaff is far too
prodigious a creature to be included in any of our usual cate-
gories.   He is a world in himself.   He has an overpowering
humour and a most wistful pathos.   He is Every-man, enlisted

in a riotous conception of life and working to his doom with a blithe, devil-may-care recklessness. Shakespeare never traced on his canvas a more wonderful being, so detestable and so lovable. But Falstaff in the *Merry Wives is* a caricature, and Tree, who accepted him as such, gave a ripe, unctuous performance of an All-fatness, oozing out drink and a maudlin sentimentality at every pore, which was quite irresistible. Malvolio belongs to the same order of humanity, the fatuous egotist, the pedantic megalomaniac. Tree was clearly doubtful whether average audiences would understand the conception, for he repeated Malvolio in the servants who formed his retinue and who, in their turn, caricatured the caricature. In the heyday of Malvolio's pompous idiocy Tree excelled ; when it came to the poor pedant, bullied, imprisoned and tortured, it was, of course, another matter. But has anyone reconciled the earlier and the later Malvolio ? Henry Ainley, who did so well in the part at the Savoy Theatre, found himself confronted with the same difficulty.

You will have gathered, of course, that versatility was Tree's chief characteristic, or, as some might say, his besetting sin. Versatile he undoubtedly was ; he tried to show his skill in very different fields of dramatic work. He essayed tragic rôles—at one time he was very anxious to act King Lear, as a pendant or culmination to his Macbeth, his Othello, his Hamlet. He was a comedian either with or without a touch of melodrama ; he made his name originally in farce, as those know who saw his *Private Secretary.* Versatility is undoubtedly a perilous gift ; you know how a so-called versatile man is supposed to waste himself and his talents in many channels of activity—and to succeed in none. I have said a " so-called versatile man " because no man is really versatile ; he only thinks he is, or is idly so reported by others. There is always one thing he does which is better than others, despite his many-sidedness, and if he is wise, he will discover what it is and cultivate it to the best of his ability. Tree liked to be considered many-sided ; indeed, he resented any suggestion to the contrary, and for this reason, I suppose, wrote two books, though he ostentatiously declared that he was not a book-reader. His restless and unbounded activity was compelled to show itself in various fields ; I do not think I ever came across any man who was more pertinaciously and assiduously alive. He was " a dragon for work," as they say, and had a greater range of vivid interests —literary, political, social, dramatic—than most of us can lay claim to. His quick alertness of spirit, his ready apprehension, his humour—which at times verged on the *macabre*—made him a most stimulating companion. He always saw objects from the less obvious standpoints and delighted in all that was unconventional and paradoxical. His wit was never mordant, nor was it always very pointed. And his epigrams were for the most part ebullitions of high spirits.

But if you ask me in what, within his own proper sphere of work, the dramatic, Tree was best, I answer without hesitation. It was, as perhaps you might gather from what has just been said, in the representation of fantastic, eccentric, bizarre characters, characters with a twist in them which made them peculiar and original. Here a long list of successes testifies to the actor's easy mastery. I take some names—just as they occur—Svengali in *Trilby* first and foremost, a fascinating study ; the hero and villain in *A Man's Shadow ;* Izard in *Business is Business ;* Captain Swift ; Montjoye in *A Bunch of Violets ;* the spectacled Russian detective Demetrius in *The Red Lamp ;* Dr. Stockmann in *The Enemy of the People*—there is so long a list that I should weary you if I gave even a tithe of them. But let me add at least the curiously sympathetic impersonation of Caliban, a really remarkable effort of imagination in the sphere of animality, which was in its way quite as illuminating as Browning's *Caliban on Setebos*. To see Tree make up for his part was a privilege I often enjoyed. There in his dressing-room you saw the artist at work, the creative artist who adds touch after touch to complete the picture, until suddenly the whole conception bursts into significant life. When Tree had thoroughly got inside the skin of a character—which often took some time—he seemed to partake of a new and alien life. A singular illustration was Zakkuri in the *Darling of the Gods*, in which by degrees Tree gave us, I do not say a true, but an extraordinarily vivid and convincing portrait of a Japanese statesman in all his horrible subtlety and coarseness. Another example was Izard in *Business is Business*. Tree was never a smoker in the true sense of the word ; he only smoked for the sake of companionship, taking a modest fourpenny cigar, while he gave his guest Coronas. But in Izard he was perpetually smoking big and black-looking cigars. I asked him how he managed to stand it ; he answered that, as it seemed natural to the character, he found it easy for himself. Off the stage he could not have done it ; on the stage it was appropriate and therefore a piece of unconscious mimicry. Svengali smoked, I think, cigarettes or long Vevey *fins*. The Duke of Guisebury smoked, quite as to the manner born, a pipe—a luxury in which Tree, the individual, not the actor, never indulged.

You must forgive me for rambling on in this desultory fashion ; I want you to understand how, for those who knew him and liked him, Tree the man, over and above all the parts he assumed, gained his great personal ascendancy. It is Tree the man I remember now, and, doubtless, my appreciation of his personality colours all my judgment of his acting. It is Tree the man who figures in my memory, and perhaps his shade—if such things can vex those who have passed into the land of shadows—is inclined to rebuke me for writing about him. For I recall an incident bearing on the point. He asked me one night at supper at the " Garrick " what I had been writing. I answered that I had been trying to write an obituary of my friend, H. D. Traill. " That must be an odious task," he said ; " the more you like a man the less ought you to write about him." I agreed, but remarked that journalism required such heavy sacrifices of feeling and affection ; and that, anyway, it was better that an obituary notice should be written by a friend than by a merely critical observer. This is my only defence now in taking up my pen. In many ways I should have preferred to be silent. To say nothing is the only becoming attitude for friendship. But however more congenial it may be to be silent and to remember, there are other considerations which are bound to be operative. " You are always a little cold when you write about me," Tree said to me once. " Is not that natural ? " I replied. " You know the old adage about a cold hand and a warm heart." " It is all very well to dissemble your love. But why did you kick me downstairs ? " Tree quoted gaily. " But, of course, I understand," he added with a genial smile. As a matter of fact, we never had even the slightest difference in all the twenty-seven years of companionship. With most men he had an open, genial manner which they found very attractive. Even his occasional affectations—which no one laughed at more heartily than Tree himself, but which obviously he could not help—did not annoy them, because they found them amusing. I am not sure, however, whether women understood him as well as men—any more than the average woman can understand why to some of us Falstaff is as great a creation as Hamlet.

Yes, I know what you are thinking at this moment. You imagine that I shrink from the main issue and that I am toying with purely subsidiary points just because I find it difficult to solve your main problem. I answer, however, that some things, perhaps subsidiary and unessential as you feel, must be understood first before we are in any position to arrive at a positive conclusion. Let us admit without reserve that Tree as a personality was greater than anything he accomplished; but you must allow me to observe that that in itself is a compliment, and in the case of many artists a very great one. Moreover, it makes no little difference in the result how and in what spirit you approach the consideration of a character. To me the important point is to ask what a man can do, not to worry yourself about what he cannot do. The latter attitude leads to purely barren criticism and an enumeration of unilluminating negatives. The former gives one interesting glimpses of psychology. It is the same with other things besides men. It is true of a piece of mechanism like a bicycle or a motor-car; it is true also of a dog or a semi-personal being, like a ship. You will never get the best out of such objects, you will never get the best out of ordinary human relations, unless the positive occupies you more than the negative, what can be done rather than what cannot. Do not smile at such truisms. So far as I can judge, they are often quite curiously and wantonly disregarded by many men, most women, and a large proportion of critics.

Somewhere—I think in " The Mirror of the Sea "—Mr. Joseph Conrad remarks that certain ship-masters are like Royal Academicians. They are eminently safe, but they never startle

you by a fresh audacity of inspiration or a touch of originality.
There are actors of a similar kind. They are quite sure of
themselves, they can be trusted to do the right thing at the
proper moment, they are recognized leaders of the profession
who will always give you the same sort of acting, quite good,
quite reputable, quite adequate (hateful word !), but devoid of
any disturbing brightness of emotion or fancy. No one could
charge Tree with belonging to this solemn order of artist. He
was always unexpected, daring, original ; he often gave one a
shock of surprise, welcome or unwelcome. He was good when
you anticipated a relative failure ; poor, when you could have
wagered on his success. His acting was never monotonous, rarely
the same from night to night. Like his conversation, it was full
of quick turns and unlooked-for spurts of vivid, graphic, picturesque, satisfying the eye, even when occasionally he failed to
satisfy the mind. When he was acting Mark Antony in the
Forum scene he broke off the famous speech in the middle, came
down from the rostrum, and finished his speech standing on a
broken pillar. I argued with him about this, suggesting that
if Mark Antony was really holding his audience he would never
have altered his position. Tree answered : " You forget the soon-
wearied eye of the spectator ; he becomes tired of one situation
and demands another. Besides," he added, with a whimsical
smile, " change is a necessity for my nature." It was indeed.
And, owing to this he became tired and bored with his part,
and sometimes broke off the run of a piece in the midst of a brilliant
success ! I anticipate what you will say, my critical friend !
You will remind me that I am describing the qualities of an
amateur, not of a professional. I do not shrink from the conclusion. Tree had all the best points of an amateur, and some
of his triumphs were gained just for that reason. He was a
glorified amateur who dared things which a professional never
would have dared, and won a shining victory. He mistrusted
all talk about technique. " I have not got technique," he once
said ; " it is a dull thing. It enslaves the imagination." And
when he established his school in Gower Street, in which I was
able to render some small help, he retained some doubts, which
were afterwards dispelled. " You cannot teach acting," he
said. No, but you can prepare the groundwork by means of which

the natural aptitude gets its chance.   And this he subsequently
recognized to be the case.

What were the positive contributions of Herbert Tree to the
English stage ?   Here, there is some room for dissent and dis-
agreement ; I will only put down certain facts in the form
in which they appear to me.   Remember, in the first place, that
he inherited a great tradition from Henry Irving, who had set a
magnificent example of stage-production at the Lyceum.   Tree
was at first content to carry on the tradition on similar lines.
He produced plays with extreme care for detail and many
appeals to the eye.   There was never anything slipshod either
in the method of stage representation or in the attention paid
to what the diplomats call " imponderabilia."   Indeed, it was
the care taken over the minutiæ which guaranteed the effectiveness of the whole.   Thanks in especial to Irving and Tree, London stage-production reached a higher level of completeness
and finish than was to be seen in foreign capitals.   Sarah Bernhardt and other foreign visitors acknowledged that in this respect
they did not do things better in France.   Gradually Tree bettered
the examples of his predecessors.   His critics said he over-
elaborated his effects ; his friends were never tired of welcoming
new grades of beauty.   I take only two instances out of many
which offer themselves in recollection.   Probably there never
was a more beautiful stage picture than Olivia's pleasaunce
in *Twelfth Night*.   We talk of the hanging gardens of Babylon
as of something legendary and rare.   Here before our eyes
were to be seen Olivia's hanging gardens, a dream of exquisite
and appealing beauty which seemed to bring out the more
clearly by contrast the vulgarity and coarseness of Sir Toby
Belch and Sir Andrew Aguecheek, while it enhanced the delicacy
of Viola and Olivia herself.   The other example I will take
from the *Midsummer Night's Dream*.   You will recall that,
though the scene is supposed to be laid in the neighbourhood
of Athens, the feeling, the atmosphere of the play belong
essentially to Stratford and England.   Accordingly, Tree gave
us, alternately with some marble seats and olive trees, splendid
glimpses of British forests in which the fairies ran wild and
Bottom and his companions rehearsed their uncouth theatricals.
Anything more restful to the eye than these glades of sylvan

beauty I have never seen on any stage. I used to drop into the theatre while the play was going on just to realize once more the solemn delightful effect of the old beeches sheltering the wayward fancies of Oberon, Titania and Puck, and providing a rehearsal ground for *Pyramus and Thisbe*. I must also add something about the elaborate scene at the end of the play when the pillars of the Duke's palace glow with internal light to enable the fairies to carry on their domestic tasks of making everything clean and sweet for the mortals. It was beautiful, but perhaps too elaborate. One missed in this case the note of simplicity, the wise sobriety of an accomplished artist who would not strive " to do better than well " lest he should " confound his skill in covetousness." There were charming pictures, too, in the *Tempest*, little sea-fairies peeping round the edges of the rocks, while Ariel sported in the pools, which one remembers with gratitude. But, indeed, the time would fail me if I were to recount half the wonders which the magician Tree displayed before our eyes in play after play. You may call him a consummate decorator, if you like, *le Tapissier de notre Théâtre*, as Luxemburg—was it not ?—was called by reason of his conquest of flags and other costly stuff, *le Tapissier de Notre-Dame*. But I maintain that he had the eye, the feeling, the touch of an artist.

It would be a small matter to decorate the outside of the vase if it did not contain within itself rare and exquisite essences. Tree soon realized that decoration in itself could only please the groundlings or the dilettantes, and that the main matter of consequence was the spirit in which the whole adventure was attempted. What was the character of the adventure ? It was to give the British stage dignity as well as charm, high seriousness as well as æsthetic adornment. It was for this reason that from time to time he put before his public—a *clientèle*, by the way, which was always steadily growing—stately performances of Shakespearean plays, incidentally proving that our great English dramatist did not necessarily spell bankruptcy, but, judiciously treated, might be made to yield a fair percentage of profit. He varied his programme with lighter fare, as a matter of course ; a man who had undertaken the responsibility of so large a theatre as His

Majesty's was bound to keep a steady eye on the booking-office
and replenish his coffers now and again by popular appeals.
Unfortunately, our public is not always spurred and exalted to
finer issues ; and though Shakespeare under special conditions
can become almost popular, a certain melodramatic blatancy
—or at least insistence—has a more distinct pecuniary appeal.
Where theatres are not supported by municipalities or the State,
the lessee and manager is forced to " go here and there and
make himself a motley to the view " for base considerations of
solvency.   But Tree did not forget the higher obligations of
the position he had attained.   As head of the profession, he
realized his responsibilities.   He was full of the idea of the importance of the theatrical art, as a main instrument of culture
and as a most necessary element in civic and social life.   He
did not work merely for his own hand, but upheld the claims
of his calling.   He instituted a Shakespearean week—a most
costly undertaking—in order to keep alive our indebtedness
to the Elizabethan stage.   He presided at meetings, made
speeches, inaugurated movements, pushed and encouraged various
policies, in order to prove that actors were important elements
in the community who had their proper functions in the body
politic.   You know how many speeches Tree made in the United
States, not because speaking was easy to him—it never was—
but because he felt it to be his duty to represent British interests and ideals in this appalling universal war.   Only a
week or two before his death he told me that he often composed
the speech he was presently going to deliver while he was de-
claiming Wolsey's long " farewell to all his greatness " before
his audience in *Henry VIII*.

   There is no doubt that the career of this well-equipped actor
and most competent manager and lessee had a beneficial effect
on the English stage ; for Tree had a great organizing ability
and admirably quick and valuable intuitions.   But you will
naturally ask me a question which has long been on the tip of
your tongue—I am writing to you as though I actually saw and
witnessed your impatience—the question as to Tree's attitude
towards the future of the dramatic art.   Granted that his
influence on his contemporary public was all to the good, what
about his relation to novel movements and to those efforts

which zealous innovators have made to " reform " the drama ?
The future of the English stage ! Ah, but will you tell me what
is the future ? There was a movement some few years back, to
which I will return presently. But what is the prospect now ?
Looking superficially at existing facts, one might give several
replies. Apparently the tendency at the present moment is
in the direction of light, frivolous entertainments, only intended
to amuse and distract men's minds from the horrible preoccupation with the war. American comedies have had their chance,
and succeeded in proportion to the farcical elements they have
contained. Revues flourish as much as ever—perhaps rather
more than they used to. Composite entertainments, musical,
droll, heterogeneous, are in vogue, especially if they have
enlisted in their company at least one clever woman and one
reputedly clever man. Mr. H. B. Irving, with admirable bold-
ness, tried *Hamlet*, but it had to be withdrawn for want of
support. Serious plays seem to be at a discount, unless, like
M. Brieux's plays, *Les Avariés* and *Les trois filles de M. Dupont*,
and Ibsen's *Ghosts*, they make an appeal which is not mainly
histrionic. Doubtless some of these phenomena are due to the
unreal conditions of the time ; they are symptomatic not of
currents of artistic or inartistic fashion running below the surface, but of our unrest, our weariness, our irrepressible feeling
that, set against the lurid background of ceaseless warfare, no
artistic effort matters very much. Meanwhile our theatres are
full—when they are full—of officers and soldiers on leave, accompanied by their sisters or cousins or lovers, who only want their
military friends to be happy—and this is not the kind of
theatrical audience which cares for dramatic art or even desires
to think at all. Tree brought back from America a piece in
which he strongly believed. *The Great Lover*, I think, was its
name. He had every intention of producing it forthwith ;
but what success it might have secured under present conditions
is an unsolved problem. The great success in London is, of
course, *Chu Chin Chow*, a piece beautifully presented and full
of elaborate and admirable pictures. But it is hardly a play in
the sense in which you and I understand the term.

Still, you remember that there was a movement going on a
few years back, which we associate with Granville Barker and

with a competent body of actors—Ainley, Nicholson, Leon Quartermaine, Lillah McCarthy, and others.*   It was an effort in the direction of greater simplicity of stage presentation and the abolition of long waits between scenes and acts.   It revealed to us, for instance, that some of Shakespeare's plays could be given in three hours without any cuts and omissions—so that we might be seeing the plays more or less as the author intended that we should.   Time was gained by making the actors speak faster, without wearisome pauses and unimpressive silences. I don't think I have ever heard an actor speak with such rapidity as Ainley achieved as Laertes in *A Winter's Tale*.   The movement included some elements of mere freakishness, as when Barker gave the fairies in *Midsummer Night's Dream* gilded faces. But the scenery, though elementary, was to a sufficient degree picturesque, and the acting was persuasively good.   A similar method applied to *Macbeth* or *Othello* would have been very instructive.   Meanwhile *Twelfth Night*, so treated, had a real effectiveness of its own.   And the daring experiment of putting Mr. Hardy's *The Dynasts* on the boards was, within the limits prescribed, a triumph.

I do not think that Tree had much sympathy with this movement.   He took a great interest in it, of course, just as he did in the Russian Ballet, which he visited as often as he could. But so far as I could make out, he preferred older methods. With regard to the Russian Ballet, he once remarked, with no little acuteness, that it struck him as " the gilded plaything of an effete autocracy ; "   and with regard to Granville Barker's productions he seemed to feel—though I do not remember a definite statement—that they were bizarre, freakish experiments, which could only appeal to a section of the public and not to the great mass of theatre-goers.   For himself, remember that he had the vast auditorium of His Majesty's resting on his shoulders, and that he was bound to consider the tastes, not of sections, but of the public at large.   He always insisted on this fact.   " I have to find something which will be agreeable to stalls, upper circle, pit, gallery—all at once."   And directly we think of the many-headed public who keep theatres going,

---

* Mr. Martin Harvey tried similar experiments in *Taming of the Shrew* and *Hamlet*.

and the difficulty there is in finding a common focus for their ardent, unsophisticated enthusiasm and their uncritical approval, we shall begin to recognize the burden laid on theatrical *entrepreneurs*, and the necessary contrast between their point of view and that of irresponsible dramatic critics.

I do not know if I have satisfied your curiosity in these few remarks of mine.   I recognize that yours is a legitimate curiosity from the standpoint of a man like yourself, who stands outside our more intimate interests and desires to view the situation in its broad and general features.   To you Herbert Tree is an actor and a manager who has done certain large things in a large way, and has either succeeded or failed.   To us he is a many-sided personality, in whose case mere histrionic success is only one element in a complex and varied whole.   On one point I think you may feel confidence.   If you admit that Tree fills a conspicuous space in our admiration and regard, you will also have to accept this as a solid fact—even though it may surprise you—with which you have to reckon.   He has had many admirers and no few devoted friends.   He was believed in as a force in our dramatic world, as a man who consistently held a high ideal for our stage, and employed his sympathy, his energy, and his own remarkable powers in a valiant attempt at its realization.   That is a simple fact which cannot be gainsaid ; and it must enter into your general estimate on the other side of the Atlantic, as it has already done and will increasingly do into ours on this side.

A high ideal for the stage ?   Perhaps you stop over this phrase and feel some hesitation in adopting it.   But if you do, you are up against one of those baffling points in psychology which affect many other men besides Tree.   How much of the ideal must be sacrificed in daily practice if anything whatever is to be achieved ?   Does the ideal cease to be an ideal if it ever be forgotten ?   Can one worship the ideal in secret and deny it in the open light of day ?   Is compromise a reputable, even if necessary, policy ?   Ah, who shall scrutinize his conscience without many pangs of self-reproach in questions like these ? That Tree produced some unworthy pieces it would be absurd to deny.   He did, and he knew he did—just as he knew also that he must keep up a great theatrical establishment and transact a vast business, for which the possession of funds was obligatory. I remember one occasion at a club after the production of a gaudy melodrama—I will not mention its name for fear of getting into trouble with the author—when some of us were chaffing—I think you call it " chipping "—Tree concerning some of its banal effects and its " popular " character. He loved being chaffed, or, at all events, he bore it with unflinching good humour, and riposted gaily on his critics. As a matter of fact, the piece was a pecuniary success. But Tree by himself was in a different mood. He knew what he was doing, and was not proud of it. " Compromise, the god of the shiftless," he used to say.

You remember Henry James's ironical little story, " The Lesson of the Master " ? In that you will find the philosophy of the matter. An older novelist preaching to a younger novelist, warns him against being seduced from his high ideals by such encumbrances as a wife and children and the obligation of keeping up a costly and hospitable house. The young writer is duly impressed until he discovers that his mentor—even after his melancholy experience of what marriage can do to deaden aspiration—deliberately marries again, and marries the very girl with whom the young disciple of the master was in love ! How shockingly cynical, one says, and then, after a moment's deliberation, how abominably true ! It is true, my friend, and true of all of us. A little clearer vision and then the clouds come down again. A glimpse of pure high æther of heaven and then the rain-splashed earth. We do what we must and not always what we can. Let him that is without sin cast the first stone. I, at all events, have no wish either to bombard you with truisms or to cast stones at Tree. His was a fine, courageous, indomitable character ; and over and over again, for his delight and ours, he drew from his intellectual instrument the finest music that nature had hidden in it, and played it as it should be played. Peace be to his ashes—he will be much and widely missed. *Multis ille bonis flebilis occidit.*

TIME SHALL NOT ALTER MEMORY

TIME shall not alter memory nor chill
The smile you wore to one of mute despair
Within our hearts, in looking back to where
Your radiant, eager face grew dim and still.
It is so small a thing that time can kill,
And there remains the solemn deathless flare
Of starry thoughts that spangle all the air,
And breathe the breath of forest and of hill.
For there remains the beauty you awoke,
The mutual love that nothing can revoke,
The dreams you beckoned and the words you spoke
That called forth gladness and that smoothed out pain.
Your smile lives still, as sunsets that retain
Their light upon some golden window-pane.

IRIS TREE.

APPENDIX I

SERMON PREACHED BY THE BISHOP OF BIRMINGHAM AT THE MEMORIAL SERVICE, 12TH JULY, 1917

A MEMORIAL SERVICE is not to be confused with the laying to rest of the one departed. I always feel that round the graveside one would only have those with whom the link of love was very close indeed, and that it is more respectful for all except the very inner circle to be absent in body, though they may be earnestly praying and sympathetic at the time of the funeral.

It is therefore good, surely, in the case of a man of many friends and of great public standing, that there should be some opportunity in the House of God of expressing certain almost uncontrollable feelings.

We are here to-day in very truth friends of the great artist and the loyal comrade who has gone so suddenly from us. We desire by our presence to show that we understand something at least of the sorrow which must be felt by those from whom much of the light of life has gone out through their bereavement.

Our friendship we find it easy to declare to-day for a reason given in regard to friendship by Sir Walter Scott : " There is no time when we are disposed to think so highly of a friend as when we find him standing high in the esteem of others." In very truth I doubt whether Sir Herbert Tree ever realized in this earthly life how fond men were of him. He had a kind of absent-mindedness, which some people thought to be almost aloofness, and which held them back at times from the kind of companionship which is the outward expression of affection, but his death has unloosed shy tongues, and as they tell of how much their owners cared for Herbert Tree, so we all are bold to bear our testimony to the fact that we know we have lost one of the small number of the greatly valued, the rare spirits with the magnetic power of making us fond, and with a breadth of sympathy which we only now fully realize.

We desire to testify in a special way to the deep respect we feel for the one in whose memory the Service is held.

We desire again to thank God publicly for the gifts He bestows upon men to enable them to do their life's work, and for the special talents He grants to some people in order to make them useful and blessed influences upon their human kind.

We wish also to mingle our prayers before the Throne of the Great Architect and Ruler of the Universe that everlasting opportunity of useful life may be given in the *other* world to the one of whom we are thinking.

This Service is not one of utter mourning : it is with " one auspicious and one dropping eye " that we are present here to-day.

Sir Herbert Tree was indeed greatly gifted, and he had been wisely guided in the choice of his profession. I am myself of opinion that for dramatic usefulness and success, the actor must be singularly and completely a personality. I do not believe that anyone who is not himself a marked individuality can enter thoroughly into great characters so as sufficiently to absorb their peculiarities to make the spectator and auditor feel the characters are being presented in their very habit, as they lived.

Mediocrity can never personify greatness.

In one of his books Sir Herbert Tree says that it seemed that to him the rarest thing in the world was independence of mind, the faculty of thinking and acting for oneself. He certainly himself exemplified the quality, for he was a man of striking individuality ; he was one to whom his craft was a sacred calling, and whilst this ensured that everything which he himself produced was put out with thoroughness, it made him revolt against anything which was shoddy or even incomplete. In fact, I suppose, now and again, it made him almost impatient with a public taste which was content with the hasty and ill-considered efforts of any who did not feel that it was all-important to give the very best in the cause of Art.

His treatment of Shakespeare on the stage has been questioned, but that he desired to honour the genius by scrupulous care in his expression of the poet's meaning all would acknowledge. His own words express the feeling : " As it is the player's chiefest joy to speak the poet's words upon the stage, so it is his high privilege to trace upon the poet's abiding monument his own fleeting name."

I am not sure that we may not acknowledge first of all as our cause of indebtedness to Sir Herbert Tree that he reminded us that whatever our lot in life may be, all work should be sanctified, and should be all done in the Great Taskmaster's eye.

And yet Sir Herbert was one who could be interested and was interested in matters outside his immediate labours. He was a man with strong national feeling. He had great gifts of expression both by tongue and pen on important matters, and in this hour of strife and of bitter feeling it is not the least of the things that we should be thankful for in Sir Herbert Tree that he was international as well as national in sympathy.

We must never forget that during his last visit to the United States he was a most successful exponent of the position of Great Britain in this awful war. He was an unofficial but most influential ambassador of right.

When sometimes I have watched actors imitating the voice and mannerisms of our friend, I have pondered over the fact that it is just those whose speech and gestures can be most easily imitated, whose depth and force are most difficult to copy. We have heard many people speak in imitation of Sir Herbert Tree, but we have none of us known any man quite like him.

Into the question of his religious feeling and belief I do not to-day intend to enter. That he did believe in the great unseen world and that he had a longing to pass within the veil for the very purpose of understanding more of the True and Eternal Life, I happen to know.

That he recognized the claim upon his loyalty and devotion of the God of all the World, his performance of his great public duties testified. To his own Master he standeth or falleth. God knows better than any of us what we feel towards Him ; nay, even if our heart condemn us, God is greater than our heart, and knoweth all things.

There was something surely typical of the mentality of Sir Herbert Tree in the last words he spoke upon this earth : " Will you open the window ? " and for him, as he uttered the words, the new vision was unveiled.

" Here we see through a glass darkly: " the window opens and we look out upon the landscape beyond and we enjoy a purer and a better air.

May we not confidently believe that as Sir Herbert felt the first freshness of the atmosphere of Paradise, things before only vaguely conceived of, became by him understood, and in very truth a fuller life began.

Our American friends have an expression which they use as to the active people of this earth—they speak of a forceful character as a " live " man. Few people were ever more fitted to that expression than was Sir Herbert Tree. It is impossible to believe in his not having a life " yon side."

> " 'Tis life of which my nerves are scant,
> 'Tis life not death for which I pant,
> More life and fuller that I want."

His imagination was full and his brain was active till that second when the clogged heart stopped. I am sure that the God who used him on this earth has for him, as for all who earnestly strive to do their best with the qualities bestowed upon them, greater and grander work in the realms of Eternity than ever they did here.

And so we leave him, believing that death is not the passing from light to darkness, but from twilight into fullest sunshine.

May we not quote in regard to his passing these lines so familiar to many of us :

> " Life, we have been long together
> In pleasant and in stormy weather ;
> 'Tis hard to part when friends are dear,
> Perchance 'twill cost a sigh, a tear ;
> Then steal away, give little warning,
> Choose thine own time, say not ' good-night,'
> But in some brighter clime bid me ' good-morning.' "

APPENDIX II

SPEECHES MADE AT THE UNVEILING OF THE MEMORIAL TABLET

[From a report in *The Times*, 28th May, 1919.]

Mr. Asquith, at the request of the subscribers, unveiled the memorial tablet to Sir Herbert Tree which has been placed on the Charles Street wall of His Majesty's Theatre.

The memorial, which was designed by Mr. W. H. Romaine-Walker, takes the form of an oval bronze tablet, wreathed with laurel and surmounted by the masks of Tragedy and Comedy. The raised letters upon it are inscribed, " This theatre was founded in 1897 by Herbert Tree, Actor, and directed by him until his death, 1917."

At a meeting inside the theatre, Mr. C. F. Gill, K.C., hon. treasurer of the committee, presided, and he was supported on the stage by Mr. Asquith, Lord Reading, the Bishop of London, Sir Squire Bancroft, and Mme. Clara Butt. The large audience included a great number of Sir Herbert Tree's personal friends, as well as comrades in the theatrical profession.

The Chairman explained that it had been felt that nothing would be more in accordance with Sir Herbert Tree's wishes than the erection of a tablet on the wall of the theatre with which he had been so long associated. No actor that ever lived had been more devoted to his art.

Mr. Asquith, who was received with loud cheers, said :

We have just unveiled, in the open air, a memorial to one of the great artists of our time, fittingly placed where every one who

273

passes by can see it, in the wall of the theatre which he himself
built and for many years directed. It is often said, and said
with truth, that of all the arts that of the actor is the most
evanescent, leaving behind it nothing but a memory which in
time fades into a tradition. Hazlitt, in my judgment one of the
best of our critics both of literature and the drama, once said
that though we have speeches of Burke, portraits of Reynolds,
writings of Goldsmith, and conversations of Johnson, and though
all those four great men were united in their admiration for the
genius of Garrick, yet nothing remained to enable us to recon-
struct and to revive the unique spell which was exercised over
his contemporaries by that most gifted of all actors.

Yet it was Dr. Johnson who said that the greatest thing
about Gárrick was his universality. It is in that sense, and
perhaps only in that sense, that it is true of the most illustrious
and historic figures of the stage that, as Theseus says in *A Midsummer Night's Dream*, " The best in this kind are but shadows."
At the same time, among all artists, there is none towards whom
among the public of his time there is the same sense of gratitude
and personal relationship as the actor. We feel that we share
with him a kind of intimacy which we do not experience with
the painter or the sculptor or even the poet.

I remember in the days of my youth, when Mr. Gladstone
was at the height of his fame and was often called the " Idol of
the Nation," that a shrewd observer once said, " If you were to
take a plebiscite as to who was the most popular man in England,
he would be easily beaten by Dr. W. G. Grace "—(laughter)—
and I cannot help thinking that he would have found a most
formidable competitor in Henry Irving.

Of all the actors of our time there have been few, if any,
for whom that sentiment not only of admiring, but also affectionate, interest has been more widely felt than for Sir Herbert
Tree. (Cheers.) It is not that he adopted catchpenny allure-
ments and artifices which, as Hamlet says, " make the judicious
grieve." He was an artist through and through, and took his
art seriously. He was perhaps the least mercenary of men ;
he was sometimes profuse almost to a fault. There was nothing
that he grudged in time, money, industry, study, even drudgery
itself to the profession to which he had given his life.

That was equally true of him as manager and as actor. The magnificence, not of vulgar display, but arising from infinite painstaking and from a passion for thoroughness, with which he put his pieces on the stage was characteristic of the man. It was the same with the scrupulous care which he gave even to the smallest *minutiæ* of the text in his productions of Shakespeare.

I remember well two years ago, when he had just come back from America, a very few weeks before his lamented death, he came to spend a night with me in the country, and he occupied a considerable time in arguing with humour, and I need not say with ingenuity and persistency, what I thought a flagrant heresy, that in the last scene in *Hamlet* what the Queen really said was not, " He is fat and scant of breath," but " He is faint and scant of breath." That was very characteristic.

It is related of Hogarth, our great painter, that he once said to Garrick, whom he had just seen in one of his most melo-dramatic parts, " You are in your element when you are begrimed with dirt or up to your elbows in blood." Many of us may have been tempted to say the same of Sir Herbert Tree, only to find him a week or two later impersonating with equal naturalness and gusto the most debonair of fine gentlemen or the most supersubtle of diplomatists. The truth is he left nothing to chance in his art, and as an actor he added to his large natural endowment of gifts and graces all the resources of elocution and make-up, and what may be called the ancillary arts of the stage. In range and versatility of parts I believe the unanimous verdict of many experts, whom I see before me, will confirm what I say, that he was unsurpassed by any actor of our time. (Cheers.)

If I may pass just for a moment from what he did as an artist and as manager to some other aspects of his personality, you will, I am sure, agree with me that long before he died he was acknowledged by the whole profession to be one of their natural leaders, a spokesman of singular and almost unique felicity of address, to whom they could always safely entrust the task of making their appeals, whether the claim to be enforced was on behalf of charity or of art. His geniality and spirit of comradeship, as they knew well, could never be too severely tasked.

What he was in the more intimate and less public relations of life only those who, like myself, were privileged for years to enjoy his friendship can realize. I will only say that there is not one of his friends, and they were many, who does not feel the poorer for the loss of that wealth of vitality and that unfailing reservoir of true kindness and affection. But here in this place and in this company let us remember him, as he would most have wished to be remembered, as a worthy, and indeed an outstanding, figure in the great procession of artists, the Burbages, the Bettertons, the Garricks, the Keans, whose memory is the treasured inheritance of the English stage. (Cheers.)

LORD READING : I thank Mr. Asquith for his address on behalf of Sir Herbert's family and of the subscribers to the memorial, and for this graceful and eloquent tribute to our dear friend. I shall only add one or two personal words about Tree. He was undoubtedly an artist in every sense of the term. He took infinite pains to stir the imagination. He was versatile in an extreme degree. One phase of that versatility has not been mentioned, and perhaps it occurs more appropriately to me because I refer to his visit to America only a little before his death. I was not there at the time, but I read of Sir Herbert's doings in the English newspapers. When I went to America soon afterwards, I heard of him not only as an actor and as an artist, but also as a patriot, taking his stand in crowded audiences, addressing the Americans, telling them of the aims and efforts of this country and its Allies, and stimulating them as he had always the power to stimulate all those who listened to him.

Tree had a great career as actor and as artist. I would fain add also that he was a true patriot. No one who knew him for even a brief space of time could fail to note his charm. He was never dull ; he was always stimulating and interesting. Let us think what it is to say that of a man through this dull and sometimes dreary life. He had a keen enjoyment of the good phrase, and he loved the *bon mot*. I am speaking the sober truth when I say that Tree had the keenest enjoyment of any phrase he had himself been able to coin, or any *bon mot* he had sped on its way. (Laughter.) No one could know him without realizing that he was a great, loyal, generous-hearted man, who loved his life, loved his art, loved his friends and associates, and took infinite pleasure in all those joys which were so rightly and properly the accompaniment of the artist's life.

SIR SQUIRE BANCROFT: While under the spell of the eloquence we have listened to, to open my lips even as a postscript calls for temerity. But as the flight of time has left me, I am told, the *doyen* of the English stage, I feel it to be my duty, as it surely is my privilege, to say how great a loss Herbert Tree was to it, and to hope that his strenuous life, his boundless courage, his splendid productions, and, above all, his brilliant imagination, may inspire his comrades to follow in the footsteps which have left such memorable marks.

After the Bancroft management came to an end, it was a relief to my wife and to me to see the Haymarket Theatre in the hands of Herbert Tree, and to feel the confidence that its traditions would be well maintained. Then followed his long and honourable career in this handsome theatre, which he built and loved.

It is men like Herbert Tree who forcibly remind us that though the orchard may not always yield its choicest fruit, and the vineyard may sometimes begrudge its most luscious grapes, the beautiful art of acting will live on; it is as undying as it is alluring—a proud possession, being " not of an age but for all time."

Mme. Clara Butt sang " The Lost Chord," one of Sir Herbert Tree's favourite songs, and a delightful ceremony ended with a Blessing pronounced by the Bishop of London.

APPENDIX III

[*On his return from America in* 1916, *Herbert Tree wrote two articles for* The Times.]

IMPRESSIONS OF AMERICA

[From *The Times*, September 8th, 1916.]

I. " NOT BAD FOR A YOUNG COUNTRY "

THE face, or shall I say the surface, of America has entirely changed since I first made its acquaintance twenty years ago. New York largely dominates the current of the nation's life, colours its atmosphere, and dictates its fashions.

The two striking impressions one receives on arriving in New York City are its architecture and its luxury. Geographical necessity was the mother of the sky-scraper. By day these giant towers convey an impression of garish splendour ; at night they are spectrally imposing. As there is no twilight in the city, so are there no half-tones in the life of the people. The dusk of Broadway is chased by the blazing electric signs which dazzle the stranger as a transformation scene of some advertising fairyland. But it has a beauty of its own. The gaiety of New York at night is most striking. Dancing proceeds in all the restaurants and hotels. But the gaiety is normal and indigenous ; it seems to be the natural outcome of the restless energy of the climate and the people. Let no one assert that there is no national American music. This new art of sound is, to the new-comer, more nerve-shattering and bewildering than that of Strauss or of the music-futurists. After the first shock the orchestral monstrosities of ragtime become haunting in their fascination. It is as though you were drawn into the depths of chaos by a maelstrom of sound. Yet in this riot of sound and movement there is always something " respectable." It has

278

the Latin exuberance of high spirits rather than the Saxon rowdiness of the flesh.

The hospitality towards English visitors is prodigal. Whereas in former times there was a tendency to depreciate the English people, their manners, their customs, and their want of humour, one is struck to-day by the sympathetic courtesy and the better understanding with which ourselves and our work are regarded. Although there is a considerable section of the community which is pro-dollar, the vast majority in the East are enthusiastically pro-Ally ; and this whole-hearted sympathy is reflected in the Press. The measures taken towards the Irish rebels did much at the time to alienate the sympathy of many Americans from the British cause. At some Irish public meetings, indeed, the " Watch on the Rhine " was sung ; but the intemperate language of the leaders of the movement was almost universally condemned.

In the Middle West and in the West the pro-Ally sentiment is less pronounced ; and certainly the newspapers in some of the cities are inclined to devote larger type to the victories of the Central Powers than to those of the Entente. This neutral tepidness may be in no small measure due to the remarkable efficiency of the German propaganda. Great applause, however, was called forth by the assertion that, but for the British Fleet, American soil would long ago have been invaded by the present enemies of the Allies ; and the conviction is daily gaining ground throughout the United States that Great Britain, in fighting for the Allies, is fighting the cause of America. There can be no better proof of this American sympathy with the Allied cause than the vast sums which have been collected—more than $50,000 having been sent to the English, French, Russian, Belgian and German funds, the vast proportion of which went to the Allies. To sum up, it is not too much to say that the sentiments of the great majority of the inhabitants and the Press of New York are no less pro-Ally than the Allies themselves.

Shortly after my arrival in America, I started for California in order to fulfil a contract to present *Macbeth* in a series of moving pictures. We spent Christmas Day at the Grand Canyon. On our arrival a blinding snowstorm blotted out the view. We turned our backs upon the mountains and were making for our hotel when the snow stopped and light came. On looking back we saw the mountains in cold, barren grandeur. At first they seemed like the habitation of some forbidding god—one was appalled by the vast uselessness of this empty waste—not a tree, not a shrub was to be seen. But Nature had surprises yet in store, and soon provided us with a feast of infinite variety. Now from the valley ascended a curtain of white mist. The act was finished. After an interlude of five minutes the curtain slowly rose ; the sun burst forth, and, shining through the dissolving mists, revealed the most wonderful transformation scene I have ever witnessed, as Nature in a frolic mood threw prismatic somersaults—three rainbows spanned the horizon. A ·voice behind me disturbed the spell : " Not bad for a young country, boss ! " it remarked. I assured the speaker that it was most promising.

We pass through New Mexico's vast desolation of uncultivated landscape, fringed with snow-capped mountains. We arrive at a railway station, where tame Indians are selling toys and painted pottery. The surrounding country is dotted with camps of Indians ; picturesque women on horseback are riding to and fro. The life of their little villages appears to be happy, and they still disdain the less picturesque civilization offered them in exchange for their freedom. The livelihood they earn suffices for their needs. Their social amenities are elemental. They have more wives than the more recent inhabitants of America ; but I am given to understand that they divorce them less frequently.

At last we are in California. There is the welcome green of the trees, the orange groves are aglow, and I smell for the first time, away from a wedding, the scent of the orange blossoms. At Los Angeles the Mayor welcomes me. I undergo the inevitable mental vivisection at the hands of the representatives of the Press, and am asked to a banquet given by the *Los Angeles Examiner*, to which the leading citizens are invited. The interviewing, which is more a cross-examination than an examination-in-chief, being overcome in an hour and a half, my next objective is the Fine Art Studio, situated at Hollywood, a suburb about seven miles out. My first step is to hire a motor-car. Life at Los Angeles would be impossible without these " perambulators." Everybody in the city seems to be possessed of a car—there are 200,000 of them in California.

At the Studio, as our car stops, we are surrounded by a motley crowd, all painted and costumed, among whom are Red Indians, cavaliers, moderns, gorgeous Babylonians, and cowboys. Suddenly there is a terrific explosion as a dozen cowboys fire their pistols into the air. This is a welcome ! Recovering from the shock, and finding myself, happily, unwounded, I raise my hat to the cheering crowd. My instinct tells me that I am in the midst of a democratic society. A fair-haired little boy of five years old approached. He is, I afterwards discovered, one of the most popular film actors. The infant phenomenon wore a long garment, on which was sewn in large letters the word " Welcome," and coming towards me with extended hand, at once put me at my ease by saying : " Pleased to meet you, Sir Tree." By way of making conversation, I ventured : " And how has the world been using you these last few years ? " With a world-weary shrug of the shoulders, it replied : " Well, I guess this world's good enough for me ! " It is a land of many babies, but few children.

I turned my eyes towards a stage of many acres—on which was raised the City of Babylon. Yes, there, solidly built, was the mimic City of Babylon. You can wander up a great street peopled by thousands of actors and stage employees, all clad in the costumes of the period. Life-sized elephants decorate the buildings and huge images of gods and goddesses confront you at every turn.

As I ascend the steps of the temple I hear in the distance a great noise as of a cheering crowd ; nearer and nearer it comes, four chariots gallop past at full tilt, followed by hundreds of soldiers on horseback, the populace escaping miraculously from the menacing hoofs and wheels. Not only are the actors expert and daring riders ; the horses, too, are marvellously trained for this kind of work. The wonder is how few accidents occur in the pageantry of this remarkable film directed by Mr. D. W. Griffith, who, it will be remembered, was responsible for *The Birth of a Nation*. The new picture beggars all description —it has taken two years to prepare, and its production must have cost between £100,000 and £150,000.

Mr. Griffith is an imaginative artist, his energy is amazing, and he apparently has a supreme indifference to money. To be a spectator of his latest work is like having gold flung in one's face. The pains taken to secure archæological accuracy in these pictures, which in the course of the play cover many periods of history, are beyond anything hitherto known to stage producers.

I imagine that this work will be the high water mark in the way of film production. Huge sums are frequently lost in these enterprises ; and it is probable that the present prodigality of outlay will not be of long duration. I believe the art of the moving picture has not yet found its feet. It has hitherto been largely imitative of the theatre. It is likely that a natural cleavage between the spoken and pictorial drama will take place. I believe that the future use of the moving pictures will be largely educational ; I believe that in coming generations history and geography will be largely taught through this fascinating medium. On the other hand, I do not think that in great cities the vogue of the cinema will be abiding as far as the drama is concerned. And a taste for the regular theatre will have been created among the millions who daily witness the primitive dramas of the " screen."

In England we have no conception of the vast influence of the moving picture industry in America, where it has become part of the national life of the people. There is at home a tendency to sneer at the serious work which is undertaken by striving artists such as Mr. Griffith—witness the brilliant ridicule by which the film of *Macbeth* was anticipated. I refer, of course, to Sir James Barrie's recent remarkable contribution to Shakespeare's Tercentenary. It is the invariable fate of any new movement to be ignored until it has taken root among the great necessities. Steam, electricity, telegraphy, wireless telegraphy, the motor-car and the airship were all scoffed at until they became part of the daily life of the people.

It is to-day impossible to ignore the moving picture, and the best thing we can all do is to see that this great new force is directed into the right channel ; in its sway over popular opinion it has an influence no less than that of the Press itself, for it makes its daily emotional appeal to millions of people, young and old. If, after the war, we are to have a Ministry of Fine Arts, one of its duties should be to see that this new power is beneficently used in the education and the humanization of the multitude. The theatre, too, should have the protection of the State. I refer not only to the higher branches of the drama, but to the lighter forms of entertainment which bring diversion and happiness to the public. Such State recognition would do much to discourage the taste for the scented hogwash which is so lavishly provided for the unthinking.

[From *The Times*, September 9th, 1916.]

IMPRESSIONS OF AMERICA

II. WHERE ALL THE WORLD'S A STAGE

I AM tempted to give a description of the life of the studios of Los Angeles, in which many thousands are employed. The community of the studio is the most democratic I have ever faced ; but from first to last, during my stay, I never met with any discourtesy from the many hundreds among whom my life was spent. The work of the pictures is done in an atmosphere of happiness and high spirits, which makes its frequent monotony bearable.

In the productions there is a systematic absence of system. Sometimes an artist will have to wait one, two, or three weeks before he is called upon to take up his share of the work ; then he will often work fifteen or sixteen hours a day. This latter was my experience in the preparations of *Macbeth*. The process of photography takes place partly in the studio by artificial light (the rays of which are somewhat trying to the eyes), partly in the open air of the studio, and partly in " locations "—that is to say, in country scenes.

When going on " location " (there obtains in California a curious love of Latin words), the entire party are driven to their destination in motor-cars. We would sometimes start for the mountains at midnight, and proceed to a country inn, be dressed by seven o'clock to catch the early sun, and ride forth on horse-back, all caparisoned and bewigged, towards the " location " of the " Blasted Heath "—there to meet the Witches. The inhabitants of California are so accustomed to fancy-dress that the approach of Macbeth, of Banquo, of Macduff, and their retinues caused no surprise, for of Los Angeles it may be said that all the world's a stage and all the men and women merely " movies."

The mimic coronation of Macbeth at Scone took place about forty miles from Los Angeles at a place called Chatsworth. Thither the actors and hundreds of supernumeraries, together with the " properties " of the occasion, were conveyed in motor-cars and motor-omnibuses. This scene was taken in brilliant sunlight, while the arrival at the King's camp of Macbeth and Banquo after the victorious battle was photographed at two in the morning, the scene being lighted by huge electric lights. Through the ranks of the cheering soldiers surrounding their camp fires and through the flaring lights projected on their faces, Macbeth and Banquo galloped with the news of victory. This nocturnal scene was deeply impressive. The interior of the Witches' Cavern was enacted in a scene built in the studio. One scene was photographed no less than a dozen times ; this ordeal was a somewhat trying one in the watches of the night.

Acting to the lens requires a peculiar. temperament, and demands much more " natural " method than that of the stage ; the great requisite in the actor is the power of momentary self-excitation. A mere resort to the technique of the theatre would not " register " satisfactorily on the film—a relentless detective. To the new-comer it is somewhat disconcerting to act a scene of carousal immediately after your death-scene. In the great studios one will often see as many as ten different plays proceeding on adjacent stages, a farce being acted in close proximity to a scene of tragedy. A quick and versatile temperament in the actor is required for the work of the " screen," and, although I had little difficulty in acclimatizing myself to the new conditions, I confess I have not outlived my preference for the spoken drama. It is only by the exercise of one's imagination in visualizing the perspective of vast crowds of spectators that one can maintain the pitch of excitement necessary for the fine frenzy of the scene. The sets for *Macbeth* were all built ; the scene of the King's Castle in the last act, solidly constructed in a " location " outside Hollywood, was fully equipped with a moat filled with water, a drawbridge, and battlements, over which the attacking army clambered, stones being hurled and boiling pitch being poured on them.

All the leading actors of America have been " immortalized " in the pictures ; and at this moment Mr. S. H. Sothern, who, after an honourable career has lately retired from the regular stage with an enviable fortune, and will shortly make his permanent home in England, is acting on the "screen." Among those whom I met in California was the renowned "Charlie Chaplin." Contrary to expectations, I found him to be a young man of a serious and sensitive disposition, who has artistic ambitions of a kind not suggested by his public records, and who in private life is thoughtful as well as versatile and entertaining.

The cost of living in California is much more reasonable than in other parts of the States. One can hire a well-appointed bungalow, surrounded by an acre of garden, filled with flowers and orange, lemon, grapefruit and eucalyptus trees, and be well attended by Japanese servants, who are excellent cooks. However hot the days may be (I never found them oppressively so), the evenings are always cool. It is pleasant to take motor drives to the coast. At Santa Monica, about twenty miles distant from the city, there is an excellent inn, nightly filled with happy revellers ; during dinner and supper all join in the dancing, and there is a rag-time band which puts high spirits into the minds and the toes of the feasters, who are composed largely of those employed in the picture-world. Driving home through the night one passes through the scent-laden orange and lemon groves.

The roads are wonderfully well-adapted for motoring. I was astonished to notice that the fields on each side of the track are decorated with roses and other flowering plants. One may pass through these herbaceous borders for twenty or thirty miles. The motor annihilates one's sense of distance. On one occasion, in response to a dinner invitation, I drove from Los Angeles to Santa Barbara, starting on a return journey after midnight, thus covering a distance of 210 miles. For ten miles the road had been washed away by flood, and we had to traverse this distance through sand. Friendship has its penalties.

Another pleasant pastime is to be found in the mountain excursions on horseback. The horses are well trained, many of them being used in the wonderful battle pictures of the films. After one becomes accustomed to the Mexican saddles, their seat is most comfortable. There is only one drawback to these equestrian exercises—the horses, which are wonderfully trained by cowboys, are apt to perform all manner of unexpected gyrations ; to their standing up proudly on their hind-legs and beating the air with their hoofs one rapidly becomes accustomed ; but when, by an unconsidered jerk of the reins, one unconsciously gives them the cue to die, they are apt to fling themselves prone on the ground ; thus a histrionic instinct is liable to bring discomfort to the rider unaccustomed to the exigencies of the film.

After the strenuous life of California, the most welcome rest I ever experienced was that passed in the railway train from Los Angeles to New York. As the coming guest was welcomed with salvos of pistols at the hands of " cowboys," so was the parting guest speeded. On my arrival in New York I drove from the station to attend the first rehearsal of *Henry VIII*. In New York the earth seems to spin more quickly round its axis ; happily, the vitalizing climate enables one to keep pace with its quickened revolutions ; and the preparations for the Shakespeare Festival were only part of the daily duties which confronted one. Many hours each day were devoted to these preparations ; interviews in the newspapers were part of the daily routine ; and every evening and most afternoons a speech was exacted, till one felt the kind of impetus which afflicts those that cannot walk but needs must run.

Our great anxiety as to the fate of the Shakespeare Festival was set at rest on the first night, when *Henry VIII*. was produced in the manner familiar to Londoners. The success of the Shakespeare representations exceeded all our most sanguine expectations and falsified the widespread predictions that New York would not tolerate Shakespeare. We were fortunate, indeed, that our season synchronized with the Tercentenary celebrations. The incense of these celebrations blew our way ; certainly the theatre was nightly filled by crowded audiences ; and the run might have been continued for the entire season of three months but that I wished to carry out the promised programme of giving a Shakespeare Festival ; separate runs of *The Merchant of Venice* and *The Merry Wives of Windsor* were accordingly given.

To celebrate Shakespeare Day a performance was organized on Monday, April 24th, for the British Red Cross Fund. A varied programme was provided, consisting of scenes from *Macbeth, Henry IV*. (Falstaff's scenes), the abdication scene from

Richard II., and scenes from *Twelfth Night.* American audiences are quickly responsive—they are very little like our cosmopolitan London audiences ; but they are quicker to leave the theatre at the end of the play, and accordingly the actor's speech (when insisted upon) has to be delivered at the end of the penultimate act. New York audiences, moreover, are more enthusiastic in the mornings than in the evenings (probably owing to the preponderance of young people and students).

Among many memorable occasions during my stay in New York, the one that made the deepest impression on my mind was that on which my comrade Sir Johnston Forbes-Robertson and I were invited to give addresses in the Cathedral of St. John the Divine on Easter Sunday, Shakespeare's birthday. It was natural that I regarded this request as a signal honour to our stage. Nothing could have been more imaginatively touching than to take part in the homage paid by this great nation to the master in whose service the better part of our artistic lives had been passed. Nor have I ever been more deeply moved than by the impressive service and the inspiring music which choired in the same hour the two men who have spiritually and humanly most influenced mankind. It was with a sense of awe and solemnity that I mounted the pulpit from which the Bishop had just spoken in such glowing words of Shakespeare's genius and of the high mission of our calling ; it was with a natural trepidation that I faced the congregation which filled the vast cathedral. I shall not readily forget the dignified beauty of the tribute delivered by my comrade Forbes-Robertson.

Though absent from the Tercentenary celebrations which took place in London, it was no small consolation to know that we were able to contribute to the general acclaim of the poet which found enthusiastic utterance in every important city throughout the United States.

[*In* 1917, *after his last visit to America, Herbert Tree wrote the following articles for the* Daily Chronicle. *Of these, together with the articles in* The Times, *and with some additional matter, he intended to make a small book. On the very last day of his life he was busy with this scheme.*]

MORE IMPRESSIONS OF AMERICA

[From the *Daily Chronicle*, June 13th, 1917.]

I

UNDER this heading I propose to set down some American impressions and experiences, and to chronicle the vast changes which have been wrought in America during the last six months.

It is a fortnight since I left New York in a riot of pro-Ally enthusiasm. Had anyone ventured to prophesy such a transformation a year ago he would have been regarded as a madman or a sensational journalist. A great tidal wave has swept from the East to the West. The awakening of America is but a part of the world-movement which caused the revolution in Russia. It has come as suddenly, its causes are no less deep-rooted, its consequences will be no less overwhelming. It is the birth of the New Life.

In recording these impressions, my point of view is human rather than political. Nor do I pretend that they are more than snapshots. But it may be claimed that the most valuable impressions are the first and the last : the interim is often but as a blurred phantasmagoria of undigested realities.

THE CONTRAST OF CITIES

A brief holiday in London during last September enabled me to receive a fleeting impression of the changed conditions at home. Black streets, men in khaki hurrying to and fro ; men in blue limping hither and thither ; women in uniform ; vice in crape dancing rag-time ; a greater simplicity of living ; the pervading irrepressible Cockney humour ; and a sense of fate somnolent and pregnant, overbrooding all.

Thence back to New York. What a contrast between these cities. Here I find no hint of impending war—it is just a frenzy of luxury, a hectic gaiety which belongs to this nervous vital climate. Here is none of the tender languor of our own dull, balmy atmosphere. Here the electric current is destructive of romance—one's impulse is to " do and do and do." In this land of light and publicity, it is the reporter who is the first to welcome the coming, as he was the last to speed the parting guest. It is from the searching questions of the reporter I learn on my arrival that for the last four days of our voyage on the steamer *Philadelphia* a fire had been raging in the hold of the ship. I tell him that I had been wholly unaware of the danger through which we had passed ; and thus the suggestion that the fire was but another instance of " frightfulness " only adds to my thankfulness that we had escaped the perils of the contending elements of fire and water. My friendly interlocutor assures me that the obituary (or " post-mortem ") which had been prepared for me was of the most flattering nature and hints that its insertion is only a pleasure deferred.

It is well at once to capitulate to the reporter—an American's home is his interviewer's castle. The average American does not luxuriate in that sacred unpublicity in which most Englishmen prefer to pass their private lives. It is the climate of New York which largely governs the lives of the inhabitants of this electric city. On each successive visit to New York, I have been struck by its vital and energizing influences. One may be worn out, but one is never tired. The electric quality in the air is, indeed, sometimes disconcerting to the new-comer. It has happened that on my being presented to a lady, a complete stranger, we have in shaking hands experienced a mutual electric shock which has caused us both to start back with an involuntary exclamation. " Pardon my electricity," seems but an inadequate apology in such moments. I have found that one's liability to this inconvenience varies with one's health. The climate demands a less vigorous diet ; the increased abstention from alcohol, although the national " cocktail " still survives, is very marked. I noticed in addressing City clubs that alcohol was not served at all at luncheon. As there are few half-tones in the landscapes, so are there few half-tones in the character of the people. There is an absence of twilight, of that mystery so characteristic of England. In the same way the houses and gardens are not surrounded by walls. They are open to the public view. The only walls I remember to have seen were those of a base-ball stadium and a lunatic asylum—the one presumably to keep people from getting in, the other to keep them from getting out. As there is a fiercer publicity, so is there a greater frankness in the life of the people. In fashionable hotels at tea-time young couples will sit hand-in-hand, feeling no awkwardness or shyness in this public intimacy. This frankness, which extends even to telegrams (most of which arrive in ungummed envelopes), may be an explanation of the " leakages " on the Stock Exchange of which we have recently heard.

Life in New York is largely that of the restaurant. The contrast between the greater simplicity of living at home and the luxury of New York is indeed striking. Here the waste of a day's food would placate an army of anarchists. At all the great hotels there are nightly dances ; and entertainments in the way of bazaars and fancy dress balls are constantly given. These are chiefly devoted to Red Cross and other War Funds. Such entertainments are given throughout the country, and everywhere women are busy in devising and carrying out movements for the relief of sufferers in the war.

ARCHITECTURE

Perhaps the most notable thing in America is its architecture. In this direction Art has made rapid strides during the past twenty years. With the famous sky-scrapers, Londoners are, of course, familiar ; these have a certain characteristic beauty of their own. But it is the public buildings and, above all, the railway stations that most impress the new-comer by their grandeur, simplicity and dignity. This applies not only to New York, but to Washington, Boston, Chicago and other cities. The modern architecture (derived, of course, from the classic) reflects the largeness and frankness of modern life. Wherever one goes, one finds the Georgian prettiness and homeliness, the ornamental irrelevancies and rococo pretentiousness of the Victorian period replaced by imposing edifices whose only decoration is that of

doors, windows and chimneys. The railway stations are built
as great Temples, and must needs be inspiring and mind-enlarging
to the incoming and outgoing travellers. The Cathedrals of
New York are of rare beauty. An imposing building, too, is the
Public Library on Fifth Avenue, though an unconscious peda-
gogic touch is given the lions, who appear to be afflicted with the
adenoid sniff of the superior person. There are many stately
buildings, too, in the Wall Street district. On the eve of my
sailing, I attended a farewell luncheon given by the " Pilgrims."
The feast took place in a large room on the fortieth floor, from
which giddy height one gets an awesome impression of the city
beneath. Such functions are frequent in this city of hospitality,
and are always accompanied by a high order of eloquence, the
late Mr. Choate until his death being a shining light of oratory.
Mr. Chauncey Depew, in his eighty-second year, still retains his
old eloquence and elegance of speech. On the occasion in question, he made an oration of glowing eulogy on England, and her
part in the war ; in brilliant metaphor he drew a picture of a
meeting between Shakespeare, George III. and George Washington in the Elysian Fields ; and ended his speech by conjuring
up in his imagination the kind of play Shakespeare would have
constructed out of the great pageant of events through which
humanity is passing : " The lesson of such a play," he concluded, " might evangelize the world."

The oratory of America is of a high order. It is a land of
a hundred million souls, mostly after-dinner speakers. Even
at an ordinary dinner-table, it is not unusual to hear speeches
by the chief guests. The hospitality extended to guests, and
especially to British guests, is extraordinary ; and the bestowal
of honorary membership of clubs is a great boon to Englishmen.
Especially agreeable are the Country Clubs which every great
city boasts ; these are not only most comfortable and well-
appointed, but afford opportunities for golf and other sports.

THE PATIENCE OF MR. WILSON

I had the good fortune to attend a historic meeting at the
Union League Club on the occasion when Ex-Presidents Roosevelt and Taft shook hands to bridge over the schism that had

rent the Republican cause. All the leading Republicans spoke, including Mr. Hughes, whose election was then regarded as a foregone conclusion. I confess I was not greatly impressed with the Candidate's oratory, which was of " the common-sense, common-place order." This memorable meeting took place immediately before the General Election. Intense excitement prevailed throughout the States, Mr. Wilson being then suspected of a policy of drift and indecision. Many of his sternest opponents have now become his closest supporters, and are loyally devoting themselves to his cause. Indeed, the evolution of political affairs in America bears a strange likeness to that of England in the early stages of the war, when the self-effacement of political parties and politicians was one of the most remarkable proofs of this country's strength in crisis.

Nor does the resemblance stop there. I believe that the people of England entered into this war to fight for an ideal—and I believe that the people of America were inspired by a like ideal, an ideal which has only latterly entered the soul of the nation. I do not say that political considerations did not in part animate the calculations of our own statesmen and those of our American allies ; but I am sure, having addressed myself daily to American audiences, that their sympathy with the cause was mainly due to a belief that the cause of England was a righteous cause, and a consciousness that the two nations were side by side in the fight for civilization. "It is honour that will bring you to our side," were words that were always greeted with enthusiasm. Gradually the feeling has come to the American people that they were too proud *not* to fight. All in all, our new Allies have reason to congratulate themselves that Mr. Wilson remained in office. Indeed, since the President's great war message, the entire country has accepted him as its official idol. One must admire the whole-hearted national faith in a leader whose patience, tact and single-mindedness have come to be recognized even by his bitterest opponents.

Wilson's action was something between a *coup d'état* and a miracle. Had he made his declaration six months ago, he would probably have called forth civil war. By appearing to be holding back, he allowed the people to push him on. In this situation the President showed the fierce patience of a Jew.

(He is at least of Scotch descent.) Six months ago seven-eighths of Congress and the country would have been against him ; to-day seven-eighths are for him. The spirit of the people had to be prepared, the proletariat had to be hypnotized. What were the various contributing causes that wrought this change one can but leave to the political psychologist to determine, as one may leave him to explain the wonder of the Russian revolution. But I cannot help thinking that the result was in no small measure due to the constant and courageous efforts of the leading Press of New York, who, year in and year out, consistently and almost without exception, championed the cause of the Allies. The war movement may be said to have been one of Press and President. It may be granted that in New York, which is a cosmopolitan city, the task of forming public opinion was not so difficult, for the cultured and travelled classes were from an early date of the war for the most part whole-heartedly on the side of the Allies. The same may be said of New England and of Washington. Not so the proletariat and the inhabitants of the Middle West and the Far West, who were too far away from the battlefield to sympathize with the sufferers or to probe the causes of the war, and who were not unnaturally guided by motives of local self-interest rather than by those of a world-patriotism ; while a very large element was undoubtedly opposed to Great Britain owing to the ever-open sore of the Irish question. Illogical as it may sound, there are many who, in their German-Irish sentiments, would have substituted the " Watch on the Liffey " for the " Wearing of the Green." I cannot help thinking that with the settlement of the Irish question would vanish the last dregs of bitterness in the cup of Anglo-American relations.

MORE IMPRESSIONS OF AMERICA

[From *Daily Chronicle*, June 19th, 1917, and June 22nd, 1917.]

II

THE personality which, after President Wilson, has the greatest national appeal, is undoubtedly that of Colonel Roosevelt, whose courage, patriotic fervour and catapultic force " get over " the people. But the situation needed a Brutus rather than an Antony. Probably no living man did more to create respect for the American flag than did Roosevelt during his Presidential term. If in his retirement he lacked something of the reticence we associate with greatness, one must remember that in captivity the lion is apt to roar at the mouse. There can be little doubt that had the Colonel cultivated cabbages and held his tongue, he would have been President of the United States at this moment. Undoubtedly this " fiery particle " has and will have a dominant influence in the creation of the American army which is in the making. The God of War has need of such a man.

It is extraordinary to reflect upon the change that has been wrought, as it were overnight, in this peace-loving people. Six months ago two men out of three (even those who were heart and soul pro-Ally) would shrug their shoulders when the question of war was mooted, believing as they did that such a consummation was out of the question. One must bear in mind that the German system of propaganda had been perfectly conducted through the Press and through pamphlets. Literature, pointing out that Great Britain had made the war for trade purposes, that the British Navy was a menace to the freedom of the seas, was put into my hand as I arrived at my hotels. There can be little doubt that this systematic flooding of the whole country was largely productive of the mistrust or indifference which was shown towards the cause of the Allies, and especially towards England, in the earlier stages of the war. And it is a fact that all along the attitude of the main body of the people was much more sympathetic to the French than to the English. To this day it is the " Marseillaise " that wins the enthusiastic applause of an assembly.

THE HUMAN TOUCH

On the other hand, there was little done in the way of spreading the gospel of the Allied Cause. It is, I suppose, due to a national trait that the English refrained from resorting to these propagandic methods, preferring to rely upon the slow assertion of the truth and the justice of their cause. But this ethical lethargy has its drawbacks. A truth that is only advertised once is apt to be prevailed over by a lie that is advertised a dozen times ; and I cannot help thinking that if England could have spared some of her great men at the beginning of the war, the understanding and cordiality which, happily, exist to-day might have been brought about many months ago. It is the human touch that tells. The American people are like children. They want to be told, they want to be understood, to be sympathized with, they want to be praised. True, the flattery must be sympathetic and sincere—the professional genialist is apt to " come a cropper."

I claim to speak with some authority on this subject, as for many months past I have daily spoken in public on Anglo-American friendship, addressing not only nightly audiences in the theatre, but several times a week have I had opportunities of addressing Universities, city clubs, bazaars, political meetings, Church congregations and, latterly, recruiting meetings. Whereas, in the earlier stages of the war, a speaker was bound to be discreet, to hang his eloquence on the peg of peace rather than of war, I latterly found that no pro-Ally sentiment was too strong for the enthusiastic applause of the public ; nor, strangely enough, did I receive a single interruption in the course of these speeches, or a single letter of complaint. I must confess to a keen delight in disconcerting my managers. The assertion that, but for the British Navy, America would have been invaded long ago and the Monroe doctrine but a scrap of paper, was regarded by my managers as unneutral in sentiment. But I found these indiscretions a solace in my exile.

If there is one force which has a more potent appeal than another in addressing American audiences, that force is humour. In that country humour is nowhere suspect—not even in the pulpit, and audiences are quick as lightning in responding to its touch. It is by the human appeal that I hear sympathy is gained. I was discussing the question of public opinion with an eminent diplomat, who said : " What we have to do is to tell them what they ought to do—not to tell them what is right, but to make them like us." The eminent diplomat proceeded to explain the situation by analogy : " We do not," he said, " love a woman for her virtue, but because she is pretty." Though I had mental reservations as to this somewhat bureaucratic view of love, I bowed to my mentor's political discernment.

Among the multitude, there certainly was not wanting in the earlier stages of the war a kind of ethical indifference. " What are we going to get out of it ? " would often be asked by the pro-dollarist. Especially was this the case in the West. " All the gold in the world is coming our way," said one. I could not refrain from reminding him that there was a certain danger in this plethora. A man should not hoard too much gold in his garden lest his neighbour look over the wall ; for property belongs to those who have the power to take it. The truth of this has recently been brought home to us in Russia, and will probably be made yet clearer after the war. It is only gradually that the American people have realized the historic aspect of this war—that America could not afford to stand by and let the other countries fight this battle—the battle of civilization. The perspective of history has been brought home to the people by the great leaders, such as Elihu Root and Choate, and, above all, by the noble message of the President.

A nation is slow to move. It is necessary to kindle into flame the ethical glow of a people—for men will not give their lives for motives of self-interest. I do not profess to know the inwardness of politics, or what may be the underlying exigencies " behind the scenes," but I am certain that these exigencies will not lead a people to sacrifice their lives and their homes. I am certain, too, that an individual has one psychology and a multitude another. There is a public and a private conscience in us all. The hearts of a multitude beat in unison. On several occasions I told audiences of the scene I witnessed in the House of Commons twenty-four hours before war was declared, when Sir Edward Grey said that Great Britain was not bound by her interests or by treaties to go to war. But when he proceeded that there was the honour, the good name, of England to be considered, the entire House rose in one mighty cheer, and history was made as Big Ben tolled forth the Amen of the Soul of England. It is, I repeat, the human touch that reaches the people. It is the sense that the British and American people are fighting for the democracy of the world that causes men to consent to universal service during the war, so infinitely preferable to voluntary service and the degrading system of involuntary service—the recruiting by the white feather of blackmail.

It was a novel experience to me to address a recruiting meeting, as I had never been afforded an opportunity of doing so in London. Such a crowded meeting was held " down Town " in New York during the luncheon hour. Early in my speech an untoward event caused an interruption. I had just uttered the words, " Wilson, like Nelson, expects that every man this day will do his duty," when there occurred a terrific explosion. There were cries from the crowd. " It has come," I said to myself, endeavouring to feel dignified in death. When the smoke cleared away, I found that the panic had been caused by the all-intruding flashlight photographer. Then there was a roar of laughter from the crowd. Happily I was able to utilize the situation by likening it to our own preparedness at the outbreak of war.

BILLY SUNDAY

One of the most effectual recruiting sergeants is Billy Sunday, the famous Revivalist, whose audience frequently number fifteen thousand people—and as he has two meetings a day, he addresses himself to a vast public. I have no doubt that in this direction of recruiting " Billy " did splendid service. I must confess that I regard his religious exercises with mixed feelings. As I believe it to be his intention to devote a campaign of some years to England, it may be interesting to give some impressions of this remarkable man, who, I understand, makes a profit of no less than $50,000 in each town he visits.

It was in Buffalo that I heard this. He certainly has the faculty of taking one's breath away. The sermon took place in a large tent-like structure, built of wood, which is erected for the purpose. The acoustics of the vast hall were perfect, and made me wish that a theatre could be thus constructed. At the back of the stage, on which thousands (including a choir of many hundreds) were seated, was the inscription in flaming letters " Buffalo for Christ," and in front of the improvised pulpit hung the Star-Spangled Banner. I must confess that I was not deeply impressed by this fanatic, whose sincerity can hardly be doubted. There were many intelligent faces among the congregation, which is made up of all classes. The people are no doubt deeply moved by the speaker, who indulges in language which, to put it mildly, is somewhat vernacular. Billy Sunday provides a cheap way of getting to Heaven—his teaching is of the " open your mouth and shut your eyes " order. His Hell is inhabited by a knock-about devil. His chief success lies in saying the obvious : " It is better to see than to be blind ; it is better to hear than to be deaf ; it is better to be healthy than to be sick ; it is better to be good than to be bad ; it is better to go to Heaven than to go to Hell." At this there was great applause, with exclamations of " How true ! " This kind of eloquence never fails of its effect—even in the theatre. I remember how Sir Augustus Harris saved a melodrama at Drury Lane Theatre many years ago by the utterance of a great truth. The play was called *A Sailor and His Lass*—the manager was himself part-author and played the leading part—that of an English midshipman with a leaning towards the fair sex. Until the end of the second act the success of the play was trembling in the balance. It was saved by a brilliant inspiration of the manager. Just before the fall of the curtain the young midshipman came to the front of the footlights and, taking off his cap, exclaimed in a stentorian voice, which brooked no contradiction : " For a British sailor is not a woman but a man ! " The audience burst into a tumult of applause at the utterance of this great and indisputable truth ; the piece was saved, and ran for many months to crowded houses.   Casuistry was dumb and humour bent its brow.

Billy Sunday has a way of shouting at the people, and is most agile upon the platform.   He is a retired base-ball player, and will frequently use the gestures of that admirable sport in making his point in the pulpit.   Never does he allow the attention of the audience to wander—and woe be to him who dares to cough, for he is at once demmed to the audience.   Yet withal there is something lovable about the man—if he is never inspiring, he is undoubtedly hypnotic.   He has the something one cannot explain, or explain away.   He is intensely sincere in his belief in hell-fire, in which he assured us that anyone who does not believe in the God of Billy Sunday will frizzle ever-lastingly.   His use of slang is inexhaustible, and appears to delight the audience.   He told us that he will have no truck with protoplasms, and was quite positive that he was not descended from monkeys.   In making this statement, he hopped about the platform with such alertness that one who had hitherto been a waverer as to the Darwinian theory embraced it upon the spot.   At one moment he bent over the platform pretending to listen to a telephonic message from Hell, and at the end of his address said : " Well, Jesus, I want to thank you for this pleasant afternoon."   At the end he shook hands with many hundreds.   This is called " hitting the trail."

Many of the foremost citizens, including Mr. Rockefeller, Junior, support Billy Sunday, and by the clergy he is very largely encouraged owing to his wide appeal and unbounded popularity.   Whether this kind of religion, with its attendant clerical " boom," is productive of abiding good, or whether it is merely hysterical and harmful to true spiritual progress, I cannot pretend to say.   Whether the sway of this kind of revivalism will prevail hereafter will depend upon the lesson of this war—on the need of mankind for a human religion, embodying the forgotten doctrines of Christ.   It will depend on the call for a new civilization, which shall forbid the sacrifice of millions of human lives on the altar of politics.   We are told, it is true, that an eminent divine has lately declared that he failed to find any utterance of Christ which disapproved of war.   If this be true, I cannot help thinking that in making this assertion the

eminent divine stood perilously between the Devil and the Holy
See. To what extent the churches have influenced the ethical
attitude of the people in this time of times, I do not know. But
a deeply impressive picture of Raemaekers' (the famous Dutch
cartoonist) has been largely helpful in bringing home to the
soul of the American nation that it is those who most love
peace who are most determined to wage this fight to the bitter
end. The picture is that of an American standing in a reverent
attitude before the crucified Saviour. Under it are the words,
" If it be Thy fight, it is my fight."

It is always good manners to accommodate oneself to the
usages of the country in which one is a guest, making due allowance for the inhabitants being " foreigners." This applies even
to languages. " Let us take the lift," said I to a prominent
citizen. " ' Elevator,' we call it," corrected my companion.
A motor was waiting outside. " Can I give you an elevator
in my car ? " I asked. And we parted friends. I found no
difficulty in " acclimatizing" myself to the more democratic
habit of the people—whether in the theatre, in the hotel, or in
general company. The employees of the theatre soon brought
home to me that the " star " system is tolerated only in the
" Spangled Banner." I have myself an inrooted conviction as
to the equality of men, but I think a kind of official respect is
calculated to expedite business on the stage as well as in other
walks of life. At first it seemed strange to get no answering
" Sir " when I gave an order. So I took to addressing the servants as " Sir." A *modus vivendi* was thus gradually established, and I found myself addressed as " Boss." Life is a
compromise.

There is a greater freedom between man and man. " Well,
boss," asked the ticket collector in the train, " are you feeling
pretty ' good ' to-day ? " I replied that I felt rather like that.
He held a green identification ticket in his hand, and, without
another word, deftly but relentlessly placed it in the brim of my
hat. Feeling rather like a book-maker, I asked him if it was
compulsory to wear it like that ? " Well," said the official,
" this is a free country, but I guess our President is liable to wear
it like that."

A pleasant little incident occurred at Buffalo Station. A

coloured porter, formerly an actor, now a " red-cap," took my luggage, and after putting it in my compartment, refused the proffered tip, saying : " Allow me to shake hands with you, comrade. I saw you as Wolsey the other night, and when in your speech you spoke about free Russia, I called out ' God bless you.' " I said, " I heard you." He continued : " I have done a bit of shouting in my time. I played Othello without paint." Then, turning to the company and the populace assembled outside, he made a little speech, referring to me as " noble and godlike." Modesty impelled me to assure him that I was but a demigod ; but my champion warmly deprecated the suggestion, saying he did not believe it.

The negroes seemed to me for the most part kindly people, and their formalities and social amenities are a perpetual source of interest and delight. They are somewhat resentful if spoken of as " blacks," preferring to be described as " darkies," or " coloured gentlemen." In an hotel I said to the female coloured attendant : " I should like to have my boots darkened." She replied : " Sir, that's not my compartment—it's de boot boy." I said : " Will you kindly ask the boot boy to darken them ? " She lamented that she was not on speaking terms with that gentleman owing to a difference in their religious views ; but she would communicate with the bell-boy on the subject, who would communicate with the " boots."

I had an interesting experience at the Negro Playhouse in New York. It is called the Lafayette Theatre. I was told that if I would consent to make a speech to the audience one Sunday night the management would give a gala performance of *Othello*. Such an invitation I could not resist, and accordingly I went to the theatre with a party of friends. I was somewhat taken aback on entering my box to find that " God save the King " was played, but I bowed as though I were accustomed to this tribute. The Othello was very powerful, the Desdemona blonde, and fair beyond the reaches of powder. The theatre was crammed (to suffocation). I made a patriotic speech, which was received with much enthusiasm.

CLOUD WITH A YELLOW LINING

No less important is the question of the Yellow races, the Japanese being still denied the proprietary citizenship extended to other nations. In California the Japanese are already largely employed in agricultural pursuits, and there a.e not lacking signs of political threatenings. Standing among the dark committee, I was a trifle disconcerted on hearing a distinguished English actress in a box remark in an audible whisper : " How fair our Herbert looks to-night." It is said that the Black question is one which will be a burning one in the near distance ; it certainly is one which will tax the political ingenuity of this democratic country, for the negro population is increasing by leaps and bounds, and the education of the people is progressing rapidly, while many members of the community are wealthy and are good substantial citizens.

MORE IMPRESSIONS OF AMERICA

[From *Daily Chronicle*, June 24th, 1917, and June 25th, 1917.]

III

In the West there has appeared a cloud with a yellow lining. At an hotel not far from Los Angeles a remarkably polite Japanese attendant took my hat and coat.

"I shall not forget you, sir," said he, dispensing with the formality of a check. I pointed him out to my host as a singularly intelligent menial. I then learned that he was a highly educated man, and that when the Japanese Fleet came to the West, it was my friend in buttons who was the host of the dinner given in honour of the officers—he it was who proposed the toast of the Japanese Navy ; it was he who helped me on with my coat !

In the Far West the Mexican and the Yellow question undoubtedly filled men's minds, so that they scarce heeded the great upheaval that shook and shocked the rest of the world. In California the feeling towards the Allies' cause was undoubtedly somewhat neutral, where it was not pro-German, although I understand a great change has now come over the spirit of the people.

Certainly, the newspapers in San Francisco and Los Angeles reflected this indifference, while the widespread German propaganda in the Press and elsewhere led the people to believe that Great Britain had made the war for trade purposes. As an illustration of this neutrality, I was confronted on entering an office with the following printed notice :

"If you want to talk war, join the Army and get paid for it."

To my surprise, I found the cities of the Middle West, which contain an enormous German population, in the main warmly pro-Ally ; it is certainly extraordinary that up to the present time the prophecies in regard to "frightfulness" in these centres have been entirely falsified. I found that many Germans were in absolute disaccord with the Germany of the Hohenzollerns, being able to estimate at this distance the true state of things with a more philosophic eye and a saner outlook than can their compatriots at home. They cannot realize at this distance why Germany, who, by her enterprises, her industry, her intelligence and her efficiency, was peacefully annexing the trade of the world, should sacrifice this bloodless conquest to the vanity of a dying dynasty.

America is a democracy of all the nations. This was borne in upon me on visiting Detroit. At his motor works in that city Mr. Ford employs 45,000 workmen belonging to fifty-three different nationalities and speaking a hundred different languages. The works themselves are like a war "in little." It is an interesting sight to watch the progress of a motor-car towards its completion. Here is a model of efficiency. The growing machine moves slowly down as on a river, on either side of which each workman adds his appointed "bit" to the perfecting of the car in making. There seemed a tragic monotony in this system, each man performing the same task each minute in the eight-hour day. Although Mr. Ford runs his great undertaking on principles of Socialism, his profit last year was $60,000,000. He apparently finds it easier to control his army of contending nationalities than to control a boatload of pacifists, few of whom were, I believe, on speaking terms when the Ship of Peace bumped against the wharf of Christiania.

The motor-car industry throughout the Western cities is stupendous. In St. Louis whole streets are devoted exclusively to this vast industry. Most of these smoke-laden cities bear a strong resemblance to Clapham Junction—life in them seems like a very busy bank-holiday. There are rag-time bands in all the restaurants; at dinner there is dancing between the courses. As the band ceases, the hall empties and the city is asleep.

In most of these cities the architecture is of a somewhat pretentious kind, and may be described as rococo Elizabethan, the houses resembling overgrown dolls'-houses, with Georgian columns supporting untreadable balconies. At Baltimore, a really delightful city, its residential quarter strongly reminiscent of Edinburgh, I had the privilege of meeting Cardinal Gibbons, one of the most influential intellects in the United States and a most fascinating and impressive personality. Though over eighty years of age, he takes a youthful interest in worldly affairs, and is beloved alike by Protestants and Catholics. He expressed his sense of the great value of the drama as teacher. " Whereas," he said, " I preach the Gospel of Christ, you actors preach the gospel of Shakespeare." Incidentally, I learned from him that Cardinal Wolsey did not wear his ring upon his index finger (Of great men one sometimes learns little things.)

One of the most characteristic cities is Chicago, which has undergone an enormous change in twenty years—it is seething with energy ; the people are warm-hearted ; there is a barbaric pagan frankness of life in strong contrast with the somewhat respectable preciosity of time-honoured Boston, a city that boasts an older and soberer culture. Boston, too, has its own characteristics. It is, in fact, very Bostonian (there is no other word that can quite do justice to it).

At Harvard University there is, I am proud to find, a section devoted exclusively to the Drama, and great attention is given to the study of Shakespeare. While at Boston I visited the town of Lexington, where, 141 years ago, the famous Earl Percy, at the head of hostile troops, entered what was then a New England village. It was his visit that brought about the revolutionary war and caused the Republic to come into being. On the way to Concord we passed the homes of Hawthorne and Alcott and Emerson, Longfellow and Lowell. Here is classic ground. These smiling houses of the eighteenth century are all built of wood and are plastered inside. The Sunday wayside markets are stocked with all kinds of vegetables, and the vivid colours of apples and pumpkins gladden the eyes of the stream of motorists. The pro-Ally sentiment of Boston is, if anything, stronger than that of New York itself, and the same may be said of Philadelphia.

Washington has a dignity and an old-world character which seem to be the natural belongings of the Capital. As the procession of the " inauguration " of the new President passed down the wide streets on its way to the White House, one felt that the scene was appropriate to the historic pageant which has brought America into line with the other great nations of the world in the fight for international progress. On the occasion of my visit to the White House, the suffrage women were stationed outside like sentries, bearing flags. I wondered how the President of the United States could be so accessible without incurring considerable personal inconvenience ; but I believe that the peaceful-looking attendants and the young men who appeared to be intent on the busy plying of the typewriter were formidable experts in the art of ju-jitsu. Mr. Wilson has a gracious presence, and is gifted with the " grand manner "—that of making people feel at ease at once. " At sight," the President paid me the compliment of saying that I reminded him of a well-known statesman. On my bowing with a deprecating self-consciousness, he remarked that he himself had often been told of his resemblance to the late Mr. Joseph Chamberlain. The likeness is indeed striking, though the President's nose lacks the aspiring lilt which characterized that of the distinguished English statesman. After me came about fifty American citizens, all intent upon shaking hands with Mr. Wilson. I wonder whether there is an ailment known as " President's cramp." As I left the " presence " I could not help overhearing the whispered words of a well-known lady who accompanied me : " Mr. President, don't forget Votes for Women." As I went through the gate in a downpour of rain, the women were relieving guard. The suffrage question is not regarded with such favour on the other side as it is here. But assuredly after the war women in America, as well as in the unfreer countries, will demand that they shall by their votes be privileged to veto the killing of their men.

America is a sudden country. She woke up one morning to find herself in the war. There was hardly any twilight in the awakening—she simply accepted the fact and settled down to the business. The coming of Balfour and Joffre was a master-stroke. Both men were the right men at the right moment— it was their coming that set light to the prairie-fire of popular enthusiasm. On the night before my departure the streets were packed with crowds waiting to see their French hero pass ; the warlike note was something new, the whole people seemed animated by a new spirit ; flags waved from every window, the streets were bright with innumerable electric lights ; the Allied anthems were played in all the theatres. Mr. Balfour appealed to the American people—perhaps because he was the most un-American thing in America. They love an Englishman to be very English.

General Joffre fills the limelight as to the manner born ; he has the genius of patting little children on the head in the patriarchal manner. His nod is compelling, he has the genial flair that almost robs the war-god of his terror. His eloquence has the rare trick of being monosyllabic. A delightful story illustrates his blazing bonhomie. A lady asked him at dinner to tell her in confidence what it really was that stopped the Germans on the Marne. Turning a beaming broadside on his interlocutress, Joffre said : " *C'était moi !* " There can be no doubt that this country should send more such ambassadors to America. The two peoples want to know each other better. There has hitherto been a certain coldness between them. The supercilious manner of many an ancient Briton has caused some resentment in the past. The Americans are a very personal people, and they enjoy being exploited ; they revel in their hospitality ; they love a " lion." There are a number of men who have done the State fine service by spreading the message of Great Britain ; among these are Sir Gilbert Parker, who has lately visited California, and whose steady and persistent work is recognized on all sides, Ian Hay, whose lectures are enormously popular, and Lord Aberdeen, who has the healing touch in dealing with the Irish question. But I cannot help thinking that more frequent visits of England's great men would have the effect of permanently cementing the friendship between the two nations.

One must remember the old grudge of the War of Liberation—and one must not ignore the Irish question, which at one time threatened the welcome to the British Commission. Many of the foremost Irish leaders have thrown themselves heart and soul into the Allies' cause, just as many of its staunchest propagators have been men of German birth or German descent. Three notable instances are Mr. James Beck, who since the beginning of the war has been untiring in his espousal of the active participation of the United States in the war, and who has published several stirring books urging the necessity upon his countrymen. Another strong adherent is Mr. Theodore Marburg, a man of great wealth and influence.

WORLD PATRIOTISM

Since I have been home I have often been asked the question whether the Americans realize the seriousness of the war and are determined to throw themselves whole-heartedly into it. My belief is that they do realize to the full the meaning of the solemn pledge into which they have entered ; they realize that the present war is the " to be " or " not to be " of the freedom of the world. The very latest pronouncement of the President gives noble utterance to this spirit which has seized the whole nation. It is no longer a question of politics. It is no longer a question of the Star-Spangled Banner. In this great hour a new note has been struck—the note of world-patriotism.

The mere politician has his ear to the ground—how should he hear the message of the stars ? The President went up into the mountain heights where dwells the soul of the American people ; there he learned the message of the stars ; and when he came down from the mountain he bore with him a tablet on which were graven the words :

" The Right is more precious than Peace."

APPENDIX IV

EXTRACTS FROM HERBERT TREE'S NOTE-BOOKS

[*Herbert Tree usually carried in his pocket a small note-book for jotting down engagements. He used it also for fixing in his memory ideas that had occurred to him, and anecdotes that he had heard or invented. After his death a great many of his old note-books were found here and there among his possessions. A selection from the entries in them is here offered to the reader.*]

An idea of what Hell may be like : Desire without hope.

A work of art should make one say " Ah ! " and not " Ugh ! "

Some are born educated ; they have that inherited knowledge which is called instinct.

Viola said, " It takes Father far less time to make himself ugly than it takes Mother to make herself beautiful."

In order to get on one must stoop to flattery. One must learn to walk backwards in order to get on.

A Russian in Marienbad was asked what he thought of the assassination of Plehve. He said, " I am very sorry for the coachman."

Put your trust in men and not in systems.

Everything comes to him who doesn't wait.

He had none of the modesty of passion.

Of all the arts love is the greatest.

A mad chaos of sea dashing drowned mermaids on a shrieking coast.

Story of the Man who did not like Tripe

It is said of Theodore Hook that, walking down the street with a friend, he made a bet that he would cause to be mobbed an inoffensive old gentleman who was passing by. He said to a little boy, " That's the old gentleman who doesn't like tripe."

The boy told a companion, and they followed the stranger, crying, " Shame, shame ! That's the old man who doesn't like tripe." The old man hastened on, trying to escape these attentions. A largeish crowd followed him. He took to his heels— the crowd running after him, crying, " Tripe ! " " Shame ! " " Stop, thief ! " He was run to earth. A policeman appeared upon the scene and arrested him. The prisoner was subsequently released, but the stigma of not liking tripe clung to him to his dying day—which was greatly hastened owing to the ignominy which he suffered. In point of fact, the old gentleman was devoted to tripe, but, whenever he endeavoured to give utterance to this truth, people only laughed. Thus we see how a light word may stamp a man for life.

It is easy to sacrifice personal morality to general expediency. That which a man would shrink from doing for his own sake he will readily excuse himself for doing when he is a member of a committee.

A man is allowed to think, but not aloud.

The qualities which we are most boastful of controlling are precisely those which we do not possess.

Flattery gives us winged feet.

On retiring from the Stage: Better an hour too soon than a minute too late.

The greatest blunders of the world have been made by common-sense people.

He was always compromising with God in order not to offend the Devil.

Iris. Dog licence. " Let by-laws be by-laws."

Never impart your humour to the humourless. They will use it in evidence against you.

Give what you must, take what you can. (Motto for Millionaires.)

In Hyde Park I heard a Socialist orator holding forth on the iniquity of the feeding system in Salvation Army shelters. " What I say is this," he kept repeating, " bring the food to our homes."

To sacrifice an epigram on the altar of tact is the last martyrdom of man.

The right to misgovern themselves is the freedom that all nations claim.

Cynicism is the humour of hatred.

Genius is an infinite faculty for not taking pains.

Freedom costs more than anything.

Silence is the wisdom of fools.

Such an egoist that he thought himself unworthy to tie his own shoe-string.

You cannot brush your teeth and say your prayers at the same time.

Oscar Wilde told me that when he went to America he had two secretaries—one for autographs, the other for locks of hair. Within six months the one had died of writer's cramp, the other was completely bald.

" You might think I want to flatter you," said the Commissionaire, " but a gentleman-born coming out of the pit said there wasn't more than a dozen or so actors in your line of business as could play the part better."

A gentleman is one who doesn't care whether he is one or not.

I cannot understand why —— should be so friendly to me. Can it be that I am failing ?

I often wake in the morning determined not to tell the truth —but before the sun has set I find myself the richer by another enemy.

He is an old bore.   Even the grave yawns for him.

A lady wrote to me : " I have played Venus in living statuary and am a total abstainer."

What do they know of Ibsen who only Ibsen know ?

It is difficult to be thoroughly appreciated until one is quite dead.

I am a man of few words but many speeches.

History is the plaything of poets.

A man never knows what a fool he is until he hears himself imitated by one.

There is a reason for everything.   I have often wondered why men's heads are of different sizes.   It is in order that one may be able to identify one's hat.

Epitaph on an Acquaintance :   He never said a tactless thing and never did a kind one.

Richard II. arriving limp on the Welsh coast—he had just come back from governing Ireland.

All men are lawyers.

Harry Kemble's telegram : " Pill, pain, pity, pardon."

" Manners ! Manners ! " as the caterpillar said to the steam-roller.

Epitaph for Atheist : J'y suis, j'y reste.

La Raison n'est que la fille naturelle de la Folie fatiguée.

In Italy I saw a courageous wistaria climbing a lightning conductor.

Gillie Farquhar's definition of a gentleman : An imperfectly equipped actor.

Eastern proverb : The dogs bark, the caravan passes.

To the gouty all things are gouty.

In our endeavour to cover the ground quickly, the ground is apt to cover us.

Imitations of Tree are all alike—except Tree's.

Falling in love is largely an affair of habit.

To respect the prejudices of others is the first law of citizenship.

When people stand on their dignity you may be sure they have no other pedestal.

I will not go so far as to say that all people who write letters of more than eight pages are mad, but it is a curious fact that all madmen write letters of more than eight pages.

Methuselah, being asked his age, said, " I am 940." It was exclaimed that he didn't look a day more than 620.

He lacks nothing but the essential.

We only do really well what we can't help doing.

The sun peeped over the horizon with an inflamed eye.

Somebody said to Tennyson what a pity it was Carlyle ever married Jane Welch. " No," replied Tennyson. " Had he not married her, then *four* people would have been made unhappy."

No sight is so sad as that of a buffoon turned preacher.

The scene of Wolsey's fall in *Henry VIII.* at His Majesty's sometimes played 29 minutes, sometimes 39. It depended on whether the nervous B—— or the phlegmatic K—— was in the prompt corner.

In their old age the humbugs are found out.   They have not the energy to keep up the game.

Fechter's fall in *Robert Macaire*.   The fall was from top to bottom of the staircase, and had the appearance of being head-long.   Watching a second time, I observed that when Macaire was shot he instantly bent sideways and clutched the hand-rail of the banister.   Then, with a writhing contortion of pain, he brought the hand forward on the rail, and, keeping his feet still on the top stair, slid both his hands down as far as he could, bringing his head lower and lower till it was somewhat below the level of his heels.   The rest was an easy jump to the lower stairs, within one or two of the bottom.   Here he fell and rolled down the stage.

An American said : " When is a joke not a joke ?   When it's told to an Englishman ! "

A man went into a store in Chicago.   " I want some powder." " Face, gun, or bug ? " asked the young lady.

An American's home is an interviewer's castle.

The German Emperor made God in his own image.

If your hat blows off, never run after it.   Somebody will always run after it for you.

A committee should consist of three men, two of whom are absent.

If we don't take ourselves seriously, who will ?

THE END